Awakening Your True Self

Awakening Your True Self

Discovering the Path to Personal Growth

David Olubiyi

Dabim Support Services Inc

CONTENTS

This book is dedicated to all those courageous souls who embark on the journey of self-discovery. May you find the strength, wisdom, and guidance to navigate the twists and turns along the way. May you embrace your authentic self with love and acceptance, and may you uncover the depths of your true potential. This dedication is a tribute to your resilience, curiosity, and unwavering commitment to personal growth. May this book serve as a source of inspiration, guidance, and support as you continue to explore, discover, and evolve on your path of self-discovery.

In the pages of "Awakening Your True Self," you hold a powerful tool for personal growth and empowerment. This book is a guide that invites you to embark on a transformative journey of self-discovery, self-acceptance, and self-empowerment.

Authored by experts in the field of personal development, this book is a compilation of wisdom, insights, and practical strategies to help you unlock your true potential. It explores various aspects of personal growth, from cultivating a positive mindset and embracing self-love to developing leadership skills and connecting with your deeper purpose.

Throughout these chapters, you will find exercises, reflection prompts, and actionable steps that encourage you to actively engage with the material. This book is not meant to be passively read but rather a resource to be used as a springboard for personal transformation. It is an invitation to go beyond theory and immerse yourself in the practices that can reshape your life.

By embracing the concepts and techniques presented in this book, you have the opportunity to create lasting change in your life. You will learn how to cultivate mindfulness, nurture resilience, embrace change, and align your actions with your values. Each chapter offers insights and tools that empower you to take ownership of your journey and create a life of meaning, fulfillment, and joy.

Remember that personal growth is a process, and there is no one-size-fits-all approach. This book serves as a guide, but it is you who will navigate the path. Be open to exploration, be kind to yourself, and trust in your own wisdom.

As you embark on this transformative journey, remember that you are not alone. Countless individuals have walked this path before you, and many will walk it after you. Embrace the connections you make along the way, seek support when needed, and share your own insights to inspire others.

Now, with an open heart and an eager mind, delve into the pages of "Awakening Your True Self" and discover the extraordinary power within you. May this book be a catalyst for your personal growth and an empowering companion on your journey to self-discovery.

Foreword by David Olubiyi

To make the most of "Awakening Your True Self: Discovering the Path to Personal Growth," consider the following steps for effectively using this book:

1. *Set an intention:* Begin by clarifying your intention for reading this book. What specific areas of personal growth and empowerment do you want to focus on? Setting a clear intention will help you stay focused and engaged throughout your journey.

2. *Read and reflect:* Read each chapter mindfully, taking the time to absorb the information and reflect on how it resonates with your own experiences. Pay attention to any insights or aha moments that arise and jot them down in a journal or notebook.

3. *Take action:* Personal growth requires action. Identify specific action steps you can take based on the principles and strategies discussed in the book. Implement these steps into your daily routine and make a commitment to follow through with them.

4. *Track your progress:* Keep a record of your progress and milestones. Celebrate your achievements and note any challenges or areas for improvement. Regularly review your progress to stay motivated and track your personal growth journey.

5. *Seek support and share insights:* Don't hesitate to seek support from others on your journey. Engage in discussions with like-minded individuals, join support groups, or seek guidance from mentors or coaches. Sharing your insights and experiences can deepen your understanding and inspire others on their own journeys.

6. *Revisit and review:* As you continue on your personal growth journey, revisit chapters or sections of the book that resonate with you. You may discover new insights or perspectives as you grow and evolve. Regularly review your notes, reflections, and action steps to reinforce your progress and maintain focus.

Remember, personal growth is a lifelong journey, and this book is a valuable resource to support and guide you along the way. Embrace the process, be patient with yourself, and enjoy the transformative power of self-discovery and empowerment.

The Awakening

In the hustle and bustle of modern life, it's easy to lose sight of our true selves amidst the expectations and demands of others. However, deep within each of us lies a wellspring of self-awareness and potential waiting to be explored. "The Awakening" sets the stage for the transformative journey of self-discovery that lies ahead.

Feeling Lost in the Maze of Life

In the vast and complex maze of life, it's not uncommon for individuals to find themselves feeling lost and disconnected. This experience of being adrift can manifest in various ways, leaving individuals questioning their purpose, direction, and overall sense of fulfillment. Feeling lost in the maze of life is a universal experience that transcends age, gender, and cultural backgrounds. In this chapter, we will delve into the depths of this common phenomenon, exploring its causes, impact, and potential paths towards finding meaning and direction.

The Experience of Disconnection

Feeling lost is an intricate emotional state that can arise when individuals find themselves detached from their true selves and disconnected from a sense of purpose. It often involves a deep longing for something more, a persistent feeling that there is an essential element missing from their lives. This disconnection can permeate various aspects, including personal relationships, career choices, and overall life satisfaction. The experience of feeling lost can be overwhelming and distressing, as individuals grapple with questions about their identity, values, and the ultimate meaning of their existence.

Causes and Contributing Factors

There are numerous factors that can contribute to the experience of feeling lost in the maze of life. Here are some common causes:

Societal and Cultural Expectations: Societal and cultural norms often dictate certain paths and milestones that individuals are expected to follow. When one feels pressured to conform to these expectations, they may lose touch with their authentic desires and aspirations, leading to a sense of disconnection.

Life Transitions and Uncertainty: Life transitions, such as graduating from school, changing careers, or going through a major personal upheaval, can disrupt our sense of stability and purpose. The uncertainty and unfamiliarity that accompany these transitions can leave individuals feeling lost and unsure of their next steps.

Lack of Clarity and Self-Awareness: A lack of self-awareness and clarity about one's values, passions, and strengths can contribute to feeling lost. Without a deep understanding of oneself, it becomes challenging to navigate the complexities of life and make choices that align with our authentic selves.

External Validation and Comparison: Relying heavily on external validation and constantly comparing oneself to others can lead to a sense of inadequacy and disconnection. When individuals base their self-worth on others' opinions or achievements, they may lose touch with their own unique path and purpose.

Unfulfilling or Misaligned Pursuits: Engaging in activities or pursuing careers that don't resonate with one's true passions and values can create a sense of emptiness and disconnection. When individuals find themselves on a path that doesn't align with their authentic selves, it can be a recipe for feeling lost and unfulfilled.

The Impact of Feeling Lost

Feeling lost can have a profound impact on an individual's well-being and overall quality of life. Some common effects include:

Emotional Turmoil: The experience of feeling lost is often accompanied by a range of intense emotions, such as frustration, anxiety, sadness, and a general sense of discontent. These emotions can create inner turmoil and impact mental health.

Lack of Motivation and Direction: When individuals feel disconnected and unsure of their purpose, they may struggle to find motivation and direction in their lives. This can result in a sense of stagnation, lack of fulfillment, and a feeling of being stuck.

Strained Relationships: Feeling lost can affect interpersonal relationships. Individuals may find it challenging to connect with others authentically when they themselves feel disconnected. This can lead to a sense of isolation and strain on personal relationships, as individuals may struggle to communicate their needs and desires effectively.

Diminished Self-Confidence: The experience of feeling lost can erode self-confidence and self-esteem. Doubts and insecurities about one's purpose and direction can overshadow personal strengths and achievements, leading to a negative self-perception.

Finding Meaning and Direction

While feeling lost in the maze of life can be disheartening, it also presents an opportunity for self-discovery and growth. Here are some strategies and paths individuals can explore to find meaning and direction:

Cultivate Self-Awareness: Self-awareness is the foundation for finding meaning and direction. Engage in introspection and self-reflection to gain a deeper understanding of your values, passions, strengths, and aspirations. Explore activities that bring you joy and a sense of fulfillment, and identify patterns or themes that emerge.

Explore New Opportunities: Break free from the familiar and venture into new experiences and opportunities. This could involve trying new hobbies, taking classes, or exploring different career paths. By stepping outside of your comfort zone, you open yourself up to new possibilities and insights about yourself.

Seek Guidance and Support: Don't hesitate to seek guidance and support from trusted mentors, coaches, or therapists. They can provide valuable insights, perspective, and tools to navigate the journey of self-discovery. Surround yourself with a supportive community that understands and encourages your quest for meaning.

Embrace Self-Compassion: Practicing self-compassion is crucial when feeling lost. Be kind to yourself and acknowledge that this is a natural part of the human experience. Treat yourself with patience and understanding, and remember that the journey towards finding meaning and direction takes time.

Set Meaningful Goals: Set meaningful goals that align with your values and aspirations. Break them down into actionable steps and celebrate each milestone along the way. Goal-setting provides direction and a sense of purpose, helping you navigate the maze of life with intention.

Embrace the Unknown: Embrace the uncertainty that comes with self-discovery. Instead of fearing the unknown, view it as an opportunity for growth and exploration. Be open to unexpected twists and turns, as they often lead to unexpected discoveries about yourself and your path.

Practice Mindfulness and Gratitude: Cultivate mindfulness to stay present and fully engaged in the journey of self-discovery. Notice and appreciate the small moments of joy and growth along the way.

Practicing gratitude can also shift your perspective and foster a sense of appreciation for the lessons and experiences that shape your path.

Take Inspired Action: Once you gain clarity and insight, take inspired action towards your goals and aspirations. Break free from analysis paralysis and start taking steps, no matter how small, to move forward. Action builds momentum and brings you closer to finding your purpose and direction.

Feeling lost in the maze of life is a common experience that can leave individuals questioning their purpose and sense of direction. However, this challenging phase also presents an opportunity for self-discovery and personal growth. By cultivating self-awareness, exploring new opportunities, seeking guidance, practicing self-compassion, and embracing the unknown, individuals can navigate their way towards finding meaning and direction in their lives. Remember, the journey of self-discovery is unique to each individual, and it is the process itself that holds transformative power. Embrace the uncertainty, trust the path, and have faith that within the maze, you will find the way.

Recognizing the Signs of Disconnection

In the midst of our busy lives, it's easy to overlook the subtle signs that indicate we may be feeling disconnected from our true selves and a sense of fulfillment. Recognizing these signs is a crucial step towards initiating the journey of self-discovery. Here, we will explore some common indicators of disconnection and the longing for something more meaningful.

Lack of Fulfillment: A persistent feeling of emptiness or a sense that something essential is missing from our lives can be a significant sign of disconnection. Despite external achievements or material possessions, there may be a lingering sense of dissatisfaction and a yearning for deeper meaning and fulfillment.

Constant Stress and Restlessness: Feeling overwhelmed, stressed, or constantly on edge can indicate a disconnection from our inner selves.

When we are out of alignment with our authentic desires and values, the external pressures of life can take a toll on our well-being, leading to chronic stress and a general sense of restlessness.

Longing for Something More: A deep longing or a persistent feeling that there must be more to life can signal a disconnection from our true purpose and a desire for a more meaningful existence. This longing may arise from a sense of unfulfilled potential or a yearning to make a positive impact on the world.

Loss of Passion and Enthusiasm: If activities or pursuits that used to bring joy and passion have become mundane or uninspiring, it could be an indication of disconnection. A loss of enthusiasm and a lack of engagement in the things we once loved may suggest a need to reconnect with our authentic passions and interests.

Sense of Isolation: Feeling disconnected can create a sense of isolation, even when surrounded by others. It may feel like nobody truly understands or sees us for who we are. This isolation can lead to a sense of loneliness and a longing for deeper connections and meaningful relationships.

Lack of Clarity and Direction: When we feel disconnected, there is often a lack of clarity about our purpose and direction in life. We may find it challenging to make decisions or set goals because we are unsure of what truly resonates with us. This lack of direction can lead to a sense of drifting aimlessly through life.

Repetitive Patterns and Stagnation: Engaging in repetitive patterns, such as staying in unfulfilling relationships or jobs, can be a sign of disconnection. We may feel trapped in a cycle of stagnation, where we are not actively growing or evolving. Breaking free from these patterns requires reconnecting with our authentic selves and embracing change.

Ignoring Intuition and Inner Wisdom: Disconnection often involves disregarding our intuition and inner wisdom. We may find ourselves seeking external validation or constantly seeking advice from others, rather than trusting our own instincts. Ignoring our inner voice can lead to a sense of disempowerment and a loss of authenticity.

Emotional Numbness or Overwhelm: Feeling emotionally numb or overwhelmed by intense emotions can be a sign of disconnection. We may find it challenging to connect with and express our emotions authentically. This disconnection can create a barrier to experiencing the full range of human emotions and connecting with our inner selves.

Recognizing these signs of disconnection is the first step towards initiating change and embarking on a journey of self-discovery. By acknowledging and honoring these indicators, we can begin to reconnect with our authentic selves, find meaning and purpose, and cultivate a more fulfilling and aligned life.

The Catalysts for Awakening

The journey of self-discovery is often initiated by catalysts—events, challenges, or moments of insight—that compel individuals to embark on a path of self-exploration and personal growth. These catalysts can vary from person to person, but they share a common theme of prompting a deeper examination of oneself and a desire for a more meaningful existence. Let's explore some of the catalysts that frequently awaken individuals to the call of self-discovery:

Major Life Changes: Significant life changes, such as starting a new chapter in education, career, or relationships, can act as powerful catalysts for self-discovery. These transitions disrupt our familiar routines and provide an opportunity for introspection and reevaluation of our values, goals, and aspirations.

Personal Crises: Crises, whether physical, emotional, or spiritual, often shake individuals to their core and force them to confront their deepest fears, vulnerabilities, and limitations. Personal crises such as illness, loss of a loved one, or the breakdown of relationships can serve as wake-up calls that ignite a profound desire for personal growth and self-understanding.

Feeling Stuck or Unfulfilled: A persistent sense of being stuck, unfulfilled, or dissatisfied with various aspects of life can act as a catalyst for self-discovery. The realization that there must be more to life than the current circumstances and the yearning for a greater sense of purpose and fulfillment can ignite a transformative journey of self-exploration.

Existential Questions: Pondering existential questions, such as the meaning of life, the nature of happiness, or the purpose of our existence, can trigger a deep introspection and desire for self-discovery. The search for answers to these profound inquiries often leads individuals to embark on a journey of self-reflection and inner exploration.

Breakdown of Beliefs or Ideologies: When long-held beliefs, ideologies, or systems that have shaped our worldview begin to crumble or no longer resonate with us, it can be a catalyst for self-discovery. The realization that our beliefs may not align with our authentic selves can trigger a process of questioning, re-evaluation, and seeking new perspectives.

Awakening to Authentic Desires: Sometimes, individuals experience a sudden or gradual awakening to their true desires and passions. This may involve recognizing that they have been living in accordance with societal or familial expectations, rather than honoring their own authentic dreams. This awakening often propels individuals to embark on a journey to align their lives with their genuine passions and values.

Inspiration from Others: Encounters with inspiring individuals, whether through personal relationships, books, or media, can act as catalysts for self-discovery. Witnessing the transformative journeys of others, their courage, and their pursuit of authenticity can ignite a spark within us, prompting us to embark on our own quest for self-understanding and personal growth.

Seeking Personal Growth: A deep desire for personal growth and a yearning to become the best version of oneself can serve as a powerful catalyst for self-discovery. This inner calling drives individuals to explore their strengths, weaknesses, and areas for improvement, seeking self-awareness and a deeper understanding of their true potential.

These catalysts, whether gentle nudges or profound upheavals, awaken individuals to the need for self-discovery and personal growth.

They act as invitations to embark on a transformative journey of self-exploration, introspection, and alignment with one's authentic self. Embracing these catalysts can lead to profound personal transformation and a more fulfilling and meaningful existence.

Embracing Discomfort as a Gateway to Change

When individuals begin to question their current path and yearn for a deeper sense of fulfillment, it often stirs up feelings of discomfort and restlessness. This discomfort is a natural response to the process of self-discovery and personal growth. It signifies that something within us is seeking expansion, change, and alignment with our authentic selves. Embracing this discomfort becomes a necessary step toward embarking on a transformative journey. Here, we will highlight the importance of embracing discomfort as a gateway to personal growth.

Stepping Outside the Comfort Zone: Growth rarely occurs within the confines of our comfort zone. To discover our true passions, purpose, and potential, we must be willing to push past our familiar boundaries and embrace the unknown. This requires facing fears, taking risks, and challenging the status quo. Discomfort arises when we confront the unfamiliar, but it is within this discomfort that real growth happens.

Stimulating Self-Reflection: Discomfort acts as a catalyst for self-reflection and introspection. When we experience a sense of unease or restlessness, it prompts us to question our current path, values, and beliefs. It invites us to examine what truly matters to us and explore the misalignments between our authentic selves and our present circumstances. In this space of discomfort, we gain clarity about our desires and aspirations.

Encouraging Learning and Adaptation: Embracing discomfort allows us to embrace a mindset of continual learning and adaptation. It opens us up to new perspectives, ideas, and possibilities. By willingly stepping into unfamiliar territory, we expose ourselves to different experiences, challenges, and opportunities for growth. Discomfort becomes a signal that we are expanding our horizons and developing new skills and insights.

Breaking Limiting Patterns: Discomfort often arises when we confront the limiting patterns and beliefs that have held us back. It prompts us to examine the narratives we've created about ourselves and the world, and to question their validity. By embracing this discomfort, we have the opportunity to challenge and break free from self-imposed limitations, allowing us to create a more fulfilling and authentic life.

Cultivating Resilience and Inner Strength: Embracing discomfort builds resilience and inner strength. It teaches us to tolerate and navigate through challenging emotions, setbacks, and uncertainties. By leaning into discomfort rather than avoiding it, we develop the resilience needed to overcome obstacles and persevere in the face of adversity. It empowers us to trust in our ability to navigate the journey of self-discovery and personal growth.

Fostering Personal Evolution: Discomfort acts as a catalyst for personal evolution. It signifies that we are no longer content with staying stagnant or settling for a life that feels disconnected from our true selves. Embracing discomfort allows us to evolve, transform, and become the best version of ourselves. It opens doors to new possibilities, experiences, and opportunities that align with our authentic desires and aspirations.

Creating Meaningful Change: Last but not least, embracing discomfort paves the way for meaningful change in our lives. It propels us to take action, make necessary adjustments, and create a life that reflects our true values and passions. Discomfort becomes the fuel that drives us toward purposeful action and allows us to manifest our authentic selves in the world.

Embracing discomfort as a gateway to change is essential for personal growth and self-discovery. It signifies a willingness to step into the unknown, question the status quo, and pursue a more authentic and fulfilling life. By leaning into discomfort, we unlock our potential, challenge our limiting beliefs, and embrace the transformative journey that leads to a life aligned with our true selves.

Seeking Meaning and Purpose

The innate human desire to find meaning and purpose in life is a powerful driving force that propels individuals to embark on a journey of self-discovery. This quest arises from a deep longing to lead a life that feels fulfilling, significant, and aligned with our true selves. It is through this exploration that we uncover our core values, passions, and authentic desires. Let's delve into the significance of aligning one's actions and choices with their core values and passions in the pursuit of meaning and purpose.

A Source of Fulfillment: Finding meaning and purpose in life provides a profound sense of fulfillment and satisfaction. When our actions and choices align with our core values and passions, we experience a deep sense of authenticity and inner harmony. This alignment connects us to a greater sense of purpose that goes beyond mere material success or external validation.

Guiding Decision-Making: When we are clear about our core values and passions, they become guiding principles in our decision-making process. They serve as a compass, helping us make choices that are in alignment with who we truly are. This alignment ensures that our actions are purposeful and meaningful, leading to a more fulfilling and intentional life.

Enhanced Well-being and Resilience: Living a life of meaning and purpose contributes to overall well-being and resilience. When our actions are driven by our core values and passions, we experience a greater sense of authenticity and personal satisfaction. This authenticity supports our mental, emotional, and even physical well-being, allowing us to navigate challenges and setbacks with greater resilience and inner strength.

Increased Motivation and Engagement: When we align our actions with our core values and passions, we tap into a deep well of motivation and engagement. The pursuit of meaning and purpose ignites a sense of enthusiasm and drive that propels us forward. We become more willing to invest our time and energy into activities and endeavors that truly matter to us, leading to a more fulfilling and inspired life.

Greater Sense of Direction: Aligning our actions and choices with our core values and passions provides a clear sense of direction. It helps us define our priorities and set meaningful goals that resonate with who we are at our core. This clarity enables us to navigate the complexities of life with intention and focus, leading us closer to our unique purpose and a life of significance.

Positive Impact on Others: Living a life of meaning and purpose has a ripple effect that extends beyond ourselves. When we align our actions with our core values and passions, we become a source of inspiration and positive influence for others. By authentically pursuing our own fulfillment, we have the capacity to inspire and uplift those around us, creating a positive impact in our communities and the world.

Greater Resonance with Authentic Self: Aligning our actions and choices with our core values and passions brings us into closer alignment with our authentic selves. It allows us to live in congruence with who we truly are, rather than conforming to societal expectations or external pressures. This resonance with our authentic self fosters a deep sense of self-acceptance, self-confidence, and self-empowerment.

In the quest for meaning and purpose, aligning our actions and choices with our core values and passions is vital. It not only brings fulfillment and satisfaction to our own lives but also has a positive impact on those around us. By embracing this alignment, we uncover the essence of who we are, unlocking our unique gifts and contributing to a more meaningful and purposeful existence.

The Power of Self-Reflection

Self-reflection is a transformative practice that allows individuals to gain clarity, deepen self-awareness, and navigate the journey of self-discovery. It is a process of turning inward, examining our thoughts, emotions, and experiences with curiosity and openness. Through self-reflection, we cultivate a deeper understanding of ourselves, our values, beliefs, strengths, and areas for growth. Let's explore the concept of self-reflection and various techniques that can facilitate this powerful practice.

Understanding Self-Awareness: Self-reflection is rooted in self-awareness—the ability to observe and understand our thoughts, emotions, and behaviors without judgment. It involves cultivating a sense of curiosity and openness toward our inner experiences, exploring the why behind our actions and reactions. By developing self-awareness, we gain insight into our patterns, triggers, and motivations, which can lead to personal growth and transformation.

Journaling: Journaling is a widely practiced technique for self-reflection. By putting pen to paper, we create a safe space to explore our thoughts, feelings, and experiences. Writing allows us to externalize our internal world, giving shape and form to our innermost thoughts and emotions. Regular journaling can uncover patterns, provide clarity, and serve as a valuable tool for self-exploration and self-understanding.

Meditation: Meditation is another powerful practice that fosters self-reflection. Through mindfulness meditation, we cultivate present-moment awareness, observing our thoughts and emotions without attachment or judgment. This practice allows us to develop a deeper understanding of our internal landscape and explore the underlying motivations behind our actions and reactions. Meditation provides a stillness and clarity that support self-reflection and self-discovery.

Asking Meaningful Questions: Engaging in self-reflection involves asking meaningful questions that invite deeper exploration. These questions can focus on various aspects of our lives, such as values, beliefs, goals, relationships, and personal growth. Examples of reflective questions include: What brings me joy? What are my core values? Am I living in alignment with my authentic self? What are the patterns I want to change? By pondering these questions, we open the door to self-discovery and personal transformation.

Seeking Feedback: In addition to introspection, seeking feedback from trusted individuals can provide valuable insights for self-reflection. Others may offer perspectives that we may have overlooked or provide feedback on our strengths and areas for improvement. This feedback can deepen our self-awareness and help us gain a more holistic understanding of ourselves.

Creating Space for Solitude: Creating dedicated time and space for solitude is crucial for self-reflection. In our fast-paced world, it is easy to get caught up in the noise and distractions. By intentionally carving out moments of solitude, we allow ourselves to disconnect from external influences and connect with our inner selves. This solitude provides the necessary space for self-reflection, introspection, and a deeper understanding of our own thoughts, emotions, and desires.

Practicing Mindful Awareness: Bringing mindful awareness to our daily activities and interactions is an effective way to incorporate self-reflection into our daily lives. By paying attention to our thoughts, emotions, and sensations as we go about our routines, we cultivate a greater sense of presence and self-awareness. This mindful awareness allows us to observe our patterns, triggers, and responses in real-time, opening the door to self-reflection and conscious choice-making.

Self-reflection is a powerful tool for gaining clarity, self-awareness, and personal growth. Techniques such as journaling, meditation, asking meaningful questions, seeking feedback, creating solitude, and practicing mindful awareness can facilitate this transformative process. By engaging in regular self-reflection, we embark on a journey of self-discovery, deepening our understanding of ourselves and our experiences.

Exploring the Gap between Who You Are and Who You Want to Be

Self-discovery involves an honest examination of who we are and who we aspire to become. It requires us to explore the gap that may exist between our current identities and our envisioned selves. This exploration prompts us to question our values, goals, and the congruence between our external lives and internal desires. By inviting individuals to reflect on this gap, we encourage a deeper understanding of themselves and the potential for personal growth and transformation. Let's delve into the process of exploring the gap between who you are and who you want to be.

Identifying Core Values: Begin by examining your core values—the fundamental principles that guide your life. Reflect on what truly matters to you and what you consider essential for a meaningful and fulfilled existence. Take time to evaluate whether your current actions and choices align with these values or if there are discrepancies that create a gap between your values and your lived experiences.

Reflecting on Personal Aspirations: Consider your aspirations and long-term goals—the vision you hold for your future self. What are the qualities, accomplishments, and experiences you desire? Reflect on whether your current path and daily actions are leading you closer to those aspirations or if they diverge from the person you aspire to be. Identify any gaps that may exist between your current reality and your envisioned self.

Examining External Expectations: Society, family, and cultural influences often shape our beliefs and expectations. Reflect on whether your current identity and choices are driven by external expectations rather than your authentic desires. Are you conforming to societal norms or living up to others' expectations, even if it contradicts your true self? Identifying any misalignments between your external life and internal desires is essential for closing the gap.

Evaluating Relationships and Environment: Our relationships and environment significantly impact our personal growth. Consider the people you surround yourself with and the spaces you inhabit. Do they support and nourish your authentic self, or do they hinder your growth and contribute to the gap between who you are and who you want to be? Assessing the influence of relationships and environments helps you determine if adjustments are necessary for alignment and growth.

Self-Reflection and Introspection: Engage in self-reflection and introspection to explore the deeper layers of your identity. Look inward and question your beliefs, fears, and limiting patterns that may contribute to the gap between your current and desired self. This introspective process allows you to uncover hidden motivations, confront self-imposed limitations, and gain insight into areas where personal growth is needed.

Setting Aligned Goals: Once you have identified the gaps and misalignments, set goals that bridge the distance between who you are and who you want to be. Break down these goals into actionable steps that align with your values, aspirations, and authentic self. By setting goals that resonate with your true desires, you create a roadmap for personal growth and closing the gap.

Embracing Change and Growth: Closing the gap between who you are and who you want to be requires a willingness to embrace change and personal growth. It may involve stepping out of your comfort zone, challenging limiting beliefs, and taking intentional actions aligned with your aspirations. Embrace the discomfort that comes with growth, knowing that it is an essential part of the journey towards becoming your authentic self.

By exploring the gap between who you are and who you want to be, you embark on a transformative journey of self-discovery. Reflecting on core values, aspirations, external expectations, relationships, and personal growth allows you to identify areas for alignment and growth. Embrace the process of self-reflection, set goals that resonate with your authentic self, and embrace change as you strive to bridge the gap and become the person you aspire to be.

Overcoming Fear and Resistance

Embarking on a journey of self-discovery can be both exciting and daunting. It is common for fears and resistance to arise as we contemplate stepping into the unknown and exploring our true selves. These fears can manifest as self-doubt, fear of judgment, fear of failure, or fear of change. It is important to address these fears and resistance head-on, as they can hinder our progress and prevent us from fully embracing the transformative power of self-discovery. Here are insights and practical strategies to help you navigate these fears and move forward on your journey.

Reframe Challenges as Opportunities for Growth: Instead of viewing challenges and obstacles as roadblocks, reframe them as opportunities for growth and self-discovery. Embrace the mindset that every setback or difficulty is a chance to learn, develop resilience, and uncover valuable insights about yourself. By reframing challenges, you shift your perspective from fear to curiosity, allowing you to embrace the transformative nature of the journey.

Cultivate Self-Compassion: Fear and resistance often stem from a fear of judgment or a harsh inner critic. Cultivate self-compassion by treating yourself with kindness, understanding, and acceptance. Acknowledge that self-discovery is a process, and it is natural to experience ups and downs along the way. Practice self-compassion in moments of self-doubt or when faced with challenges, reminding yourself that you are worthy of growth and self-exploration.

Create a Support System: Surround yourself with a supportive network of individuals who uplift and encourage your journey of self-discovery. Seek out like-minded individuals, friends, or mentors who can offer guidance, share their own experiences, and provide a safe space for you to express your fears and concerns. Having a support system can provide the encouragement and reassurance needed to overcome resistance and keep moving forward.

Embrace Mindset Shifts: Shift your mindset from one of fear and limitation to one of possibility and growth. Recognize that embarking on a journey of self-discovery is an act of courage and self-empowerment. Embrace the belief that you have the capacity to grow, evolve, and create a life that aligns with your authentic self. Emphasize the opportunities for self-expression, fulfillment, and personal transformation that await you on this path.

Take Incremental Steps: Break down the journey into manageable steps and set achievable goals. Taking small, incremental steps allows you to build confidence, overcome resistance, and gradually expand your comfort zone. Celebrate each milestone along the way, acknowledging your progress and growth. Remember that self-discovery is a continuous process, and it is the cumulative effect of small steps that leads to significant transformation.

Practice Mindfulness and Self-Reflection: Cultivate mindfulness and self-reflection as regular practices in your life. Mindfulness helps you stay present, observe your fears and resistance without judgment, and develop a deeper understanding of their underlying causes. Self-reflection allows you to explore the thoughts, emotions, and beliefs that contribute to your fears, enabling you to challenge and reframe them. Incorporating these practices into your daily routine supports your journey of self-discovery and helps you navigate fear and resistance with greater clarity and compassion.

Trust the Process: Finally, trust in the process of self-discovery. Understand that it is a unique and personal journey that unfolds at its own pace. Trust that as you commit to exploring your true self, the answers and insights you seek will reveal themselves. Embrace the unknown and have faith in your ability to navigate the challenges that arise along the way. Trust that by overcoming your fears and resistance, you will discover a deeper sense of self and create a life that aligns with your authentic desires.

Remember, fear and resistance are natural parts of the journey of self-discovery. By reframing challenges, cultivating self-compassion, creating a support system, embracing mindset shifts, taking incremental steps, practicing mindfulness and self-reflection, and trusting the process, you can overcome these obstacles and move forward with courage and determination. Embrace the transformative power of self-discovery and allow yourself to grow, evolve, and create a life that is aligned with your authentic self.

The Importance of Self-Honesty

Self-honesty is a cornerstone of the journey of self-discovery. It is the willingness to confront our fears, insecurities, and limiting beliefs with honesty and compassion. When we are honest with ourselves, we create a foundation of authenticity, clarity, and personal growth. Here, we explore the significance of self-honesty and provide encouragement for readers to embrace this vital aspect of their journey.

Embracing Authenticity: Self-honesty is synonymous with embracing authenticity. It requires us to face our true thoughts, emotions, desires, and values without judgment or denial. By being honest with ourselves, we acknowledge our authentic selves and honor our individuality. This authenticity is the key to living a fulfilled and purposeful life aligned with our core being.

Unveiling Limiting Beliefs: Self-honesty empowers us to confront our limiting beliefs—the thoughts and beliefs that hold us back from reaching our full potential. By honestly acknowledging and examining these beliefs, we can challenge and replace them with empowering and supportive beliefs. This process liberates us from self-imposed limitations and opens up new possibilities for growth and self-discovery.

Confronting Fears and Insecurities: Fear and insecurity often prevent us from fully embracing our true selves. Self-honesty encourages us to face these fears head-on and examine their origins and impact on our lives. By acknowledging our fears and insecurities with honesty and compassion, we can work through them and move forward with courage and self-empowerment.

Recognizing Patterns and Behaviors: Self-honesty allows us to recognize recurring patterns and behaviors in our lives. By honestly examining these patterns, we gain insights into their underlying causes and the ways they may be hindering our personal growth. This awareness enables us to make conscious choices and take proactive steps to break free from unhealthy patterns and cultivate new, empowering ones.

Cultivating Self-Compassion: Self-honesty is not about self-judgment or criticism but about cultivating self-compassion. It involves acknowledging our imperfections, vulnerabilities, and areas for growth with kindness and understanding. Self-compassion allows us to approach our self-discovery journey with patience, acceptance, and forgiveness, fostering an environment of love and growth within ourselves.

Deepening Self-Awareness: Self-honesty is intricately connected to self-awareness. By being honest with ourselves, we deepen our understanding of who we are—our strengths, weaknesses, desires, and fears. This self-awareness forms the foundation for personal growth and guides us in making choices that align with our authentic selves.

Creating Authentic Connections: When we are honest with ourselves, we are better equipped to form authentic connections with others. By being true to ourselves, we attract like-minded individuals who resonate with our genuine nature. Honest self-expression fosters deeper and more meaningful relationships, as it allows us to connect on a genuine and authentic level.

Embracing self-honesty throughout the journey of self-discovery is crucial for personal growth, authenticity, and creating a fulfilling life. By confronting our fears, insecurities, and limiting beliefs with honesty and compassion, we empower ourselves to break free from self-imposed limitations and embrace our true potential. Let self-honesty be your guiding principle as you navigate the path of self-discovery, and remember to approach this journey with love, acceptance, and a commitment to living a life true to yourself.

Embracing Curiosity and Openness

As readers embark on their journey of self-discovery, it is essential to cultivate a curious and open mindset. This mindset allows for exploration, growth, and a broader understanding of oneself and the world. By approaching the journey with curiosity and openness, readers can embrace new perspectives, ideas, and experiences, fostering personal transformation and a deeper connection to their authentic selves. Here, we emphasize the importance of curiosity and openness and encourage readers to embrace these qualities throughout their self-discovery journey.

Expanding Perspectives: Curiosity and openness enable us to expand our perspectives and challenge our existing beliefs. By approaching our journey of self-discovery with an open mind, we invite new ideas, insights, and experiences that broaden our understanding of ourselves and the world around us. Embrace the opportunity to explore different viewpoints, cultures, and philosophies, as this can lead to personal growth and a more inclusive perspective.

Embracing Learning and Growth: A curious and open mindset fosters a love for learning and personal growth. When we approach our self-discovery journey with curiosity, we seek out new knowledge, skills, and experiences. We recognize that every encounter, whether positive or challenging, holds an opportunity for learning and growth. Embrace the mindset of a lifelong learner and see each moment as a chance to expand your understanding and evolve as an individual.

Questioning Assumptions: Curiosity and openness encourage us to question our assumptions about ourselves and the world. By challenging our preconceived notions, we create space for self-reflection and personal development. Ask yourself why you hold certain beliefs, what assumptions underlie your thoughts and actions, and whether these beliefs serve your authentic self. By questioning assumptions, you gain clarity and the freedom to redefine your values and priorities.

Embracing New Experiences: Curiosity and openness prompt us to seek out new experiences and step outside our comfort zones. Embrace the opportunity to try new activities, explore different cultures, and engage in diverse communities. Each new experience presents an opportunity for self-discovery, self-expression, and personal growth. Embrace the unknown with an open heart and a willingness to embrace the transformative power of novel experiences.

Practicing Mindful Presence: Cultivate a sense of mindful presence as you embark on your self-discovery journey. Curiosity and openness are heightened when we are fully present in the moment, allowing us to observe and engage with our surroundings and inner experiences without judgment. Mindfulness enables us to deepen our connection to ourselves and the world, fostering curiosity and openness as we explore our thoughts, emotions, and desires.

Embracing Vulnerability: Curiosity and openness require vulnerability—the willingness to be authentic, exposed, and receptive to new experiences and perspectives. Embrace vulnerability as a strength, as it allows for deeper connections, growth, and self-discovery. Recognize that vulnerability is an essential ingredient in cultivating curiosity and openness, and it paves the way for meaningful and transformative encounters.

Cultivating Self-Discovery as a Continuous Journey: Approach self-discovery as a lifelong, continuous journey. Cultivate curiosity and openness as ongoing qualities that shape your relationship with yourself and the world. Embrace the idea that self-discovery is not a destination but a process of constant exploration and growth. Allow curiosity and openness to guide you on this journey of self-discovery, and remain open to the ever-unfolding possibilities of personal transformation.

By embracing curiosity and openness throughout your self-discovery journey, you open yourself to new experiences, perspectives, and personal growth. Cultivate a mindset that values learning, questions assumptions, and embraces vulnerability. Remember that self-discovery is an ongoing process, and each moment presents an opportunity for exploration and connection. Embrace curiosity and embrace the unknown. Allow yourself to be curious about who you are, what you desire, and what brings you joy and fulfillment. Explore different aspects of yourself and be open to discovering new passions and interests. Seek out experiences that expand your horizons and challenge your beliefs.

Surrendering to the Journey of Self-Discovery

In the journey of self-discovery, it is important to let go of rigid expectations and attachments, and instead embrace the unknown with openness and surrender. Self-discovery is not a linear path with predetermined outcomes; it is a dynamic and transformative process that requires trust and faith in oneself. Here, we explore the need to surrender and let go, and encourage readers to trust the journey of self-discovery.

Embracing the Unknown: Self-discovery often involves venturing into uncharted territory. It requires a willingness to step outside of your comfort zone and embrace the unknown. By surrendering to the journey, you open yourself to new experiences, perspectives, and possibilities that may not align with your preconceived notions. Embrace the uncertainty with an open heart and a sense of adventure, knowing that it is within the unknown that true growth and self-discovery reside.

Letting Go of Rigid Expectations: Surrendering to the journey of self-discovery means letting go of rigid expectations. Release the need for a specific outcome or a predefined timeline. Instead, allow yourself to be guided by the unfolding of the process. Let go of societal pressures, comparisons, and external validations. Embrace the freedom of exploring your authentic self without the constraints of expectations. By releasing attachments to specific outcomes, you create space for unexpected discoveries and profound personal transformation.

Trusting the Process: Trust is an essential element of surrendering to the journey of self-discovery. Trust in your own inner wisdom, intuition, and ability to navigate the twists and turns that arise. Have faith that the journey is leading you exactly where you need to be. Trust that even in moments of uncertainty or perceived setbacks, there are valuable lessons and growth opportunities. Embrace the belief that the process is unfolding perfectly, guiding you towards self-realization and personal fulfillment.

Embracing Detours and Setbacks: On the journey of self-discovery, detours and setbacks are inevitable. Surrendering to the process means embracing these moments as valuable learning experiences. Rather than viewing them as failures or obstacles, see them as opportunities for growth, self-reflection, and course correction. Embrace the wisdom that comes from navigating challenges, and trust that even detours contribute to the richness and depth of your self-discovery journey.

Cultivating Patience and Self-Compassion: Surrendering to the journey of self-discovery requires patience and self-compassion. Recognize that self-discovery is a lifelong journey, and growth takes time. Be gentle with yourself, celebrating your progress and accepting your imperfections along the way. Cultivate patience as you navigate the highs and lows of the journey, trusting that each phase serves a purpose in your personal evolution.

Embodying Mindfulness: Mindfulness is a powerful practice that supports surrendering to the journey of self-discovery. By cultivating present-moment awareness, you become attuned to the subtle shifts, insights, and guidance that arise. Embody mindfulness as you engage in self-reflection, make choices, and embrace new experiences. By staying present, you can fully immerse yourself in the journey and connect with the deeper aspects of your being.

Honoring Your Authentic Self: Above all, surrendering to the journey of self-discovery means honoring your authentic self. Trust your inner voice, passions, and desires. Allow your true essence to guide you on the path of self-discovery. By surrendering to your authentic self, you align with your deepest values and aspirations, creating a life that is true to who you are.

Surrendering to the journey of self-discovery is an act of courage, trust, and faith in oneself. Let go of preconceived notions, expectations, and attachments that may hinder your self-discovery journey. Surrender to the process and trust that it will unfold in its own time and in its own way.

The Role of Intuition in Awakening

Intuition is a powerful and innate aspect of our being that plays a vital role in guiding individuals on their path of self-discovery. It is the deep knowing and inner wisdom that transcends logic and reasoning. In this chapter, we introduce the concept of intuition and explore its significance in awakening. We also provide practical ways to tap into and trust one's intuition.

Understanding Intuition:

Intuition is often described as a "gut feeling" or a sense of inner knowing. It is a form of direct knowledge that arises without conscious reasoning or analysis. Intuition bypasses the limitations of the rational mind and connects us to a deeper wisdom that resides within us. It is a valuable resource that can guide us toward our authentic selves and help us navigate the complexities of life.

Cultivating Inner Stillness:

One way to access intuition is through cultivating inner stillness. Practices like meditation and mindfulness allow us to quiet the constant chatter of the mind and create space for intuition to arise. By stilling the mind, we become more attuned to the subtle whispers of our inner wisdom, enabling us to tap into our intuition with greater clarity and ease.

Listening to the Body:

Our bodies are powerful sources of intuitive wisdom. Pay attention to the physical sensations that arise in different situations or when making decisions. Notice any tension, relaxation, or subtle shifts that occur within the body. Your body often provides valuable signals that can guide you in the direction of your authentic self. Trust the sensations you feel and honor the wisdom of your body.

Honoring Emotional Resonance:

Emotions are another gateway to intuition. Notice the emotions that arise in different situations, interactions, or when contemplating certain choices. Pay attention to feelings of expansion or contraction, lightness or heaviness. Your emotions can act as an intuitive compass, guiding you toward alignment with your authentic self. Trust the emotional resonances that you experience and use them as guideposts on your journey.

Journaling for Intuitive Insight:

Journaling is a powerful tool for accessing and understanding your intuition. Set aside time to write freely and without judgment, allowing your intuition to flow onto the pages. Write down your thoughts, feelings, and observations. Reflect on the patterns, themes, and insights that emerge. Journaling helps to deepen your self-awareness and strengthens your connection to your intuitive guidance.

Trusting Your Inner Voice:

Trusting your intuition requires developing a sense of trust in your own inner voice. It involves letting go of doubt, fear, and external validation. Cultivate self-trust by acknowledging and honoring the times when your intuition has proven accurate and beneficial. Remind yourself that you possess the wisdom and guidance within to navigate your journey of self-discovery.

Taking Inspired Action:

Intuition is not just about receiving guidance; it is also about taking inspired action based on that guidance. When your intuition speaks, listen and have the courage to follow its guidance. Trust that your intuition will lead you toward experiences, opportunities, and choices that align with your authentic self. Embrace the unknown and take steps forward, even when they may seem uncertain.

By tapping into and trusting your intuition, you invite a deeper level of self-discovery and personal growth. Embrace practices that cultivate stillness, listen to the wisdom of your body and emotions, and journal to gain intuitive insights. Trust your inner voice and take inspired action aligned with your intuition. As you do so, you will navigate your journey of self-discovery with greater clarity, purpose, and authenticity.

Letting Go of External Validation

In the journey of self-discovery, it is crucial to free oneself from the constant need for external validation. Relying on the approval and validation of others can hinder personal growth and prevent individuals from truly connecting with their authentic selves. In this chapter, we highlight the importance of letting go of external validation and encourage readers to cultivate self-acceptance and rely on their own inner compass for guidance and fulfillment.

Recognizing the Illusion of External Validation:

External validation refers to seeking approval, recognition, and acceptance from others as a measure of one's self-worth. It is important to understand that external validation is often transient and conditional. Relying on it for validation can be disempowering, as it places one's sense of self-worth in the hands of others. Realize that true fulfillment comes from within, through self-acceptance and self-validation.

Cultivating Self-Acceptance:

Self-acceptance is the foundation for freeing oneself from the need for external validation. It involves embracing all aspects of oneself, including strengths, weaknesses, imperfections, and vulnerabilities. Practice self-compassion and let go of self-judgment. Embrace the truth that you are inherently worthy and deserving of love and acceptance, regardless of external opinions.

Connecting with Your Inner Compass:

Each individual possesses an inner compass, a deep intuitive knowing that guides them toward their authentic path and purpose. By cultivating self-awareness and deepening the connection to your inner self, you can tap into this inner compass. Trust your intuition and allow it to guide your decisions, choices, and actions. Rely on your own values, passions, and desires to navigate your journey of self-discovery.

Embracing Authenticity:

Authenticity lies in embracing and expressing your true self, without seeking validation or approval from others. Embrace your unique qualities, perspectives, and experiences. Let go of the need to conform to societal expectations or the opinions of others. When you align your actions and choices with your authentic self, you experience a sense of wholeness and fulfillment that transcends external validation.

Celebrating Personal Growth:

Focus on your personal growth and inner transformation, rather than seeking external validation. Celebrate your progress, accomplishments, and milestones along your journey of self-discovery. Acknowledge your efforts, learning experiences, and the courage it takes to explore and evolve. By shifting your focus to internal growth and self-improvement, you cultivate a sense of empowerment and intrinsic fulfillment.

Building a Supportive Network:

Surround yourself with a supportive network of individuals who appreciate and value you for who you truly are. Seek out relationships and communities that foster growth, authenticity, and mutual support. Connect with like-minded individuals who understand and respect your journey of self-discovery. Having a strong support system can help reinforce your sense of self-worth and reduce the need for external validation.

Nurturing Your Inner Happiness:

Find joy and fulfillment within yourself, independent of external circumstances or validation. Engage in activities that bring you happiness, practice self-care, and cultivate a positive mindset. Develop a deep connection with your inner self and nurture your own well-being. When you prioritize your own happiness and fulfillment, external validation becomes less significant.

By letting go of the need for external validation and embracing self-acceptance, you reclaim your power and live authentically. Cultivate your inner compass, celebrate personal growth, and build a supportive network. Nurture your own happiness and find fulfillment from within. As you rely on your own inner validation, you will discover a deep sense of self-worth and live a more fulfilling and authentic life.

Trusting the Inner Voice

Reconnecting with and trusting your inner voice is essential on the journey of self-discovery. Your inner voice serves as a guiding force, offering wisdom, insight, and clarity as you navigate life's complexities. In this chapter, we encourage readers to develop and strengthen their connection with their inner voice. We explore practical ways to cultivate trust in this innate guidance, such as practicing self-reflection, mindfulness, and creating space for inner quiet.

Cultivating Self-Reflection:

Self-reflection is a powerful practice for reconnecting with your inner voice. Set aside regular time for introspection and self-inquiry. Create a quiet and undisturbed space where you can engage in deep self-reflection. Ask yourself meaningful questions and listen for the subtle responses that arise within. Through self-reflection, you deepen your understanding of yourself and access the wisdom of your inner voice.

Embracing Mindfulness:

Mindfulness is a valuable tool for developing a strong connection with your inner voice. Practice being fully present in the present moment, without judgment or attachment. Pay attention to your thoughts, emotions, and sensations as they arise. By cultivating mindfulness, you create space to listen to your inner voice and discern its guidance amidst the noise of external distractions. Mindfulness allows you to tap into the inherent wisdom within.

Quieting External Distractions:

In our modern, fast-paced world, external distractions can drown out the voice of our inner wisdom. Take intentional steps to quiet external noise and create moments of stillness. Turn off electronic devices, spend time in nature, or engage in activities that bring you peace and calm. By intentionally creating space for inner quiet, you allow your inner voice to be heard more clearly.

Honoring Intuitive Prompts:

Your inner voice often communicates through intuitive prompts, nudges, or gut feelings. Pay attention to these subtle signals and honor them. Trust the wisdom they carry. When faced with decisions or choices, listen to the intuitive guidance that arises within you. Recognize that your inner voice knows what is best for you and can guide you toward alignment with your authentic self.

Journaling as a Dialogue:

Journaling can serve as a powerful tool for engaging in a dialogue with your inner voice. Use journaling as a means to have a conversation with yourself. Write down your questions, concerns, or dilemmas, and allow your inner voice to respond through your writing. This process can deepen your connection with your inner wisdom and provide valuable insights and guidance.

Trusting the Process:

Trusting your inner voice requires an element of surrender and faith in the process of self-discovery. Let go of the need for instant answers or immediate clarity. Recognize that self-discovery is a journey, and insights may unfold gradually over time. Trust that your inner voice will reveal itself and provide guidance when the time is right. Embrace the journey with patience and openness.

Taking Aligned Action:

Trusting your inner voice involves taking aligned action based on its guidance. When your inner voice speaks, listen and have the courage to follow its guidance. Trust that your inner voice is guiding you toward experiences, choices, and paths that align with your authentic self. Take steps forward, even when they may seem uncertain, and trust that your inner wisdom will lead you in the right direction.

As you reconnect with and trust your inner voice, you tap into a wellspring of guidance and wisdom. Cultivate self-reflection, mindfulness, and create space for inner quiet. Honor intuitive prompts and engage in a dialogue with your inner voice through journaling. Trust the process and take aligned action. By trusting your inner voice, you navigate your journey of self-discovery with greater clarity, authenticity, and fulfillment.

Embracing Uncertainty as a Stepping Stone to Self-Discovery

Uncertainty is an inherent part of the journey of self-discovery. It is the fertile ground where personal growth takes root and transformation flourishes. In this chapter, we explore the inevitability of uncertainty on the path of self-discovery and highlight its potential as a catalyst for growth. We encourage readers to embrace the unknown, step outside their comfort zones, and view uncertainty as an opportunity for self-exploration and personal transformation.

Understanding the Nature of Uncertainty:

Uncertainty is a natural and constant aspect of life. It arises from the unpredictability of the future, the ambiguity of choices, and the complexity of personal growth. Recognize that certainty is an illusion and that embracing uncertainty is essential for expanding your horizons and discovering new aspects of yourself.

Embracing the Unknown:

Embracing the unknown requires a shift in perspective. Instead of fearing uncertainty, view it as a source of possibility and growth. Embrace the idea that the unknown holds infinite potential for self-exploration and personal transformation. Cultivate a mindset of curiosity and openness toward the unknown, allowing it to be a stepping stone on your journey.

Stepping Outside the Comfort Zone:

Growth and self-discovery often occur when you step outside your comfort zone. Embrace the discomfort and challenges that accompany uncertainty. Recognize that by stretching your boundaries and trying new experiences, you create opportunities for self-exploration and learning. Be willing to take calculated risks and explore unfamiliar territories.

Developing Resilience:

Embracing uncertainty requires developing resilience—the ability to bounce back from setbacks and adapt to changing circumstances. Cultivate a resilient mindset by reframing challenges as opportunities for growth. Recognize that setbacks and obstacles are valuable lessons that can lead to personal transformation. Embrace the uncertainty as a chance to build resilience and inner strength.

Practicing Mindfulness:

Mindfulness is a powerful tool for navigating uncertainty. When faced with uncertainty, practice being fully present in the present moment. Notice your thoughts, emotions, and physical sensations without judgment. By grounding yourself in the present, you can better manage anxiety and fear associated with uncertainty. Mindfulness helps you develop a sense of calm and clarity amidst the unknown.

Cultivating Flexibility:

Flexibility is crucial when embracing uncertainty. Be willing to adapt and adjust your plans as new information emerges. Let go of rigid expectations and attachments to specific outcomes. Trust that the journey of self-discovery may take unexpected turns, and each detour presents an opportunity for growth. Cultivate the flexibility to flow with the changing tides of uncertainty.

Viewing Uncertainty as an Opportunity:

Shift your perspective on uncertainty, viewing it as an opportunity for self-exploration and personal transformation. Uncertainty invites you to question your beliefs, values, and assumptions. It encourages self-reflection, introspection, and a deeper understanding of yourself. Embrace the unknown as an invitation to uncover hidden strengths, passions, and possibilities.

By embracing uncertainty, stepping outside your comfort zone, and viewing it as an opportunity, you open yourself to a world of self-exploration and personal transformation. Embrace the unknown with curiosity and openness. Cultivate resilience, practice mindfulness, and be flexible in your approach. View uncertainty as a catalyst for growth and trust in the process of self-discovery. As you do so, you will uncover new dimensions of yourself and embark on a transformative journey of self-discovery.

2

The Call to Adventure

Meeting the Mysterious Mentor

On the journey of self-discovery, we often find ourselves encountering mysterious mentors who play a significant role in guiding and shaping our path. These mentors may appear in various forms, offering their wisdom, experience, and guidance to help us navigate the challenges and uncertainties that lie ahead.

Recognizing the Mysterious Mentor: The first step in meeting the mysterious mentor is developing awareness and openness to the possibility of their presence in our lives. Sometimes, they may arrive unexpectedly, appearing in the form of a wise teacher, a supportive friend, or a stranger who crosses our path at the right moment. It is important to be attuned to the subtle synchronicities and signs that may indicate the presence of a mentor in our lives.

The Role of the Mysterious Mentor: The mysterious mentor serves as a guide, offering insights, perspectives, and knowledge that can deepen our self-understanding and illuminate our path. They have often walked a similar journey themselves and have acquired wisdom through their own experiences. Their presence is not about providing all the answers or solving our problems but rather about nudging us in the right direction and empowering us to discover our own truths.

The Gift of Perspective: One of the most valuable gifts a mysterious mentor offers is a fresh perspective. They help us see beyond our limited view and challenge our assumptions and beliefs. By sharing their own stories and experiences, they broaden our horizons and open us up to new possibilities. They may ask thought-provoking questions or offer alternative viewpoints, inspiring us to question and explore our own beliefs and desires.

Building Trust and Connection: Trust is essential in the mentor-mentee relationship. We must trust that the mentor has our best interests at heart and that their guidance comes from a place of genuine care and wisdom. Building this trust requires open and honest communication, mutual respect, and a willingness to be vulnerable. By sharing our fears, doubts, and aspirations with the mentor, we create a safe space for guidance and growth.

Learning from the Mentor's Wisdom: The mysterious mentor's wisdom can be gleaned through conversations, shared experiences, and observing their way of being in the world. Their guidance may come in the form of practical advice, insightful questions, or profound teachings. It is important to approach the mentor's wisdom with openness and a willingness to learn, as their insights can help us gain clarity, overcome obstacles, and make informed decisions on our journey.

Applying the Mentor's Wisdom: While the mentor's guidance is valuable, it is ultimately up to us to apply it in our own lives. We must take responsibility for our own growth and actively incorporate the mentor's wisdom into our actions and choices. This requires self-reflection, discernment, and a willingness to step out of our comfort zones. By aligning our actions with the mentor's guidance, we can make progress on our path of self-discovery.

Embracing the Mentor Within: As we continue our journey, it is essential to recognize that the mentor resides not only outside of us but also within. We each have an inner mentor, an inner wisdom that can guide us if we learn to listen and trust ourselves. The mysterious mentor serves as a catalyst for awakening this inner mentor, reminding us of the power and wisdom that lie within us.

Maintaining the Mentor-Mentee Relationship: The mentor-mentee relationship is a dynamic and evolving connection. It is important to cultivate gratitude for the mentor's presence in our lives and to express our appreciation for their guidance. Regular check-ins and conversations can help nurture and strengthen the relationship. It is also essential to recognize that mentors may come and go as our journey unfolds, and new mentors may appear along the way.

Meeting the mysterious mentor is an integral part of the call to adventure on the journey of self-discovery. The mysterious mentor represents a guide or teacher who provides wisdom, support, and guidance as you navigate the challenges and revelations of your personal quest. The encounter with the mysterious mentor often occurs at a crucial point in your journey, when you are seeking answers, direction, or a deeper understanding of yourself. This mentor may appear in various forms, such as a wise elder, a spiritual teacher, a therapist, or even a book or a piece of art that resonates with you deeply.

Recognizing Synchronicities and Divine Timing

In our journey of self-discovery, we often come across moments of synchronicity and experience the workings of divine timing. These occurrences, seemingly coincidental but deeply meaningful, hold valuable messages and guidance for us. By recognizing and embracing synchronicities, we can navigate our path with greater trust and awareness.

Understanding Synchronicity: Synchronicity, a concept introduced by Swiss psychologist Carl Jung, refers to the meaningful coincidences that occur in our lives. These are events that seem to be unrelated on the surface but are connected through their deeper significance. Synchronicities often serve as signposts, pointing us in the direction of our authentic path and purpose.

Paying Attention to Signs: Synchronicities can manifest in various forms, such as repetitive numbers, symbols, unexpected encounters, or even a series of events unfolding in a significant sequence. By cultivating mindfulness and presence, we become more attuned to these signs and can interpret their messages. It is important to approach synchronicities with curiosity and open-mindedness, allowing them to guide us on our journey.

Trusting Divine Timing: Divine timing refers to the notion that there is a greater intelligence or cosmic order at work in our lives. It suggests that events and experiences unfold in a precise and perfect manner, aligning with our highest good and growth. Trusting in divine timing means surrendering the need for control and accepting that things happen at the right time and in the right way, even if it may not align with our immediate desires.

Navigating the Flow of Life: Recognizing synchronicities and trusting divine timing requires us to attune ourselves to the flow of life. It involves surrendering to the natural rhythm and pace of our journey, rather than forcing or rushing things. By relinquishing resistance and embracing the unfolding of events, we allow space for synchronicities to occur and divine guidance to reveal itself.

Listening to Intuition: Our intuition serves as a bridge between our conscious mind and the greater intelligence of the universe. By honing our intuitive abilities and listening to our inner voice, we can better recognize and interpret synchronicities. Our intuition acts as a guiding compass, helping us discern which signs and events hold deeper significance for our personal growth and self-discovery.

Reflecting on Personal Experiences: Looking back on our personal experiences, we often find instances of synchronicity that have shaped our path. Reflecting on these moments allows us to gain clarity and insight into the patterns and themes that have emerged. By journaling or engaging in introspection, we can uncover the hidden messages and lessons that synchronicities have presented to us.

Cultivating Trust and Faith: Trusting in synchronicities and divine timing requires cultivating trust and faith in the unseen forces at play. It involves surrendering to the unknown and embracing the mystery of life. By letting go of the need to control every aspect of our journey, we open ourselves up to the magic and serendipity that synchronicities bring.

Taking Aligned Action: Recognizing synchronicities and divine timing is not merely about observing and interpreting signs but also about taking aligned action. As we receive guidance from these meaningful coincidences, it is important to act upon them. By aligning our thoughts, intentions, and actions with the messages we receive, we move closer to our authentic selves and the fulfillment of our purpose.

Recognizing synchronicities and embracing divine timing invites us to deepen our connection with the greater forces at play in our lives. By paying attention to the signs, trusting the unfolding journey, and taking aligned action, we align ourselves with the flow of life. Through this alignment, we navigate our path of self-discovery with grace, trust, and a sense of divine guidance.

Synchronicities are meaningful coincidences or events that seem to be perfectly timed and aligned with our thoughts, intentions, or desires. They are often seen as signs from the universe or the divine, guiding us along our path of self-discovery. When we open ourselves to recognizing and acknowledging these synchronicities, we deepen our connection to the greater wisdom and guidance that is available to us.

Embracing the Unknown

In the journey of self-discovery, embracing the unknown is a transformative step that invites us to release our need for certainty and control. It is an act of surrendering to the mysteries of life and opening ourselves to new possibilities, growth, and self-exploration. By embracing the unknown, we embark on a path of discovery and invite the magic of uncertainty into our lives.

Letting Go of Certainty:

Certainty provides a sense of security and stability, but it can also limit our potential for growth and transformation. Embracing the unknown requires us to let go of our attachment to knowing all the answers and having a predetermined outcome. It is a willingness to step into the realm of uncertainty and trust that the journey itself will reveal what we need to know.

Cultivating Curiosity:

Curiosity is the gateway to embracing the unknown. By cultivating a sense of wonder and fascination, we become open to exploring new territories and possibilities. Instead of viewing the unknown as something to be feared, we approach it with curiosity, eager to discover what lies beyond our comfort zone. Curiosity allows us to engage with the world and ourselves in a playful and open-minded way.

Embracing Growth and Expansion:

Embracing the unknown is an invitation to step outside our comfort zone and expand our horizons. It is in the unknown that we encounter new experiences, perspectives, and challenges that foster personal growth. By willingly embracing the unknown, we create opportunities for self-exploration and the discovery of hidden strengths and passions.

Navigating Fear and Resistance:

Fear and resistance often accompany the unknown. It is natural to feel apprehensive or hesitant when faced with uncertainty. However, by acknowledging and embracing our fears, we can move through them and discover the courage within ourselves. It is through confronting and transcending our fears that we can truly embrace the unknown and experience its transformative power.

Trusting the Journey:

Trusting the journey is an essential aspect of embracing the unknown. It is the belief that life has a way of guiding us and providing what we need at the right time. Trusting the journey involves surrendering to the process and having faith in our own resilience and ability to navigate the unknown. It is a deep knowing that the unknown holds infinite possibilities for growth and self-discovery.

Embracing Serendipity:

Serendipitous moments and unexpected events often arise when we embrace the unknown. These seemingly random occurrences can lead to profound insights, connections, and opportunities. By remaining open and receptive to the synchronicities and serendipities that come our way, we allow the unknown to guide us toward new paths and experiences.

Embracing Self-Exploration:

The unknown is an invitation for self-exploration and self-discovery. It encourages us to question our beliefs, desires, and aspirations. Through self-reflection, introspection, and engaging in practices such as journaling, meditation, or creative expression, we can deepen our understanding of ourselves and uncover hidden aspects of our being. Embracing the unknown is an act of self-empowerment and self-awareness.

Finding Comfort in Uncertainty:

While the unknown may initially feel uncomfortable, it is within this space of uncertainty that we can find true freedom and authenticity. By embracing the unknown, we liberate ourselves from the constraints of societal expectations and conditioning. We give ourselves permission to explore our passions, follow our intuition, and create a life that aligns with our true selves.

Conclusion:

Embracing the unknown is a courageous and transformative step on the journey of self-discovery. It requires us to let go of certainty, cultivate curiosity, and navigate fear and resistance. By trusting the journey, embracing serendipity, and engaging in self-exploration, we open ourselves to new possibilities, growth, and self-understanding. Embracing the unknown is not about seeking a destination but rather about immersing ourselves in the process of self-discovery and allowing ourselves to be shaped by the journey.

Embracing the unknown invites us to break free from the confines of our comfort zone and venture into uncharted territory. It is in these unexplored realms that we encounter new experiences, perspectives, and opportunities for personal and spiritual growth. By embracing the unknown, we challenge ourselves to expand our limits, face our fears, and tap into our untapped potential.

The unknown holds the potential for profound transformation. It is a space where we can let go of old patterns, beliefs, and limitations that no longer serve us. It is an invitation to explore different aspects of ourselves and discover hidden strengths, passions, and talents. Embracing the unknown allows us to evolve and become more authentic versions of ourselves.

Embracing the unknown also teaches us valuable life skills. It cultivates resilience as we learn to navigate uncertainty and adapt to changing circumstances. It strengthens our ability to think creatively and problem-solve as we encounter new challenges along the way. Embracing the unknown fosters a growth mindset, where we view obstacles as opportunities for learning and growth.

Stepping Out of the Comfort Zone

In the journey of self-discovery, stepping out of our comfort zones is an essential and transformative step. It is through challenging ourselves and embracing discomfort that we expand our horizons, develop resilience, and tap into our hidden potential. Stepping out of the comfort zone allows us to break free from limitations and embark on a path of growth and self-discovery.

Recognizing the Comfort Zone: The comfort zone refers to a psychological state in which we feel safe, familiar, and at ease. It is a place where routines and familiarity prevail, but personal growth and transformation are limited. Recognizing our comfort zones is the first step in understanding the areas of our lives that may benefit from exploration and expansion.

Embracing Discomfort: Stepping out of the comfort zone requires us to embrace discomfort and willingly confront the unknown. It means acknowledging that growth often occurs outside of our familiar boundaries. By embracing discomfort, we open ourselves up to new experiences, challenges, and opportunities for self-discovery.

Setting Realistic Goals: Setting realistic goals can help us navigate the process of stepping out of our comfort zones. By breaking down our aspirations into smaller, achievable steps, we can gradually expand our comfort zones without overwhelming ourselves. Setting realistic goals allows us to build momentum and confidence as we make progress towards our larger objectives.

Taking Calculated Risks: Taking calculated risks is a key element of stepping out of the comfort zone. It involves weighing the potential rewards against the potential consequences and making informed decisions. By taking calculated risks, we push ourselves beyond our perceived limits and open ourselves up to new possibilities and growth.

Embracing Failure as a Learning Opportunity: Failure is an inevitable part of stepping out of the comfort zone. However, rather than seeing failure as a setback, we can choose to view it as a valuable learning opportunity. Embracing failure allows us to grow, learn from our mistakes, and develop resilience. It teaches us that setbacks are not indicative of our worth but rather stepping stones on the path to success.

Seeking Support and Encouragement: Stepping out of the comfort zone can be challenging, and it is essential to seek support and encouragement along the way. Surrounding ourselves with individuals who believe in our potential and provide constructive feedback can bolster our confidence and motivate us to continue taking courageous steps forward. Seeking support from mentors, coaches, or like-minded individuals can provide guidance and accountability.

Cultivating a Growth Mindset: A growth mindset is crucial when stepping out of the comfort zone. It is the belief that our abilities and intelligence can be developed through dedication and effort. By cultivating a growth mindset, we approach challenges as opportunities for growth rather than obstacles. This mindset allows us to embrace the unknown and persist in the face of setbacks or obstacles.

Celebrating Progress: Celebrating progress, no matter how small, is important when stepping out of the comfort zone. Recognizing and acknowledging our achievements along the way boosts our motivation and self-confidence. By celebrating progress, we reinforce the positive impact of our efforts and encourage ourselves to continue pushing beyond our comfort zones.

Stepping out of the comfort zone is an integral part of the journey of self-discovery. By embracing discomfort, setting realistic goals, taking calculated risks, and cultivating a growth mindset, we expand our horizons and tap into our hidden potential. Through seeking support, embracing failure, and celebrating progress, we navigate the challenges and discover the transformative power of stepping outside our comfort zones.

Cultivating a Growth Mindset

In the journey of self-discovery, cultivating a growth mindset is a fundamental mindset shift that propels us forward. It is the belief that our abilities and intelligence can be developed through dedication and effort. A growth mindset allows us to overcome self-limiting beliefs, embrace challenges as opportunities for growth, and unleash our full potential. This chapter explores the power of a growth mindset and provides practical strategies for cultivating it.

Understanding Fixed and Growth Mindsets: A fixed mindset is the belief that our abilities and intelligence are fixed traits that cannot be changed. It leads to a fear of failure, avoidance of challenges, and a tendency to give up easily. On the other hand, a growth mindset is the belief that our abilities can be developed through effort, learning, and perseverance. It fosters resilience, a love for learning, and a willingness to embrace challenges.

Challenging Self-Limiting Beliefs: Cultivating a growth mindset re-quires challenging and reframing self-limiting beliefs. By questioning our assumptions about our abilities and potential, we can break free from the constraints of a fixed mindset. Recognize that abilities can be developed and improved with practice and effort, and that failures and setbacks are opportunities for learning and growth.

Embracing Challenges and Persistence: A growth mindset embraces challenges as opportunities for growth and development. Rather than avoiding difficulties, we seek them out to stretch our capabilities. Embracing challenges involves setting goals that push us outside our comfort zones, maintaining a positive attitude in the face of obstacles, and persisting even when the going gets tough.

Viewing Failure as a Stepping Stone: Failure is an inevitable part of any journey of self-discovery. In cultivating a growth mindset, we reframe failure as a stepping stone toward success. Rather than seeing failure as a reflection of our abilities, we view it as an opportunity to learn, adapt, and improve. By embracing failure, we become more resilient and develop a deeper understanding of ourselves.

Cultivating a Love for Learning: A growth mindset fosters a love for learning and continuous improvement. Embrace a lifelong learning mentality and seek out new knowledge and experiences. Recognize that learning is not limited to formal education but can occur through various avenues, such as reading, engaging in new activities, and seeking feedback from others.

Adopting a Positive Self-Talk: Our inner dialogue has a significant impact on our mindset. Cultivate a positive self-talk by challenging negative self-perceptions and replacing them with affirming and empowering statements. Practice self-compassion and encourage yourself during times of difficulty. By nurturing a positive inner dialogue, we foster a growth mindset and support our self-discovery journey.

Seeking Feedback and Learning from Others: Feedback from others provides valuable insights and perspectives that can enhance our growth and self-discovery. Be open to receiving feedback and view it as an opportunity for growth rather than criticism. Seek out mentors, coaches, or trusted individuals who can provide constructive feedback and guidance along your journey.

Celebrating Effort and Progress: In cultivating a growth mindset, it is important to celebrate effort and progress, not just outcomes. Recognize and acknowledge your efforts, perseverance, and the steps you take toward your goals. By celebrating progress, no matter how small, you reinforce the value of growth and motivate yourself to continue pushing forward.

Cultivating a growth mindset is a transformative shift that empowers us to embrace challenges, view failure as a stepping stone, and develop a love for learning. By challenging self-limiting beliefs, adopting a positive self-talk, seeking feedback, and celebrating effort and progress, we nourish a growth mindset that fuels our journey of self-discovery. Through the power of a growth mindset, we unlock our full potential and embark on a path of continuous growth and self-discovery.

Seizing Opportunities for Personal Growth

Life is a constant source of opportunities for personal growth and self-discovery. It is through actively seizing these opportunities that we can accelerate our journey of self-discovery and unlock our full potential. This chapter explores how to recognize and embrace opportunities for personal growth, whether they come in the form of challenges, new experiences, or relationships.

Embracing Challenges as Opportunities: Challenges often serve as catalysts for personal growth. Rather than shying away from challenges, embrace them as opportunities to learn, develop new skills, and expand your comfort zone. Challenges push us beyond our limits, helping us discover our strengths and develop resilience. By reframing challenges as growth opportunities, we cultivate a mindset that welcomes and seeks out such experiences.

Embracing New Experiences: New experiences provide fertile ground for personal growth. Stepping out of familiar routines and comfort zones allows us to broaden our perspectives, gain new insights, and discover hidden passions and talents. Embrace opportunities to try new activities, explore different cultures, or learn new skills. Each new experience presents a chance to learn more about ourselves and deepen our self-discovery.

Nurturing Relationships and Connections: Relationships can be profound catalysts for personal growth. Surround yourself with individuals who inspire, challenge, and support you. Seek out mentors, friends, or communities that foster personal growth and provide a safe space for exploration and self-expression. Engage in meaningful conversations, listen to different viewpoints, and learn from the experiences of others. By nurturing relationships, we create a fertile ground for personal growth and self-discovery.

Stepping Into the Unknown: The unknown holds immense potential for personal growth. Embrace uncertainty and step outside of your comfort zone. Take calculated risks and explore uncharted territories. This could involve pursuing a new career, traveling to unfamiliar places, or embracing new roles and responsibilities. By venturing into the unknown, we challenge ourselves, discover hidden strengths, and expand our sense of what is possible.

Learning from Setbacks and Failures: Setbacks and failures are invaluable opportunities for personal growth and self-reflection. Embrace them as stepping stones rather than roadblocks. When faced with setbacks, take time to reflect on the lessons learned, identify areas for improvement, and adjust your approach. By reframing setbacks as learning experiences, we develop resilience and acquire wisdom that propels us forward.

Seeking Personal Development Resources: Personal development resources such as books, courses, workshops, and online platforms offer a wealth of knowledge and tools for self-discovery. Seek out resources that align with your interests, goals, and values. Engage in continuous learning and self-reflection to deepen your understanding of yourself and expand your personal growth journey.

Setting Goals for Personal Growth: Goal setting provides direction and focus for personal growth. Set specific, achievable goals that align with your values and aspirations. Break them down into actionable steps and track your progress along the way. Setting goals helps you stay motivated, accountable, and intentional in your personal growth journey.

Embracing Lifelong Learning: Embrace a mindset of lifelong learning and continuous improvement. Be open to new ideas, perspectives, and feedback. Engage in self-reflection and self-assessment to identify areas for growth and development. By committing to lifelong learning, we foster personal growth that transcends specific goals or achievements.

Seizing opportunities for personal growth is a conscious choice that propels us on our journey of self-discovery. By embracing challenges, new experiences, nurturing relationships, stepping into the unknown, learning from setbacks, seeking resources, setting goals, and embracing lifelong learning, we actively cultivate personal growth. Through this proactive approach, we accelerate our self-discovery and unleash our full potential. Seize the opportunities that come your way and embrace them as invitations for personal growth and self-discovery.

The Power of Intention and Setting Goals

Intention and goal setting serve as powerful tools in our journey of self-discovery. They provide a roadmap that guides our actions and helps us align with our authentic selves. This chapter explores the transformative power of intention and effective goal-setting strategies.

Understanding Intention: Intention is the conscious choice to align our thoughts, emotions, and actions with our deepest desires and values. It is the guiding force that directs our energy and attention towards what truly matters to us. By setting clear intentions, we create a focused mindset and cultivate a sense of purpose in our self-discovery journey.

Clarifying Your Intentions: Take time to reflect on what truly matters to you and what you aspire to achieve in your self-discovery journey. Clarify your values, passions, and the areas of growth and development you wish to explore. Write down your intentions in a concise and meaningful way, capturing the essence of what you want to manifest in your life.

Setting Meaningful Goals: Goals provide direction and purpose in our self-discovery journey. When setting goals, ensure they are specific, measurable, attainable, relevant, and time-bound (SMART). Break down larger goals into smaller, actionable steps that are manageable and align with your intentions. This approach enables you to track your progress and stay motivated along the way.

Aligning Goals with Your Authentic Self: Ensure that your goals align with your authentic self and values. Reflect on whether each goal resonates with your true desires and aspirations or if it stems from external expectations. Aligning goals with your authentic self fosters a sense of fulfillment and supports your overall well-being.

Visualizing Success: Visualization is a powerful tool for goal achievement. Take time to visualize yourself successfully accomplishing your goals. Engage your senses and immerse yourself in the experience. This practice helps create a clear mental image of your desired outcomes, enhances motivation, and aligns your subconscious mind with your conscious intentions.

Creating an Action Plan: An action plan provides a roadmap for achieving your goals. Break down your goals into actionable steps and create a timeline for completion. Identify resources, skills, or support you may need along the way. Regularly review and adjust your action plan as needed to ensure it remains aligned with your intentions and goals.

Tracking Progress and Celebrating Milestones: Regularly track your progress toward your goals. This allows you to celebrate milestones, recognize your accomplishments, and stay motivated. Use tools such as journals, calendars, or progress trackers to monitor your journey. Celebrate each step forward, no matter how small, as it represents progress in your self-discovery.

Staying Flexible and Adapting: While setting goals is important, it is equally crucial to remain flexible and adaptable. Recognize that the journey of self-discovery may bring unexpected opportunities or challenges. Be open to adjusting your goals and intentions as you gain new insights and experiences along the way. Embrace the evolving nature of your journey and allow space for growth and exploration.

Revisiting and Reflecting on Goals: Regularly revisit and reflect on your goals and intentions. Are they still aligned with your authentic self? Have your priorities or aspirations shifted? Adjust and refine your goals as needed to ensure they continue to support your self-discovery journey. Reflection allows for self-awareness and course correction, promoting continuous growth and evolution.

Intention and goal setting provide a transformative framework for our journey of self-discovery. By clarifying our intentions, setting meaningful goals, visualizing success, creating action plans, tracking progress, and staying flexible, we empower ourselves to align our actions with our authentic selves. Embrace the power of intention and goal setting as catalysts for self-discovery and personal transformation. Intention and goal setting serve as powerful tools on our journey of self-discovery. They provide us with a clear direction and purpose, guiding our actions and choices in alignment with our authentic selves. By setting intentions, we declare our heartfelt desires and aspirations, and by setting goals, we create tangible milestones to work towards.

Creating a Vision for Self-Discovery

A vision acts as a guiding light, illuminating our path and inspiring us on our journey of self-discovery. By envisioning our ideal selves and lives, we ignite a sense of purpose and motivation. This chapter explores the process of creating a vision for self-discovery and harnessing its transformative power.

Understanding the Power of Vision: A vision is a vivid, compelling image of the future we desire to create for ourselves. It goes beyond mere goals and encompasses the essence of who we want to be and how we want to live. By creating a vision, we tap into our inner desires and aspirations, providing a sense of direction and inspiration.

Reflecting on Your Authentic Self: To create a meaningful vision, it is essential to reflect on your authentic self. Take time to explore your values, passions, strengths, and dreams. What brings you joy and fulfillment? What legacy do you want to leave behind? By connecting with your authentic self, you lay the foundation for a vision that aligns with your truest aspirations.

Imagining Your Ideal Life: Close your eyes and imagine your ideal life. Visualize yourself living authentically, in alignment with your values and passions. Picture the various aspects of your life, such as relationships, career, health, personal growth, and contribution to the world. Allow yourself to dream without limitations or judgments, letting your imagination run wild.

Clarifying Your Vision: Once you have a sense of your ideal life, clarify your vision by putting it into words. Write a vision statement that encapsulates the essence of your desired future. Be specific and vivid in describing the life you envision, using sensory details to bring it to life. Make your vision statement personal, heartfelt, and inspiring.

Making Your Vision Compelling: To make your vision compelling, connect it to your deepest desires and motivations. Reflect on why this vision is meaningful to you. How does it align with your values and purpose? How will it bring you joy, fulfillment, and a sense of purpose? By infusing your vision with emotional significance, you cultivate a deep sense of commitment and determination.

Visualizing Your Vision: Visualization is a powerful tool to reinforce your vision. Set aside regular time to visualize yourself living your vision. Close your eyes and immerse yourself in the experience, engaging your senses and emotions. Imagine the sights, sounds, and feelings associated with your ideal life. This practice strengthens your connection to your vision and empowers you to manifest it in reality.

Integrating Your Vision into Daily Life: Integrate your vision into your daily life by aligning your actions with it. Break down your vision into actionable steps and set goals that move you closer to its real-ization. Infuse your routines, habits, and decisions with the values and aspirations of your vision. By consciously living in alignment with your vision, you create momentum and bring it closer to reality.

Revisiting and Evolving Your Vision: As you grow and evolve, your vision may also evolve. Regularly revisit and reflect on your vision to ensure it remains aligned with your authentic self. Adjust and refine it as needed to accommodate new insights, aspirations, or changes in your life circumstances. Allow your vision to evolve as you do, embracing the continuous process of self-discovery.

Sharing and Enlisting Support: Share your vision with trusted indi-viduals who can support and encourage you on your journey. Seek out like-minded communities or mentors who resonate with your vision and can offer guidance. Surrounding yourself with a supportive net-work strengthens your commitment and provides accountability and encouragement.

Creating a vision for self-discovery is a powerful act of self-expression and manifestation. By envisioning our ideal selves and lives, we infuse our journey with purpose and inspiration. Through reflection, visual-ization goal setting, and daily alignment with our vision, we actively shape our path of self-discovery.

Embracing Imperfections and Embracing Growth

In our journey of self-discovery, it is important to recognize and embrace our imperfections. No one is perfect, and our imperfections contribute to our individuality and growth. Embracing imperfections requires a shift in perspective, from viewing them as shortcomings to seeing them as opportunities for learning and development.

When we accept our imperfections, we free ourselves from the burden of unrealistic expectations and self-judgment. We recognize that making mistakes, facing challenges, and experiencing setbacks are natural parts of the learning process. Instead of dwelling on our perceived flaws, we can focus on self-improvement and personal growth.

Embracing imperfections also involves practicing self-compassion. We extend kindness, understanding, and forgiveness to ourselves when we fall short or make mistakes. Rather than being critical and harsh, we treat ourselves with the same compassion and empathy we would offer to a friend facing similar challenges. Self-compassion allows us to cultivate a nurturing and supportive relationship with ourselves, fostering an environment conducive to growth and self-discovery.

Imperfections can serve as powerful catalysts for growth. They highlight areas where we have room for improvement, skills we can develop, or beliefs we can challenge. By embracing imperfections, we open ourselves to growth opportunities and actively seek ways to enhance our abilities, expand our knowledge, and evolve as individuals.

A growth-oriented mindset is key to embracing imperfections and fostering personal growth. Instead of viewing our abilities and qualities as fixed traits, we believe in our capacity to learn, adapt, and improve. We approach challenges with a curiosity and willingness to learn from both successes and failures. Embracing imperfections becomes an empowering process that propels us forward on our journey of self-discovery.

It is important to remember that embracing imperfections does not mean settling for mediocrity or complacency. It is about acknowledging and accepting our current state while actively working towards self-improvement and growth. Embracing imperfections does not imply a lack of ambition or aspiration; rather, it is an acknowledgment that growth and progress are ongoing and that perfection is an unattainable ideal.

By embracing imperfections and viewing them as opportunities for growth, we create an environment that fosters self-acceptance, resilience, and personal development. We learn to celebrate our strengths, appreciate our uniqueness, and cultivate a sense of authenticity. Through this process, we discover that imperfections are not obstacles but stepping stones on our path of self-discovery and fulfillment.

Embodying Courage and Resilience

On the path of self-discovery, embodying courage and resilience is essential. Courage allows us to face our fears, step outside our comfort zones, and embrace the unknown. Resilience empowers us to bounce back from setbacks, adapt to challenges, and persevere in the face of adversity. Together, these qualities provide the inner strength and determination needed to navigate the twists and turns of our journey.

Cultivating courage begins with acknowledging our fears and understanding that they often indicate areas of growth and expansion. It requires a willingness to confront and overcome our fears, even when it feels uncomfortable or uncertain. By taking small steps outside our comfort zones, we gradually build our courage muscle and expand our capacity for personal growth.

One way to cultivate courage is by reframing failure as a stepping stone to success. Embrace the mindset that failure is not a reflection of our worth or abilities, but rather an opportunity to learn, grow, and improve. By reframing failure as feedback and using it as a catalyst for growth, we can approach challenges with resilience and a willingness to try again.

Resilience is the ability to bounce back from setbacks and adapt to changing circumstances. It involves developing a mindset that embraces challenges as opportunities for growth and views setbacks as temporary obstacles on the path to success. Resilience is nurtured through self-care practices that support our physical, emotional, and mental well-being. Taking care of ourselves allows us to recharge, maintain balance, and better cope with adversity.

Building resilience also involves cultivating a positive mindset and reframing negative thoughts. Instead of dwelling on limitations or failures, focus on strengths, accomplishments, and possibilities. By shifting our perspective and embracing an optimistic outlook, we build resilience and increase our ability to overcome challenges.

Surrounding ourselves with a supportive network is another key aspect of cultivating resilience. Connecting with like-minded individuals who understand and support our journey can provide valuable encouragement, guidance, and perspective. Seek out mentors, friends, or communities that foster resilience and provide a safe space for vulnerability and growth.

Embodying courage and resilience requires perseverance and a growth-oriented mindset. It involves embracing discomfort, facing challenges head-on, and trusting in our abilities to navigate the unknown. As we embody these qualities, we not only strengthen our resilience and courage but also inspire others to do the same.

Remember that embodying courage and resilience is not about being fearless or invulnerable. It is about acknowledging our fears, setbacks, and vulnerabilities while choosing to move forward with determination, adaptability, and a belief in our ability to grow. By embodying courage and resilience, we cultivate the inner strength needed to overcome obstacles, embrace our authenticity, and continue on our transformative journey of self-discovery.

Navigating Resistance and Obstacles

On the journey of self-discovery, we often encounter resistance and obstacles that can hinder our progress. These roadblocks may come from within ourselves, such as self-doubt, fear, or limiting beliefs, or they may manifest externally through societal expectations, naysayers, or challenging circumstances. Navigating resistance and obstacles requires resilience, determination, and a mindset that embraces challenges as opportunities for growth.

One of the first steps in navigating resistance is to recognize and acknowledge its presence. Self-awareness is key to understanding the underlying causes of resistance and identifying the thoughts, emotions, or behaviors that may be holding us back. By shining a light on our internal resistance, we gain clarity and insight into the areas that require attention and growth.

Next, it is important to reframe obstacles as opportunities for growth. Instead of seeing challenges as insurmountable barriers, view them as stepping stones on the path to self-discovery. Embrace the mindset that every obstacle presents an opportunity for learning, personal development, and building resilience. By shifting our perspective, we can turn adversity into a catalyst for transformation.

Developing strategies to overcome resistance is another crucial aspect of navigating obstacles. This may involve breaking down larger goals into smaller, manageable steps, creating action plans, and setting realistic expectations. By focusing on incremental progress, we build momentum and gain confidence in our ability to overcome challenges. It is also helpful to cultivate a positive and growth-oriented mindset, fostering self-belief and an unwavering determination to push through resistance.

Seeking support is an essential part of navigating obstacles. Reach out to trusted friends, mentors, or support groups who can provide guidance, encouragement, and accountability. Sharing our challenges and aspirations with others who have experienced similar obstacles can provide valuable insights and a sense of camaraderie. Collaborating with others who are on a similar path can also offer new perspectives and strategies for overcoming resistance.

Self-care practices play a vital role in navigating resistance and obstacles. Taking care of our physical, emotional, and mental well-being strengthens our resilience and equips us to face challenges head-on. Prioritize activities that replenish your energy, reduce stress, and foster self-compassion. This may include exercise, meditation, spending time in nature, journaling, or engaging in creative outlets.

It is important to remember that navigating resistance and obstacles is not a linear process. There will be ups and downs, moments of progress and setbacks. Embrace the journey as a whole, recognizing that each step, including the challenges and detours, contributes to your growth and self-discovery. Stay patient and kind to yourself, celebrating even the smallest victories along the way.

Ultimately, navigating resistance and obstacles is an opportunity for personal growth and self-transformation. By reframing challenges, developing strategies, seeking support, and prioritizing self-care, we can navigate resistance with resilience, determination, and a deep commitment to our journey of self-discovery. Embrace the challenges as opportunities for growth, and let your unwavering determination lead you to new levels of authenticity and fulfillment.

Harnessing the Power of Commitment

Commitment is the anchor that keeps us grounded on our journey of self-discovery. It is the conscious decision to prioritize our personal growth and transformation, and the dedication to stay committed even when faced with obstacles and setbacks. Harnessing the power of commitment empowers us to overcome challenges, maintain focus, and make consistent progress towards our authentic selves.

One of the first steps in harnessing the power of commitment is to clarify our purpose and values. Take time to reflect on what truly matters to you and what you aspire to become. Define your core values and align your commitment with them. When our commitment is rooted in our deepest values and aspirations, it becomes more meaningful and sustainable.

Setting clear and achievable goals is another important aspect of commitment. Break down your journey of self-discovery into smaller, actionable goals that you can work towards. These goals should be specific, measurable, attainable, relevant, and time-bound (SMART goals). By having a clear roadmap and measurable milestones, you can track your progress and stay motivated.

Maintaining accountability is crucial in sustaining commitment. Find an accountability partner or join a supportive community that shares similar goals and values. Regular check-ins, sharing progress, and discussing challenges with others can provide encouragement and help you stay on track. Additionally, hold yourself accountable by regularly reviewing your goals, reflecting on your progress, and making adjustments as needed.

Cultivating discipline and perseverance is essential when facing obstacles and setbacks. Commitment requires consistent effort and resilience. Practice self-discipline by creating daily habits and routines that support your growth. Embrace challenges as opportunities for learning and growth, rather than as deterrents. Develop a mindset that sees setbacks as temporary and use them as stepping stones for progress.

Self-care is an important component of maintaining commitment. Take care of your physical, emotional, and mental well-being to sustain your energy and motivation. Prioritize activities that recharge and nourish you, such as exercise, healthy eating, quality sleep, and engaging in activities that bring you joy. Remember that self-care is not selfish; it is necessary to sustain your commitment and show up fully in your journey.

Revisit your commitment regularly and make adjustments as needed. As you evolve and grow, your goals and aspirations may change. It is important to periodically reassess your commitment and make necessary adjustments to stay aligned with your authentic self. This flexibility allows you to adapt to new insights and experiences along the way.

Finally, celebrate milestones and acknowledge your progress. Recognize and celebrate even the smallest victories on your journey. Each step forward, no matter how small, is an achievement worth acknowledging. Celebrating milestones boosts motivation, reinforces commitment, and encourages you to keep moving forward.

In harnessing the power of commitment, remember that it is a conscious choice you make every day. It is normal to face challenges and moments of doubt, but staying committed means persevering through those moments and trusting in the process of self-discovery. By nurturing your commitment and staying dedicated to your growth, you empower yourself to unlock your true potential and live a fulfilling and authentic life.

Embracing the Journey, Not Just the Destination

Embracing the journey of self-discovery is about savoring each moment, being fully present, and finding joy in the process. It's easy to become fixated on reaching a specific destination or achieving certain outcomes, but true fulfillment comes from immersing ourselves in the present moment and embracing the growth and learning that happens along the way.

One way to embrace the journey is by practicing mindfulness. Mindfulness involves intentionally paying attention to the present moment, without judgment or attachment. By cultivating mindfulness, we can fully engage with our experiences, emotions, and thoughts as they arise. This allows us to deepen our self-awareness, appreciate the small moments of growth, and find joy in the process of self-discovery.

Another aspect of embracing the journey is practicing gratitude. Taking time to reflect on and express gratitude for the lessons, experiences, and people we encounter on our journey can shift our perspective and help us find joy in even the smallest things. Gratitude fosters a sense of appreciation for the present moment and cultivates a positive mindset that enhances our overall well-being.

Embracing the journey also means being open to detours and unexpected experiences. Life is full of surprises and unplanned moments that often lead to profound self-discovery. By remaining open and adaptable, we allow ourselves to explore new paths, learn from different perspectives, and uncover hidden aspects of ourselves. Embracing the unexpected can lead to profound personal growth and a deeper understanding of who we truly are.

Additionally, it's important to acknowledge and learn from the challenges and setbacks we encounter along the journey. They provide valuable opportunities for growth, resilience, and self-reflection. By reframing obstacles as opportunities and viewing setbacks as stepping stones, we can approach them with curiosity and embrace the lessons they offer. Each challenge becomes an opportunity to develop new skills, expand our perspectives, and cultivate inner strength.

Finding joy in the process of self-discovery also involves finding balance and taking care of ourselves along the way. It's important to prioritize self-care, nourish our bodies and minds, and create space for rest and rejuvenation. When we take care of ourselves, we enhance our capacity for growth, creativity, and resilience. Self-care allows us to approach the journey with vitality and enthusiasm.

Lastly, remember that self-discovery is a lifelong journey. Embracing the journey means understanding that personal growth is a continuous process that unfolds over time. It's not about reaching a final destination but rather about embracing the ever-evolving nature of our authentic selves. Embrace the beauty of ongoing exploration, learning, and self-evolution, knowing that the journey itself holds infinite possibilities.

By embracing the journey of self-discovery, we deepen our self-awareness, cultivate a sense of joy and gratitude, and open ourselves up to transformative experiences. Each moment becomes an opportunity for growth and a chance to connect with our authentic selves. So, let go of the attachment to outcomes and embrace the richness of the journey, for it is in the journey that we truly find ourselves.

Finding Inspiration in Others' Stories

Finding inspiration in others' stories is a powerful way to gain insights, learn from their experiences, and find guidance on our own journey of self-discovery. The stories of others can provide us with inspiration, encouragement, and a sense of connection as we navigate our own path. Here are some ways to find inspiration in others' stories and apply their wisdom to our own journey:

Seek out diverse stories: Look for stories that resonate with your interests, values, and aspirations. Explore different mediums such as books, biographies, documentaries, podcasts, or online platforms that share personal narratives and experiences. Seek out stories from a diverse range of backgrounds and perspectives to gain a broader understanding of the human experience.

Identify common themes: As you engage with others' stories, pay attention to the common themes, challenges, and triumphs that emerge. Reflect on how these resonate with your own journey and the insights they offer. Look for patterns, lessons, and wisdom that can be applied to your own self-discovery process.

Extract lessons and inspiration: Take the time to reflect on the key lessons and insights from the stories you encounter. What can you learn from the struggles, triumphs, and growth of others? How can their experiences inform your own choices, mindset, and actions? Extract the wisdom that resonates with you and integrate it into your own journey.

Engage in dialogue: Engage in discussions with others who have shared similar experiences or have knowledge in areas that interest you. Share your own journey and listen to theirs. Through dialogue, you can gain new perspectives, receive guidance, and form connections that support your personal growth.

Apply lessons to your own life: Once you have identified valuable lessons and insights from others' stories, consider how you can apply them to your own life. Reflect on how you can integrate these lessons into your mindset, choices, and actions. Experiment with new approaches and strategies inspired by the stories you've encountered, and observe how they impact your own self-discovery journey.

Be discerning and authentic: While finding inspiration in others' stories is valuable, it's important to remain true to your own unique journey. Recognize that each person's path is individual and that what works for others may not necessarily work for you. Be discerning in the lessons you choose to apply and ensure they align with your own values, aspirations, and circumstances.

Share your own story: As you embark on your journey of self-discovery, consider sharing your own story with others. By sharing your experiences, insights, and growth, you not only contribute to the collective wisdom but also inspire and support others on their own paths. Your story has the power to impact and connect with others in profound ways.

Remember that finding inspiration in others' stories is not about comparison or trying to replicate their experiences. Instead, it is about seeking guidance, broadening your perspective, and drawing wisdom that resonates with your own journey. By integrating the lessons and inspiration you find, you can navigate your path with greater clarity, resilience, and authenticity.

Celebrating Milestones and Progress

Celebrating milestones and progress is a vital practice in the journey of self-discovery. It allows us to acknowledge our growth, honor our efforts, and reinforce our commitment to personal development. By celebrating milestones, we cultivate a positive mindset and maintain motivation along our path. Here are some suggestions for honoring milestones and creating meaningful rituals to mark our progress:

Set meaningful milestones: Define specific milestones that align with your goals and aspirations. Break down your journey into smaller, achievable steps, and assign milestones to each stage of your progress. These milestones can be personal achievements, overcoming challenges, acquiring new skills, or reaching significant turning points in your self-discovery process.

Reflect on achievements: Regularly reflect on your accomplishments and progress. Take time to appreciate how far you have come and the growth you have experienced. Celebrate both the big milestones and the small victories, as every step forward is significant.

Create a milestone journal: Maintain a milestone journal to record and document your achievements. Write down your reflections, insights, and lessons learned along the way. Capture the moments of breakthroughs, challenges overcome, and personal transformations. Reviewing your milestone journal can serve as a powerful reminder of your progress and the obstacles you have conquered.

Share your milestones with others: Share your milestones and progress with trusted friends, family, or a supportive community. By sharing your journey with others, you invite encouragement, validation, and celebration. This external recognition can reinforce your sense of accomplishment and provide valuable support as you continue on your path.

Create meaningful rituals: Develop meaningful rituals to commemorate your milestones. These rituals can take various forms, such as lighting a candle, writing a gratitude letter to yourself, engaging in a personal reflection practice, or treating yourself to a special activity or experience. Choose rituals that resonate with you and align with your values, providing a sense of significance and meaning.

Cultivate a positive mindset: Celebrating milestones and progress is an opportunity to cultivate a positive mindset. Embrace a mindset of gratitude, focusing on the progress you have made rather than comparing yourself to others. Recognize that growth is a continuous process, and each milestone is a testament to your dedication and commitment to self-discovery.

Set new goals and aspirations: As you celebrate your milestones, use them as stepping stones to set new goals and aspirations. Reflect on what you have learned, the insights gained, and how you want to continue growing. Set new intentions and create a roadmap for the next phase of your self-discovery journey.

Practice self-care: Celebrating milestones also involves taking care of yourself. Engage in self-care activities that replenish your energy and nourish your well-being. It could be spending time in nature, practicing mindfulness or meditation, engaging in creative pursuits, or simply taking a break to rest and rejuvenate. Self-care supports your continued growth and enables you to approach new milestones with clarity and vitality.

Remember that celebrating milestones is not about comparison or seeking external validation. It is about acknowledging your progress, honoring your efforts, and nurturing a positive mindset. By regularly celebrating your milestones and progress, you reinforce your commitment to self-discovery and inspire yourself to continue the journey with enthusiasm and resilience. From meeting mysterious mentors to recognizing synchronicities, stepping out of our comfort zones, and cultivating a growth mindset, each step contributes to our journey of self-discovery. By embracing the unknown, seizing opportunities, setting intentions, and navigating obstacles, we develop resilience and courage. By celebrating milestones and finding inspiration in others' stories, we stay motivated and connected to the transformative power of the journey.

3

Exploring the Depths

In the journey of self-discovery, delving into the depths of our being is essential. This chapter focuses on exploring various aspects of ourselves and gaining a deeper understanding of who we are. By uncovering our core values, passions, strengths, and desires, we pave the way for living an authentic and fulfilling life. Here are the key sections covered in this chapter:

Uncovering Core Values and Beliefs: The Journey to Self-Alignment

In the quest for self-discovery, one of the fundamental aspects is uncovering our core values and beliefs. These underlying principles and beliefs serve as a compass, guiding our actions, decisions, and interactions with the world. When we align our lives with our core values, we experience a profound sense of clarity, purpose, and fulfillment.

Our core values are the deeply held beliefs and principles that shape who we are and how we show up in the world. They reflect what we consider to be important, meaningful, and non-negotiable in our lives. Core values vary from person to person, as they are influenced by our unique experiences, cultural backgrounds, upbringing, and personal philosophies. Some common examples of core values include integrity, compassion, honesty, growth, family, authenticity, justice, freedom, and love.

Discovering and understanding our core values is a transformative journey that requires introspection, self-reflection, and self-awareness. It involves peeling back the layers of societal conditioning, external expectations, and the influence of others to uncover our own deeply held beliefs and principles. When we engage in this process, we gain a deeper understanding of ourselves, our motivations, and the driving forces behind our choices and actions.

One way to begin uncovering our core values is to reflect on the experiences, people, and moments that have had a significant impact on our lives. Consider the times when you felt the most alive, fulfilled, and aligned with your true self. What values were at play during those moments? What principles were guiding your thoughts, decisions, and actions? By examining these experiences, we can start to identify the core values that were present and learn more about what truly matters to us.

Another approach to uncovering core values is to examine the aspects of life that evoke strong emotional responses within us. Pay attention to the situations, events, and behaviors that trigger intense feelings, whether positive or negative. These emotional reactions often point to the values that are being violated or upheld. For example, if you feel a deep sense of injustice when witnessing unfairness, it could indicate that fairness and justice are important core values for you.

Self-reflection exercises, such as journaling, can be powerful tools for uncovering core values. Set aside dedicated time to reflect on questions such as: What are the guiding principles that inform my decisions and actions? What qualities do I admire and aspire to embody? What principles do I consider non-negotiable in my personal and professional life? By writing freely and without judgment, you can tap into your inner wisdom and gain insights into your core values.

It's important to note that core values can evolve and change over time as we grow, learn, and gain new experiences. It's a dynamic process that requires ongoing self-awareness and reflection. Regularly reassessing and reaffirming our core values ensures that we stay true to ourselves and make choices that align with our authentic selves.

Once we have identified our core values, the next step is to align our lives and actions with them. Living in alignment with our values requires conscious intention and commitment. It means making choices that reflect our core values, even in the face of challenges or conflicting external pressures. It may involve setting boundaries, making difficult decisions, and having courageous conversations.

Aligning our lives with our core values brings a sense of integrity, congruence, and authenticity. It allows us to live with purpose and meaning, as our actions and choices are grounded in what truly matters to us. When we live in alignment with our values, we experience a deep sense of fulfillment and a greater sense of self-acceptance.

Uncovering our core values and beliefs is a profound journey of self-discovery and self-alignment. It requires deep introspection, and an honest exploration of our inner landscape. It invites us to question societal norms and expectations, and to listen to the wisdom that arises from within.

Identifying Passions and Interests: Nurturing the Flame Within

Passions and interests are the sparks that ignite our enthusiasm and bring us joy. They are the activities, hobbies, and pursuits that make us come alive and connect us to our authentic selves. Exploring and embracing our passions and interests is an integral part of the journey of self-discovery, as they provide a pathway to fulfillment and a deeper understanding of who we are.

Passions can manifest in various forms, ranging from creative endeavors to intellectual pursuits, physical activities, or areas of service to others. They are the activities that energize us, captivate our attention, and create a sense of flow where time seems to stand still. Engaging in activities aligned with our passions allows us to tap into our natural talents, creativity, and zest for life.

To identify your passions and interests, start by reflecting on the activities that have brought you joy and fulfillment throughout your life. Think back to moments when you felt a deep sense of engagement and enthusiasm. What were you doing? What made those experiences special? These reflections can help you identify recurring themes and patterns that point to your passions.

Consider both longstanding passions that have been with you for years, as well as those you may have recently discovered or developed an interest in. Our passions can evolve and change over time, and it's important to remain open to new experiences and interests that may ignite our enthusiasm.

Exploring different areas of interest is key to uncovering new passions. Be curious and open-minded, and allow yourself to try new things without preconceived judgments or expectations. Take classes, attend workshops, join groups, or simply dedicate time to experimenting with activities that pique your interest. Through exploration, you may stumble upon new passions that resonate deeply with your authentic self.

Pay attention to the activities that bring you a sense of joy, fulfillment, and purpose. Notice how your energy and enthusiasm are sparked when engaging in these activities. Reflect on the qualities and elements of these pursuits that resonate with you. What aspects of these activities make them meaningful and enjoyable? By identifying these patterns, you can gain insights into the underlying values, strengths, and interests that drive your passions.

It's important to give yourself permission to pursue your passions and make time for them in your life. Often, we may neglect our passions due to other responsibilities or the belief that they are merely hobbies with no practical value. However, honoring our passions is essential for our well-being and personal growth. By devoting time and energy to our passions, we nourish our souls and tap into our unique gifts and talents.

Don't be discouraged if your passions and interests differ from those around you or if they don't align with societal expectations. Embrace your unique passions, even if they seem unconventional or uncommon. Your passions are an expression of your authentic self, and they have the power to bring you immense joy, fulfillment, and a sense of purpose.

As you uncover and embrace your passions, consider how you can integrate them into your daily life. Find ways to incorporate your passions into your work, hobbies, relationships, or even community involvement. By infusing your life with activities that align with your passions, you create a sense of harmony and alignment that enhances your overall well-being.

Remember, the journey of self-discovery is an ongoing process, and your passions and interests may continue to evolve and change as you grow and learn. Stay open to new experiences and be willing to adapt your pursuits as you gain new insights about yourself. Embracing and nurturing your passions is a lifelong commitment to self-fulfillment and a deep connection with your authentic self.

Reconnecting with Childhood Dreams and Desires

Reconnecting with our childhood dreams and desires is a powerful exercise in self-discovery. Our early years are often filled with boundless imagination, uninhibited creativity, and a sense of wonder. Revisiting the dreams and desires we had as children can unlock hidden passions and provide a window into our authentic selves.

To reconnect with your childhood dreams, take time to reflect on your early memories and experiences. Think back to what brought you joy, excitement, and a sense of purpose during those formative years. What activities or pursuits captured your imagination? What did you aspire to become or achieve? Allow yourself to tap into the innocence and curiosity of your younger self and explore the dreams and desires that were most significant to you.

Engage in activities that reconnect you with the spirit of your childhood dreams. This could involve revisiting hobbies or interests you enjoyed as a child, such as painting, playing a musical instrument, or engaging in imaginative play. Allow yourself to experience the joy and wonder that these activities once brought you.

Consider how your childhood dreams may have influenced your present-day interests and ambitions. Reflect on the underlying themes or values that were present in your childhood dreams. Do they align with your current passions or aspirations? Are there elements from your childhood dreams that you can incorporate into your life today?

Journaling can be a helpful tool for exploring your childhood dreams and desires. Write freely about your memories, emotions, and reflections related to your early dreams. Consider the impact those dreams may have had on your life choices, and whether they still hold significance for you. Use this reflective process to gain insights into your authentic desires and how they can shape your present and future.

Engaging in conversations with trusted friends, family members, or mentors can also provide valuable insights. Share your reflections on your childhood dreams and desires and ask for their perspectives. They may offer fresh perspectives, observations, or memories that can shed light on aspects of yourself that you may have overlooked.

Remember that reconnecting with your childhood dreams is not about clinging to the exact aspirations you had as a child. It is about tapping into the essence of those dreams and understanding the underlying values, passions, and interests they represent. Use this process of reconnecting to uncover the authentic desires and aspirations that resonate with your present self.

As you reconnect with your childhood dreams and desires, be open to the possibility of rediscovering passions that may have been buried or neglected over the years. Embrace the sense of wonder, curiosity, and playfulness that characterized your childhood and allow it to guide you in exploring new avenues and possibilities.

Reconnecting with your childhood dreams and desires is a journey of self-discovery that can bring a renewed sense of purpose, joy, and alignment with your authentic self. By tapping into the dreams of your younger self, you can uncover the passions and aspirations that hold the key to living a fulfilling and meaningful life. Embrace this exploration with curiosity and openness, and allow the wisdom of your childhood dreams to shape your present and future endeavors.

Exploring Personal Strengths and Talents

Exploring our personal strengths and talents is a crucial aspect of self-discovery. Each of us possesses a unique set of abilities and qualities that can contribute to our personal growth, success, and overall well-being. By identifying and celebrating these strengths, we can harness our full potential and find fulfillment in our pursuits.

To begin exploring your personal strengths and talents, take time for self-reflection and introspection. Consider the activities, tasks, or areas in which you excel or find joy. What skills or abilities do you naturally possess? What comes easily to you? Reflect on moments when you have felt a sense of accomplishment, pride, or satisfaction in your achievements. These moments often indicate areas where your strengths lie.

Pay attention to the feedback and compliments you receive from others. Sometimes, others can see our strengths more clearly than we can ourselves. Take note of the qualities and abilities that others recognize and appreciate in you. Their observations can offer valuable insights into your unique strengths and talents.

Engage in self-assessment exercises or online assessments that can help you identify your strengths. These tools provide structured frameworks and questionnaires designed to uncover your innate abilities and qualities. They can serve as a starting point for deeper exploration and self-awareness.

Consider seeking feedback from trusted friends, family members, or mentors. Ask them about the qualities or strengths they see in you.

Their perspectives can offer different angles and shed light on aspects of yourself that you may not have fully recognized.

Embrace a growth mindset as you explore your strengths and talents. Recognize that strengths can be developed and refined through practice and dedication. Be open to the possibility of discovering new strengths or nurturing existing ones to a higher level of proficiency.

Once you have identified your strengths and talents, find ways to leverage them in your life. Seek opportunities that allow you to apply your strengths and bring them to the forefront. This could involve pursuing projects or activities that align with your strengths, seeking roles or careers that capitalize on your abilities, or even finding ways to incorporate your strengths into your daily life and relationships.

Celebrate and appreciate your strengths. Recognize that your unique qualities contribute to the tapestry of humanity. Embrace and own your strengths, and let go of any comparison or self-doubt. Embracing your strengths with confidence allows you to show up authentically and make meaningful contributions in your personal and professional spheres.

However, it is important to note that self-discovery is an ongoing process, and our strengths and talents may evolve and change over time. Be open to exploring new interests, skills, and areas of growth. Continually reassess and rediscover your strengths, and be willing to adapt and expand your understanding of what you are capable of.

Remember that the exploration of personal strengths and talents is not just about personal achievement or success but also about finding alignment and fulfillment. When we engage in activities that leverage our strengths, we often experience a sense of flow, meaning, and joy. By embracing and nurturing our strengths, we can live a more authentic and purposeful life.

In conclusion, exploring our personal strengths and talents is an integral part of the journey of self-discovery. By identifying and celebrating our unique abilities and qualities, we can tap into our full potential and find fulfillment in our pursuits. Embrace the process of self-exploration, and use your strengths to make a positive impact on yourself and the world around you.

Assessing Personal Preferences and Dislikes

Assessing our personal preferences and dislikes is an important aspect of self-discovery. Our preferences and dislikes are reflections of our unique tastes, values, and desires. By taking the time to reflect on what resonates with us and what doesn't, we gain valuable insights that can guide us in making choices that align with our authentic selves and lead to a more fulfilling life.

To begin the process of assessing your personal preferences and dislikes, set aside dedicated time for self-reflection. Create a calm and quiet space where you can explore your thoughts and feelings without distractions. Consider different areas of your life, such as work, relationships, hobbies, leisure activities, and lifestyle choices.

Reflect on the activities, experiences, and environments that bring you joy, satisfaction, and a sense of fulfillment. What do you genuinely enjoy doing in your free time? What type of work or tasks make you feel engaged and motivated? Are there particular environments or settings in which you feel most comfortable and at ease? Pay attention to the aspects that consistently resonate with you and bring a sense of alignment and authenticity.

On the other hand, reflect on the experiences, activities, or situations that you find draining, unfulfilling, or contrary to your values. What tasks or responsibilities do you often procrastinate or feel a lack of enthusiasm towards? Are there certain relationships or social dynamics that leave you feeling drained or unhappy? Are there specific environments or circumstances that trigger stress or discomfort? Take note of these dislikes as they provide valuable information about your boundaries, values, and areas where you may need to make adjustments.

Consider how your preferences and dislikes align with your values and aspirations. Do your preferences support your personal growth, well-being, and the fulfillment of your goals? Are your dislikes rooted in values or beliefs that are important to you? Reflect on any patterns or themes that emerge as you assess your preferences and dislikes. These patterns can provide valuable insights into your authentic self and the choices that will bring you the most satisfaction.

It can also be helpful to observe your emotional and physical responses to different situations and experiences. Pay attention to your gut feelings, intuitive reactions, and bodily sensations when engaging in activities or making choices. Our bodies often provide valuable cues that can help us discern what resonates with us and what doesn't. Notice when you feel a sense of excitement, enthusiasm, or alignment, as well as when you experience tension, discomfort, or a lack of energy.

Engage in experimentation and exploration. Try new activities, experiences, or environments that align with your preferences to further validate and refine your understanding of what resonates with you. Similarly, be open to revisiting dislikes and exploring them with a fresh perspective. Our preferences and dislikes can evolve and change over time, so it is important to stay curious and open to new possibilities.

Use the insights gained from assessing your preferences and dislikes to guide your decision-making process. Seek opportunities and make choices that align with your authentic self, values, and aspirations. This may involve making adjustments in your daily routines, career path, relationships, or lifestyle choices. By honoring your preferences and avoiding situations that consistently clash with your dislikes, you create a life that is more in tune with who you truly are.

Remember that self-discovery is a continual process, and our preferences and dislikes may evolve as we grow and change. Be patient and compassionate with yourself as you navigate this exploration. Embrace the journey of self-discovery with an open mind and heart, and trust that by aligning your choices with your authentic preferences, you will create a more fulfilling and meaningful life.

The Power of Self-Awareness

Self-awareness is a powerful tool that enables us to cultivate a deeper understanding of ourselves and live more authentically. It involves being present and attuned to our thoughts, emotions, and behaviors, and gaining insights into our patterns, triggers, and reactions. By developing self-awareness, we become more conscious of who we are, how we show up in the world, and the impact of our choices.

To cultivate self-awareness, begin by creating moments of stillness and reflection in your daily life. Set aside time for quiet introspection, meditation, or journaling. This allows you to observe your thoughts and emotions without judgment, gaining clarity about your inner world. Pay attention to your thoughts, noticing any recurring patterns or themes. Observe your emotions and how they fluctuate throughout the day, identifying what triggers positive or negative reactions within you. By becoming more aware of your thoughts and emotions, you can better understand the underlying beliefs, values, and desires that shape your experiences.

Another way to cultivate self-awareness is through self-observation in social interactions and relationships. Notice how you communicate, how you respond to others, and the dynamics that arise. Pay attention to any recurring behavioral patterns or tendencies that may arise. This reflection can provide valuable insights into your interpersonal dynamics and help you identify areas for growth and improvement.

Practicing self-compassion is essential in the process of self-awareness. It is important to approach self-observation and reflection with kindness and non-judgment. Instead of criticizing yourself for certain thoughts or emotions, view them as opportunities for learning and growth. Recognize that self-awareness is a lifelong journey, and it is natural to have areas where you may still be developing awareness.

Self-awareness can also be enhanced through seeking feedback from trusted individuals in your life. Ask for honest perspectives and reflections on your behaviors and interactions. This feedback can provide valuable insights into blind spots or patterns that you may not have been aware of on your own.

Emotional intelligence is closely linked to self-awareness. It involves understanding and managing your emotions, as well as empathizing with the emotions of others. Cultivating emotional intelligence allows you to navigate relationships and situations with greater empathy, compassion, and self-regulation. Practices such as mindfulness, deep listening, and empathy can enhance your emotional intelligence and deepen your self-awareness.

Incorporate regular self-reflection and evaluation into your routine. Set aside time to assess your progress, goals, and alignment with your authentic self. Reflect on the choices you have made and how they have contributed to your growth and well-being. This self-evaluation allows you to course-correct and make adjustments as needed, ensuring that your actions are aligned with your true self and values.

Journaling is a powerful tool for self-awareness. Write down your thoughts, emotions, and observations regularly. Use journaling prompts to delve deeper into specific aspects of your life, such as your values, goals, or challenges. Through the process of writing, you can gain clarity, identify patterns, and explore your inner landscape with greater depth.

Finally, embrace the process of self-discovery with curiosity and openness. Recognize that self-awareness is an ongoing journey, and it requires patience, self-compassion, and a willingness to confront uncomfortable truths. Be open to exploring different perspectives and challenging your own assumptions and biases. By continually deepening your self-awareness, you can make conscious choices that align with your true self, leading to greater fulfillment, authenticity, and personal growth.

In conclusion, self-awareness is a transformative practice that empowers us to live authentically and make choices aligned with our true selves. By cultivating self-awareness through introspection, observation, feedback, and self-reflection, we gain valuable insights into our thoughts, emotions, and behaviors.

Cultivating Emotional Intelligence

Cultivating emotional intelligence is a powerful skill that can greatly enhance our personal and professional lives. It involves developing an awareness and understanding of our own emotions, as well as the emotions of others. By enhancing our emotional intelligence, we can navigate relationships with greater empathy, communicate more effectively, and make decisions that align with our values and aspirations.

The first step in cultivating emotional intelligence is to become more aware of our own emotions. Take the time to observe and identify your emotions as they arise. Notice the physical sensations, thoughts, and behaviors associated with each emotion. This self-awareness allows you to better understand the triggers and patterns that influence your emotional responses.

Next, work on developing emotional self-regulation. This involves managing and expressing your emotions in a healthy and constructive way. Practice techniques such as deep breathing, mindfulness, and self-reflection to create space between the emotion and your response. By cultivating emotional self-regulation, you can make more conscious choices and avoid impulsive or harmful reactions.

Empathy is another key component of emotional intelligence. Seek to understand and connect with the emotions of others. Practice active listening, putting yourself in their shoes, and validating their experiences. By cultivating empathy, you can strengthen your relationships, build trust, and create a supportive and collaborative environment.

Effective communication is essential for developing emotional intelligence. Learn to express your emotions assertively and respectfully, while also being open to receiving and understanding the emotions of others. Use active listening, non-verbal cues, and empathy to foster clear and compassionate communication.

Social awareness is another aspect of emotional intelligence. It involves being attuned to the emotions and needs of others in social settings. Pay attention to verbal and non-verbal cues, and be mindful of the impact of your words and actions on those around you. Developing social awareness allows you to navigate social dynamics more effectively and build positive and meaningful connections.

Finally, emotional intelligence encompasses the ability to make decisions that align with your values and aspirations. By understanding your own emotions and recognizing how they influence your decision-making, you can make choices that are in line with your authentic self. Consider the emotional implications of your decisions and strive for integrity and alignment with your values.

Cultivating emotional intelligence is an ongoing practice that requires self-reflection, empathy, and a commitment to personal growth. Seek opportunities to develop and refine these skills, such as attending workshops or seeking feedback from trusted individuals. Embrace challenges as opportunities for growth and learning, and approach each interaction with curiosity and an open mind.

In conclusion, cultivating emotional intelligence is a valuable endeavor that can positively impact all areas of our lives. By developing self-awareness, emotional self-regulation, empathy, effective communication, social awareness, and decision-making skills, we can navigate relationships and situations with greater empathy, authenticity, and success. Embrace the journey of developing emotional intelligence, and you will reap the rewards of deeper connections, improved communication, and a more fulfilling and purposeful life.

Practicing Gratitude and Mindfulness

Practicing gratitude and mindfulness are transformative practices that can bring greater joy, contentment, and inner peace to our lives. They allow us to cultivate a deeper appreciation for the present moment and the abundance that surrounds us.

Gratitude involves consciously acknowledging and appreciating the blessings, big and small, in our lives. It is about shifting our focus from what is lacking to what we already have. By regularly practicing gratitude, we train our minds to notice and savor the positive aspects of life, fostering a sense of abundance and fulfillment.

There are various ways to cultivate gratitude. One simple practice is keeping a gratitude journal, where you write down things you are grateful for each day. This practice helps you become more attuned to the positive moments and experiences in your life. You can also express gratitude verbally or through acts of kindness, such as sending a heartfelt thank-you note or offering assistance to someone in need.

Mindfulness, on the other hand, is the practice of being fully present in the moment, without judgment or attachment. It involves directing our attention to the present experience, whether it's our thoughts, emotions, bodily sensations, or the environment around us. By practicing mindfulness, we cultivate a deeper sense of self-awareness and acceptance, allowing us to navigate life's ups and downs with greater clarity and equanimity.

To cultivate mindfulness, you can engage in formal meditation practices, such as focused breathing or body scan exercises. These practices help train your mind to stay present and observe your thoughts and emotions without getting caught up in them. Additionally, you can incorporate mindfulness into your daily activities by bringing your full attention to simple tasks like eating, walking, or listening to others.

Both gratitude and mindfulness complement each other and support our overall well-being. When we practice gratitude, it becomes easier to cultivate mindfulness because we are more attuned to the present moment and the positive aspects of life. And when we practice mindfulness, we deepen our ability to experience and appreciate the blessings around us.

Together, gratitude and mindfulness allow us to break free from the autopilot mode of our busy lives and connect with the richness of each moment. They help us cultivate a positive mindset, reduce stress, and enhance our relationships. By incorporating these practices into our daily lives, we can cultivate a greater sense of inner peace, contentment, and joy.

So, take a moment to pause, breathe, and reflect on the things you are grateful for. Practice being fully present in the here and now, savoring the beauty and richness of the present moment. Embrace gratitude and mindfulness as powerful tools for enhancing your well-being and living a more fulfilling life.

Tapping into Inner Wisdom

Tapping into our inner wisdom and intuition is a powerful way to gain guidance and insight on our self-discovery journey. Our inner wisdom is an innate knowing that comes from a deeper level of awareness beyond our rational mind. It can provide valuable guidance, clarity, and a sense of direction.

To tap into your inner wisdom, it's important to create space for stillness and reflection. This can be done through practices such as meditation, journaling, or simply taking quiet moments of solitude. By quieting the noise of the external world and tuning into your internal landscape, you create an opportunity to connect with your inner wisdom.

Trust is an essential aspect of tapping into your inner wisdom. Trust that the answers and guidance you seek are within you. Trust that your intuition is a reliable compass that can navigate you towards your authentic self. It may take time and practice to develop this trust, but by cultivating a sense of openness and receptivity, you allow your inner wisdom to speak to you more clearly.

Pay attention to your gut feelings, intuitive nudges, and subtle sensations in your body. These are often indicators of what aligns with your true self and what doesn't. Practice listening to and honoring these signals, even if they may not always align with logic or external expectations. Your inner wisdom knows what is right for you.

Another way to tap into your inner wisdom is through the practice of self-reflection and introspection. Set aside regular time to reflect on your experiences, emotions, and thoughts. Journaling can be a helpful tool in this process, allowing you to explore your inner world and gain insights into your desires, values, and aspirations.

It's important to note that tapping into your inner wisdom doesn't mean dismissing rational thinking or external input. It's about finding a balance between logical analysis and intuitive knowing. By integrating both, you can make decisions and choices that are aligned with your true self.

Be patient and gentle with yourself as you embark on this journey of tapping into your inner wisdom. It's a process that unfolds over time, and it's okay to have moments of uncertainty or doubt. Trust that your inner wisdom will guide you in the right direction and that each step you take brings you closer to your authentic self.

As you cultivate a deeper connection with your inner wisdom, you will find that it becomes a trusted ally and a valuable resource on your self-discovery journey. Embrace this inner guidance and allow it to illuminate your path and empower you to make choices that align with your truest desires and aspirations.

Journaling and Self-Reflection Exercises

Journaling and self-reflection exercises are powerful tools for self-discovery and personal growth. They provide a safe and private space for you to explore your thoughts, emotions, and experiences, gaining deeper insights into yourself and your journey. Here are some ways to incorporate journaling and self-reflection into your practice:

Start a journal: Set aside regular time to write in a journal. Use it as a personal space to express yourself freely, without judgment or filters. Write about your thoughts, feelings, dreams, and aspirations. Reflect on your experiences, challenges, and successes. Explore your values, beliefs, and goals. The act of putting your thoughts on paper can help clarify your emotions, bring hidden patterns to light, and provide a sense of release and self-expression.

Prompts and questions: Use prompts or questions to guide your journaling and self-reflection. These can be specific questions about your values, dreams, fears, or life experiences. Some examples include: "What brings me joy and fulfillment?", "What are my strengths and how can I leverage them?", "What are the limiting beliefs that hold me back?", or "What lessons have I learned from my past experiences?". Such prompts encourage deeper self-inquiry and offer a starting point for reflection.

Reflect on challenging situations: When faced with challenges or difficult emotions, use journaling as a tool for self-reflection. Explore the root causes of the challenge, how it makes you feel, and what lessons you can learn from it. Consider alternative perspectives or strategies for moving forward. Journaling can help you gain clarity, process emotions, and identify patterns or triggers that may be hindering your growth.

Gratitude journaling: Dedicate a section of your journal to gratitude. Each day, write down things you are grateful for, both big and small. This practice helps shift your focus to the positive aspects of your life and cultivates a mindset of gratitude. Reflecting on gratitude can also reveal patterns and themes that bring you joy and fulfillment, guiding you towards activities and experiences that align with your authentic self.

Self-reflection exercises: In addition to journaling, engage in self-reflection exercises to deepen your understanding of yourself. These can include activities like creating vision boards, mapping out your life values, or writing letters to your past or future self. These exercises provide a visual and interactive way to explore your desires, aspirations, and personal growth.

Remember that journaling and self-reflection are personal practices, so feel free to customize them to suit your needs and preferences. Experiment with different techniques and find what resonates with you. Consistency is key, so aim for regular practice, whether it's daily, weekly, or whenever you feel the need to delve deeper into self-exploration.

Through journaling and self-reflection, you create a space for self-discovery, self-expression, and personal growth. Embrace the process with curiosity and openness, and allow the insights gained from these practices to guide you on your journey of self-understanding and transformation.

Exploring Different Perspectives and Worldviews

Exploring different perspectives and worldviews is a powerful way to broaden your understanding of the world and deepen your self-discovery journey. By stepping outside of your own cultural and belief framework, you gain new insights and experiences that challenge your assumptions and expand your horizons. *Here are some ways to embrace and explore different perspectives:*

Seek out diverse voices: Actively seek out diverse voices and perspectives through books, podcasts, documentaries, and other media sources. Engage with authors, speakers, and creators from different cultures, backgrounds, and disciplines. This exposure will help you gain a broader understanding of various viewpoints and experiences.

Travel and immerse yourself in different cultures: Traveling to different countries and immersing yourself in different cultures allows you to experience firsthand the richness and diversity of the world. Engage with locals, learn about their traditions, customs, and values. By experiencing different cultures, you can challenge your own assumptions, expand your understanding, and develop a more nuanced perspective.

Engage in meaningful conversations: Initiate conversations with people who have different perspectives and beliefs. Approach these conversations with curiosity, empathy, and an open mind. Listen actively and seek to understand their viewpoints, even if they differ from your own. Engaging in respectful dialogue can broaden your understanding and foster personal growth.

Join diverse communities: Engage with communities or groups that embrace diversity and inclusivity. Participate in activities or events that celebrate different cultures, languages, and traditions. Interacting with individuals from diverse backgrounds provides opportunities for learning, sharing, and fostering mutual understanding.

Reflect and challenge your own beliefs: Take time to reflect on your own beliefs, values, and biases. Examine the origins and influences of your beliefs and question whether they still align with your authentic self. By critically evaluating your own perspectives, you can gain a deeper understanding of yourself and be open to embracing new ideas and perspectives.

Practice empathy and active listening: Cultivate empathy by putting yourself in others' shoes and seeking to understand their experiences and perspectives. Practice active listening by giving your full attention and suspending judgment. This allows you to genuinely hear and appreciate different viewpoints, fostering personal growth and building meaningful connections.

Embrace discomfort and uncertainty: Exploring different perspectives requires stepping outside of your comfort zone and embracing uncertainty. Be open to challenging your own beliefs and being exposed to new ideas that may initially feel unfamiliar or uncomfortable. Embracing discomfort can lead to personal growth and expanded understanding.

Remember, exploring different perspectives and worldviews is an ongoing process. It requires an open mind, humility, and a willingness to learn from others. Embracing diversity and engaging with different perspectives enriches your self-discovery journey, deepens your understanding of yourself and the world, and promotes personal growth and empathy.

Seeking Feedback and Self-Assessment

Seeking feedback and engaging in self-assessment are valuable practices that can enhance your self-discovery journey and personal growth. They provide valuable insights and perspectives on your strengths, areas for improvement, and blind spots. *Here's how you can effectively seek feedback and engage in self-assessment:*

Identify trusted individuals: Choose individuals who know you well, have your best interests at heart, and can provide honest and constructive feedback. These can be mentors, coaches, friends, or colleagues whom you respect and trust.

Ask specific and open-ended questions: When seeking feedback, ask specific questions that focus on areas you want to explore or develop. For example, you can ask about your communication skills, problem-solving abilities, or leadership style. Encourage open and honest feedback by asking open-ended questions that invite thoughtful responses.

Be open and receptive: Approach feedback with an open mind and a willingness to listen and learn. Avoid becoming defensive or dismissive of feedback, even if it may be challenging to hear. Remember that feedback is an opportunity for growth and improvement.

Reflect and integrate feedback: Take time to reflect on the feedback you receive. Consider how it aligns with your self-perception and goals for personal development. Identify patterns or recurring themes in the feedback and use them as insights to guide your growth journey.

Engage in self-assessment exercises: Self-assessment exercises allow you to gain a comprehensive view of yourself. These exercises may include personality assessments, values clarification exercises, or strengths assessments. Reflect on the results and consider how they align with your experiences and self-perception.

Embrace a growth mindset: Approach feedback and self-assessment with a growth mindset, believing that you have the capacity to learn and improve. Embrace feedback as an opportunity for growth and view self-assessment as a means to understand yourself better and make intentional choices for personal development.

Set goals for improvement: Use the insights gained from feedback and self-assessment to set specific and actionable goals for personal growth. Break down these goals into smaller steps and create a plan to work towards them. Regularly review and adjust your goals as needed.

Practice self-reflection: Engage in regular self-reflection to assess your progress, identify areas for improvement, and celebrate your successes. Journaling, meditation, or contemplative exercises can help facilitate self-reflection and deepen your understanding of yourself.

Remember, seeking feedback and engaging in self-assessment are ongoing processes. Embrace them as valuable tools for self-discovery and personal growth. By seeking feedback, reflecting on insights, and taking intentional action, you can continuously evolve and cultivate your authentic self.

Honoring Personal Boundaries

Honoring personal boundaries is a crucial aspect of self-discovery and maintaining overall well-being. It involves recognizing and respecting your needs, values, and limits, and communicating them effectively to others. *Here are some key points to consider when it comes to honoring personal boundaries:*

Self-awareness: Start by cultivating self-awareness and understanding your own needs, values, and limits. Reflect on what feels comfortable and uncomfortable for you in different situations, relationships, and interactions. Take the time to identify your physical, emotional, and mental boundaries.

Communicate your boundaries: Once you have a clear understanding of your boundaries, it is essential to communicate them effectively to others. Clearly and assertively express your needs, limits, and expectations. Use "I" statements to express how certain behaviors or situations make you feel and what you require in order to feel respected and comfortable.

Practice self-care: Honoring personal boundaries means prioritizing self-care. Take the time to nurture yourself physically, emotionally, and mentally. Engage in activities that replenish your energy, set aside time for relaxation, and establish healthy routines that support your well-being.

Learn to say no: Saying no when necessary is an important part of honoring personal boundaries. Understand that it is okay to decline requests or obligations that do not align with your values, interests, or available time and energy. Practice setting boundaries around your commitments and responsibilities, ensuring that you allocate time for yourself.

Evaluate and adjust: Regularly assess your boundaries to ensure they continue to align with your evolving needs and values. Be open to adjusting your boundaries as you gain new insights about yourself and your desires. Give yourself permission to make changes that support your growth and well-being.

Seek support: If you find it challenging to establish or maintain boundaries, seek support from trusted friends, family members, or professionals such as therapists or coaches. They can provide guidance, insights, and tools to help you navigate boundary-setting with confidence and clarity.

Respect others' boundaries: Just as it is important to establish and communicate your own boundaries, it is equally important to respect the boundaries of others. Practice active listening, empathy, and understanding when someone communicates their limits or needs to you.

Remember that honoring personal boundaries is a continuous practice that requires self-awareness, self-compassion, and ongoing communication. By establishing and respecting your boundaries, you create a foundation of self-respect, authenticity, and healthy relationships in your journey of self-discovery.

Embracing Vulnerability as a Path to Growth

Embracing vulnerability is a powerful way to unlock personal growth and self-discovery. While vulnerability may initially feel uncomfortable or risky, it opens the door to profound transformation and connection. *Here are some key points to consider when it comes to embracing vulnerability as a path to growth:*

Authenticity and self-acceptance: Embracing vulnerability starts with being true to yourself and accepting all aspects of who you are, including your imperfections and insecurities. It requires letting go of the need to appear perfect or invulnerable and instead embracing your authentic self.

Courage to be seen: Vulnerability involves having the courage to be seen and heard as your genuine self, even when it feels challenging or uncertain. It means allowing yourself to be open, honest, and transparent with others about your thoughts, feelings, and experiences.

Building deep connections: Vulnerability fosters genuine and meaningful connections with others. When you allow yourself to be vulnerable, you invite others to do the same. This creates a safe space for authenticity, empathy, and understanding, strengthening the bonds of trust and fostering deeper relationships.

Emotional growth and self-awareness: Embracing vulnerability allows you to explore and understand your emotions more deeply. It opens up the opportunity for self-reflection and self-awareness, helping you to identify patterns, triggers, and areas for growth. By leaning into vulnerability, you can develop emotional resilience and expand your capacity for empathy and compassion.

Learning from setbacks and failures: Vulnerability involves taking risks and being willing to experience setbacks or failures. It is through these moments of vulnerability that we often learn the most valuable lessons and gain the resilience to keep moving forward. Embracing vulnerability allows you to reframe setbacks as opportunities for growth and to cultivate a growth mindset.

Creativity and innovation: Vulnerability is closely linked to creativity and innovation. When you allow yourself to be vulnerable, you free yourself from self-imposed limitations and open up to new ideas, perspectives, and possibilities. Vulnerability encourages a mindset of exploration and experimentation, fueling creativity and innovation in various areas of life.

Self-compassion and self-acceptance: Embracing vulnerability requires practicing self-compassion and self-acceptance. It means treating yourself with kindness and understanding when you feel exposed or make mistakes. By embracing vulnerability, you learn to embrace yourself fully, flaws and all, and to cultivate a sense of worthiness and self-love.

Remember that embracing vulnerability is a continuous journey and a practice that requires courage, self-compassion, and self-awareness. By opening yourself up to vulnerability, you create space for growth, connection, and a deeper understanding of yourself and others on your path of self-discovery.

Discovering Your Authentic Voice

Discovering and embracing your authentic voice is a transformative journey of self-expression and self-discovery. Your authentic voice is the unique combination of your thoughts, beliefs, values, experiences, and perspectives that shape how you communicate and express yourself. Here are some key points to consider when it comes to discovering your authentic voice:

Self-reflection and self-awareness: Take time to reflect on who you are, what matters to you, and what makes you unique. Explore your values, passions, strengths, and the experiences that have shaped you. Self-awareness is the foundation for discovering and expressing your authentic voice.

Embrace your uniqueness: Recognize that your authentic voice is unlike anyone else's. Embrace your individuality and the qualities that make you distinct. Your perspective and experiences are valuable, and your authentic voice is an essential contribution to the world.

Honesty and vulnerability: Authenticity requires being honest with yourself and others. It involves embracing vulnerability and sharing your thoughts and emotions genuinely. Allow yourself to express your true feelings and opinions, even if they may be unpopular or contrary to societal expectations.

Explore different modes of expression: Your authentic voice can manifest in various forms of expression, such as writing, speaking, art, music, or any other creative outlet. Experiment with different modes of expression to discover which ones resonate most authentically with you.

Listen to your inner guidance: Pay attention to your intuition and inner wisdom. Your authentic voice often arises from a deep knowing within you. Trust your instincts and listen to the inner guidance that nudges you towards your true expression.

Overcome self-doubt and fear of judgment: Embracing your authentic voice requires overcoming self-doubt and the fear of judgment from others. Remember that your voice matters, and sharing it authentically can inspire and impact others positively. Surround yourself with supportive and encouraging individuals who value your authenticity.

Practice self-expression: Engage in activities that allow you to express yourself freely and authentically. Write in a journal, engage in creative endeavors, speak up in conversations, or join communities that appreciate and encourage self-expression. The more you practice expressing your authentic voice, the more it will strengthen and become natural to you.

Continual growth and evolution: Your authentic voice may evolve and change over time as you grow and gain new experiences. Embrace the ongoing process of self-discovery and self-expression, allowing your authentic voice to evolve with you.

Remember that discovering your authentic voice is a deeply personal and individual journey. It may take time and self-exploration to fully understand and express your authentic self. Trust the process, be patient with yourself, and embrace the beauty of your unique voice as you contribute to the world authentically.

4

Embracing the Shadows

In the journey of self-discovery, it is essential to acknowledge and embrace the shadows within ourselves. The concept of shadows refers to the parts of ourselves that we tend to suppress, deny, or reject. These shadows often manifest as dark emotions, limiting beliefs, and unresolved wounds. By exploring and embracing our shadows, we gain a deeper understanding of ourselves and open the door to profound personal growth and transformation. This chapter explores various aspects of embracing the shadows and offers strategies for integrating them into our journey.

Understanding the Concept of Shadows

In the realm of psychology, the concept of shadows holds profound significance. Coined by renowned Swiss psychologist Carl Jung, the term "shadows" refers to the unconscious aspects of our personality that remain hidden from our conscious awareness. These shadows encompass a wide range of elements, including fears, insecurities, repressed emotions, unresolved traumas, and aspects of ourselves that we perceive as negative or undesirable.

The shadows are like dark corners within our psyche, where our hidden emotions and rejected parts of ourselves reside. They are often formed through early life experiences, societal conditioning, and the internalization of cultural norms. These unconscious aspects can exert a significant influence on our thoughts, feelings, and behaviors, shaping our self-perception, relationships, and life choices.

Acknowledging and exploring our shadows is a transformative journey that leads us to self-discovery, self-acceptance, and wholeness. It requires a willingness to confront and embrace the parts of ourselves that we may have suppressed or denied. By shining a light on these shadows, we bring them into our conscious awareness and create an opportunity for healing and personal growth.

One of the key aspects of understanding shadows is recognizing that they are not inherently negative or something to be feared. Shadows are an integral part of the human experience, and they hold valuable insights and lessons for our personal development. They can serve as gateways to self-understanding, self-compassion, and ultimately, self-transformation.

Exploring our shadows involves delving into the depths of our psyche with curiosity and openness. It requires self-reflection, introspection, and a willingness to confront the uncomfortable and unfamiliar aspects of ourselves. Through this process, we gain a deeper understanding of the layers that make up our identity and the factors that have shaped us.

Acknowledging and accepting our shadows is a vital step towards achieving wholeness and self-acceptance. It involves embracing the totality of who we are, including the parts that we may have labeled as "bad" or "unacceptable." By integrating these rejected aspects into our conscious awareness, we begin to heal the rift between our conscious and unconscious selves.

Furthermore, exploring our shadows allows us to release the power that these unconscious elements hold over us. When left unexamined and unacknowledged, shadows can manifest in destructive ways, influencing our thoughts, emotions, and behaviors without our conscious consent. By bringing them into the light of awareness, we gain the ability to make conscious choices and transform these shadow aspects into sources of strength and wisdom.

Self-compassion plays a crucial role in the process of exploring shadows. It involves treating ourselves with kindness, understanding, and non-judgment as we navigate the complexities of our inner world. Self-compassion allows us to embrace our shadows with empathy and love, fostering an environment of healing and growth.

Examining cultural and social conditioning is another important aspect of understanding shadows. Society and culture play a significant role in shaping our beliefs, values, and self-perception. Often, societal norms and expectations create shadows within us, as we internalize messages that certain aspects of ourselves are undesirable or unworthy. By critically examining these cultural influences, we can challenge the validity of these shadows and reclaim our authentic selves.

Healing inner wounds and unresolved traumas is an integral part of the journey of embracing shadows. Shadows often stem from past experiences that have left a deep emotional impact on us. By addressing and processing these wounds with compassion and support, we can release the emotional charge associated with them and begin the process of healing and integration.

Cultivating forgiveness and letting go is essential in the process of embracing shadows. This involves forgiving ourselves and others for past hurts and releasing any lingering resentments or attachments that keep us bound to the shadows. Forgiveness opens the door to healing and allows us to move forward with greater clarity, freedom, and peace.

Embracing the imperfections within ourselves is a key aspect of working with shadows. It involves accepting that we are not meant to be flawless beings, but rather, complex and multifaceted individuals. Embracing our imperfections allows us to let go of the need for perfection and unrealistic expectations, and instead, embrace our humanity with all its strengths and weaknesses.

Integrating shadow aspects for wholeness is a transformative process that requires courage and self-reflection. It involves acknowledging and embracing the parts of ourselves that we have rejected or disowned. By integrating these shadow aspects, we become more whole and authentic, tapping into the full range of our potentials and capabilities.

Embracing change and adaptability is essential in the journey of working with shadows. As we explore and integrate our shadows, we undergo profound transformations within ourselves. This process often brings about shifts in our perspectives, beliefs, and behaviors. Embracing change allows us to embrace the growth and expansion that comes with working through our shadows, rather than resisting or fearing it.

Exploring the connection between fear and growth is an important aspect of shadow work. Shadows often arise from fear-based beliefs and experiences that we have internalized. By exploring the roots of our fears and understanding how they have shaped our lives, we can consciously choose to move beyond them and embrace growth and expansion.

Finding strength in vulnerability is a powerful aspect of working with shadows. Vulnerability involves allowing ourselves to be seen and expressing our true selves authentically, even in the face of potential judgment or rejection. By embracing vulnerability, we tap into our inner strength and resilience, and create deeper connections with others.

Cultivating a supportive network is crucial in the journey of working with shadows. Surrounding ourselves with compassionate and understanding individuals who can provide support, guidance, and validation is invaluable. A supportive network helps us feel seen, heard, and accepted as we navigate the complexities of our shadow work.

Transforming fear into fuel for action is a transformative approach in working with shadows. Fear often holds us back and keeps us stuck in patterns of avoidance or resistance. By reframing fear as an opportunity for growth and stepping into the unknown with courage, we can harness its energy to propel us forward on our path of self-discovery.

Embracing self-expression and authenticity is the ultimate goal of working with shadows. It involves fully embracing and expressing our true selves, without fear of judgment or rejection. By embracing our shadows and integrating them into our authentic expression, we create a sense of wholeness and live in alignment with our deepest values and desires.

In conclusion, understanding and embracing shadows is a profound and transformative journey of self-discovery. It requires courage, self-compassion, and a willingness to explore the depths of our psyche. By acknowledging and integrating our shadows, we move closer to wholeness, self-acceptance, and authentic living. Through this journey, we tap into our inner strength, wisdom, and capacity for growth, ultimately experiencing a profound sense of liberation and fulfillment.

Acknowledging and Accepting Dark Emotions

Dark emotions, often referred to as negative emotions, are an inherent part of our human experience. They encompass feelings such as anger, sadness, fear, and shame. While these emotions are often seen as undesirable or uncomfortable, acknowledging and accepting them is crucial for our overall well-being and personal growth.

Acknowledging dark emotions means recognizing their presence within us without judgment or resistance. It involves allowing ourselves to fully experience and express these emotions, rather than suppressing or denying them. By acknowledging dark emotions, we validate our own inner experiences and honor the complexity of our emotional landscape.

Accepting dark emotions goes hand in hand with acknowledging them. Acceptance means embracing these emotions as a natural part of our human experience, without trying to push them away or label them as "good" or "bad." It involves creating space within ourselves to hold these emotions with compassion and understanding.

When we acknowledge and accept dark emotions, several benefits emerge. Firstly, it allows us to develop emotional resilience. By facing and working through these emotions, we build the capacity to navigate challenging situations and adapt to adversity. Instead of being overwhelmed by dark emotions, we learn to recognize them as signals for self-reflection and growth.

Acknowledging and accepting dark emotions also fosters self-awareness. Through this process, we gain insight into the root causes of our emotions and can identify patterns or triggers that contribute to their emergence. This self-awareness enables us to make conscious choices about how we respond to these emotions and take steps towards emotional healing and well-being.

Furthermore, embracing dark emotions creates an opportunity for healing and transformation. When we allow ourselves to fully experience and express these emotions, we release the energy associated with them, leading to emotional catharsis and a sense of relief. This process promotes emotional integration and supports our overall psychological well-being.

It is important to note that acknowledging and accepting dark emotions does not mean indulging in them or allowing them to control our actions. Instead, it involves developing healthy coping mechanisms and emotional regulation strategies to navigate these emotions constructively. This may include seeking support from trusted friends or professionals, engaging in self-care practices, or engaging in creative outlets such as art, writing, or physical activities.

In summary, acknowledging and accepting dark emotions is a vital aspect of self-discovery and personal growth. By embracing these emotions, we create space for healing, self-awareness, and emotional resilience. It is through this process that we can fully embrace our authentic selves and cultivate a greater sense of well-being and fulfillment.

Examining Cultural and Social Conditioning

Examining cultural and social conditioning is a crucial step in our journey of self-discovery. From an early age, we are influenced by the beliefs, values, and behaviors that are prevalent in our culture and society.

These influences shape our perceptions, shape our understanding of the world, and influence our choices and actions.

Cultural and social conditioning can be both explicit and implicit. Explicit conditioning includes direct messages and teachings from family, education, media, and other societal institutions. Implicit conditioning refers to the subtle norms, expectations, and assumptions that we absorb from our surroundings without conscious awareness.

To embark on a path of self-discovery, it is essential to examine and question these influences. This process involves critically evaluating the beliefs, values, and behaviors that have been ingrained in us. We need to ask ourselves whether these beliefs and values truly resonate with our authentic selves or if they are simply a product of external influences.

One way to examine cultural and social conditioning is to reflect on the messages we have received about various aspects of our identity, such as gender, race, religion, and social status. We can explore the expectations placed upon us and consider whether they align with our true desires and values. By recognizing the societal pressures that have influenced our self-perception, we can begin to reclaim our authenticity.

Challenging societal norms and expectations is an integral part of this process. It requires courage and a willingness to question the status quo. By critically evaluating the messages we have internalized, we can identify limiting beliefs that may be holding us back from fully expressing ourselves and pursuing our true passions and aspirations.

As we examine cultural and social conditioning, it is important to remember that this does not mean rejecting all aspects of our culture or society. It is about becoming aware of the influences that have shaped us and consciously choosing which beliefs and values align with our authentic selves. This process allows us to cultivate a sense of agency and authorship over our own lives.

In challenging societal norms, we open ourselves up to new possibilities and alternative ways of being. We free ourselves from the constraints of conformity and create space for self-expression, creativity, and personal growth. By embracing our uniqueness and questioning the norms that no longer serve us, we pave the way for greater authenticity and fulfillment.

It is worth noting that examining cultural and social conditioning is an ongoing process. As we continue to evolve and grow, new layers of conditioning may come to light. Embracing self-discovery requires us to remain open-minded and receptive to new perspectives and experiences.

In conclusion, examining cultural and social conditioning is a transformative step in the journey of self-discovery. By critically evaluating the influences that have shaped us, challenging societal norms, and aligning our beliefs and values with our authentic selves, we create the space for personal growth, self-expression, and a more fulfilling life.

The Power of Self-Compassion

The power of self-compassion cannot be overstated in our journey of self-discovery. It is a practice that involves treating ourselves with kindness, understanding, and acceptance, especially during moments of difficulty, failure, or pain. Self-compassion allows us to nurture and care for ourselves in a way that promotes healing, growth, and well-being.

In our quest for self-discovery, we often encounter challenges, setbacks, and moments of self-doubt. During these times, it is easy to fall into self-criticism, self-judgment, and self-blame. We may be harsh on ourselves, expecting perfection or comparing ourselves to others. This negative self-talk and lack of self-compassion only perpetuate feelings of unworthiness and hinder our personal growth.

Cultivating self-compassion involves several key elements. First, it requires acknowledging and validating our pain, struggles, and emotions. Instead of dismissing or suppressing them, we recognize that these experiences are a part of being human and deserving of our compassion.

Second, self-compassion involves responding to ourselves with kindness and understanding, just as we would to a close friend or loved one facing similar challenges. We extend empathy and compassion towards ourselves, offering words of encouragement, support, and reassurance.

By treating ourselves with kindness, we create a nurturing and safe space for growth and healing.

Third, self-compassion involves embracing our imperfections and accepting ourselves as flawed yet worthy individuals. We recognize that making mistakes, experiencing failures, and having shortcomings are all part of the human experience. Rather than judging ourselves harshly, we practice self-acceptance and remind ourselves that we are deserving of love and compassion, regardless of our perceived flaws or mistakes.

Self-compassion is not about self-indulgence or avoiding personal responsibility. It is about acknowledging our humanness, embracing our vulnerabilities, and responding to ourselves with care and understanding. By practicing self-compassion, we develop resilience and inner strength to face challenges and setbacks with greater self-care and self-support.

Research has shown that self-compassion is associated with numerous psychological and emotional benefits. It has been linked to increased well-being, reduced anxiety and depression, improved emotional regulation, and enhanced self-esteem. By treating ourselves with compassion, we create a positive and supportive inner environment that fosters personal growth, self-acceptance, and authentic living.

Practicing self-compassion requires intention, awareness, and self-reflection. It involves paying attention to our self-talk, challenging self-critical thoughts, and replacing them with more compassionate and supportive ones. It also involves engaging in self-care activities that promote our physical, mental, and emotional well-being.

In moments of difficulty or when facing our shadows, self-compassion becomes even more essential. It allows us to navigate through challenging emotions and experiences with gentleness and understanding. It enables us to embrace our shadows and unresolved wounds, offering them love and compassion rather than judgment or avoidance.

In summary, the power of self-compassion lies in its ability to nurture our growth, heal our wounds, and embrace our shadows with love and understanding. By cultivating self-compassion, we develop resilience, foster self-acceptance, and create a supportive inner environment for our journey of self-discovery. As we treat ourselves with kindness and compassion, we open ourselves up to deeper self-understanding, personal growth, and a greater sense of wholeness.

Exploring Limiting Beliefs and Self-Sabotage

Exploring and overcoming limiting beliefs and self-sabotage are vital steps in our journey of self-discovery and personal growth. Limiting beliefs are deeply ingrained thoughts or beliefs that hinder us from realizing our true potential, while self-sabotage refers to patterns of behavior that undermine our own success or well-being. Both are often rooted in fear, insecurity, and negative self-perception.

Limiting beliefs can take many forms, such as "I'm not good enough," "I don't deserve success," or "I'll never be able to achieve my goals." These beliefs create a negative framework through which we view ourselves and our abilities. They limit our aspirations, undermine our confidence, and prevent us from taking risks or pursuing our dreams.

Self-sabotage, on the other hand, involves engaging in behaviors that undermine our progress or success. This can manifest as procrastination, self-doubt, perfectionism, fear of failure, or self-sabotaging relationships. These behaviors often arise from a subconscious desire to protect ourselves from disappointment, criticism, or rejection.

To overcome limiting beliefs and self-sabotage, we must first become aware of their presence in our lives. This requires self-reflection, introspection, and honest examination of our thoughts, beliefs, and behaviors. Journaling, therapy, or coaching can be helpful tools in uncovering and challenging these patterns.

Once we identify our limiting beliefs, it is essential to question their validity and challenge their accuracy. We can ask ourselves:

What evidence do I have to support this belief?

Is this belief serving me or holding me back?

What alternative perspectives or beliefs can I adopt?

By actively challenging our limiting beliefs, we create space for new, empowering beliefs to emerge. We can reframe our thoughts, replacing negative self-talk with positive affirmations and empowering statements. Affirmations such as "I am capable," "I deserve success," or "I am enough" can help reprogram our subconscious mind and reinforce positive self-perception.

In addition to addressing limiting beliefs, it is crucial to recognize and address self-sabotaging behaviors. This requires self-awareness and self-discipline. We can start by identifying the specific behaviors or patterns that undermine our progress. For example, if we tend to procrastinate, we can develop strategies to manage our time effectively, break tasks into smaller, manageable steps, and hold ourselves accountable.

Overcoming self-sabotage also involves addressing the underlying fears and insecurities that drive these behaviors. It may be helpful to explore the root causes of our fears and work on healing any unresolved emotional wounds. Seeking support from a therapist, coach, or support group can provide guidance and tools for overcoming self-sabotage.

Building a mindset that supports growth and success requires on-going effort and practice. It involves cultivating self-belief, resilience, and a willingness to step outside of our comfort zones. Surrounding ourselves with positive influences, such as supportive friends, mentors, or role models, can provide encouragement and inspiration.

Remember that personal growth is a journey, and it takes time and patience to overcome limiting beliefs and self-sabotage. Be compassionate with yourself as you navigate this process, and celebrate your progress along the way. By actively challenging and replacing limiting beliefs, addressing self-sabotaging behaviors, and fostering a growth mindset, you empower yourself to reach your full potential and create a life aligned with your authentic self.

Healing Inner Wounds and Trauma

Healing inner wounds and trauma is a crucial aspect of our journey towards self-discovery and personal growth. Unresolved wounds and traumas from the past can have a significant impact on our emotional well-being, relationships, and overall quality of life. They can create emotional pain, limit our potential, and prevent us from fully embracing our authentic selves.

The process of healing inner wounds and trauma requires courage, self-compassion, and a willingness to confront and process painful experiences. While healing is unique to each individual, there are several strategies that can support the healing process:

Seeking professional help: Working with a qualified therapist or counselor who specializes in trauma can provide a safe and supportive environment for exploring and processing past wounds. Therapists can offer various therapeutic approaches, such as cognitive-behavioral therapy (CBT), Eye Movement Desensitization and Reprocessing (EMDR), or somatic experiencing, to help individuals heal from trauma and develop healthy coping mechanisms.

Practicing self-care: Engaging in self-care activities that promote physical, emotional, and mental well-being is essential for healing. This can include activities such as exercise, getting enough sleep, practicing mindfulness or meditation, spending time in nature, and engaging in creative outlets. Self-care helps to reduce stress, promote relaxation, and enhance self-compassion.

Engaging in healing modalities: Exploring alternative healing modalities can be beneficial for healing inner wounds and trauma. These modalities may include art therapy, music therapy, dance therapy, acupuncture, yoga, or energy healing practices like Reiki. These approaches can help individuals process and release emotional pain, connect with their bodies, and promote healing on a holistic level.

Building a support network: Surrounding yourself with a supportive network of friends, family, or support groups can provide a sense of belonging and understanding. Sharing your experiences with others who have gone through similar struggles can create a space for validation, empathy, and healing. Supportive relationships can offer encouragement, guidance, and perspective throughout the healing journey.

Cultivating self-compassion: Practicing self-compassion is crucial during the healing process. This involves treating yourself with kindness, understanding, and patience as you navigate the emotions and challenges that arise. Self-compassion allows you to acknowledge your pain without judgment, and it fosters a sense of acceptance and healing.

Embracing forgiveness and letting go: Forgiveness, both for oneself and others, is a powerful tool for healing. It involves releasing resentment, anger, and blame and allowing yourself to move forward with compassion and understanding. Forgiveness does not mean forgetting or condoning past actions; rather, it is a way of freeing yourself from the emotional burden associated with the wounds or traumas.

Engaging in inner child work: Exploring and healing the wounds of our inner child can be transformative. Inner child work involves reconnecting with the younger versions of ourselves and addressing any unmet needs or emotional wounds. Through inner child work, we can offer love, nurturing, and validation to our inner child, fostering healing and integration.

It is important to note that healing inner wounds and trauma is a gradual and non-linear process. It requires patience, self-compassion, and an understanding that healing may take time. It is also essential to respect your own boundaries and pace throughout the healing journey.

Remember that healing is possible, and as you embark on this journey, be gentle with yourself and celebrate each step of progress. By addressing and healing inner wounds and trauma, you create space for transformation, self-discovery, and a life of greater authenticity and joy.

Cultivating Forgiveness and Letting Go

Cultivating forgiveness and letting go is a transformative practice that liberates us from the burdens of resentment, anger, and pain. It involves releasing the grip that past hurts have on us and choosing to move forward with a compassionate and open heart. By embracing forgiveness and letting go, we create space for healing, personal growth, and deeper connections with ourselves and others.

Forgiveness is not about condoning or forgetting the actions that caused us pain. It is a conscious decision to release the negative emotions associated with those actions and to free ourselves from the ongoing suffering they create. When we hold onto resentment and anger, we keep ourselves trapped in the past, replaying the hurtful experiences over and over again. It becomes an emotional weight that hinders our personal well-being and prevents us from fully embracing the present moment.

To cultivate forgiveness and let go, consider the following steps:

Acknowledge and accept your emotions: Begin by acknowledging and accepting the pain, anger, and resentment you are feeling. Allow yourself to fully experience these emotions without judgment or suppression. Recognize that it is natural to feel hurt when someone has wronged you.

Understand the power of forgiveness: Reflect on the impact that holding onto resentment and anger has on your well-being. Recognize that forgiveness is not about excusing the actions of others or denying your own pain. It is about freeing yourself from the emotional burden and reclaiming your power.

Shift your perspective: Try to see the situation from a different perspective. Consider the factors that may have contributed to the other person's actions or behaviors. This doesn't mean justifying their actions, but rather gaining a broader understanding of the circumstances involved.

Practice empathy and compassion: Cultivate empathy by putting yourself in the shoes of the person who hurt you. This doesn't mean condoning their actions, but rather seeking to understand the complexities of their experiences and motivations. Extend compassion to yourself as well, acknowledging your own pain and offering yourself kindness and understanding.

Make a conscious decision to forgive: Forgiveness is a choice that you make for yourself. Decide that you are ready to let go of the resentment and anger that is holding you back. Write a letter to the person who hurt you (you don't have to send it) expressing your feelings and your intention to forgive. Alternatively, you can engage in a forgiveness meditation or ritual that resonates with you.

Practice self-forgiveness: Along with forgiving others, it is crucial to extend forgiveness to yourself. Recognize that you are human and capable of making mistakes. Release self-blame and self-criticism, and offer yourself the same empathy and compassion you would extend to others.

Set boundaries and seek support: Forgiving someone doesn't mean forgetting or enabling harmful behavior. It is essential to set boundaries and take steps to protect yourself from further harm. Seek support from trusted friends, family, or professionals who can provide guidance and understanding throughout your forgiveness journey.

Embrace the present moment: Embracing forgiveness and letting go allows you to fully embrace the present moment and create space for new experiences and relationships. Focus on nurturing your own well-being, cultivating positive relationships, and pursuing your personal growth and aspirations.

Remember that forgiveness is a process that takes time and patience. It is normal to experience setbacks or moments of resistance. Be gentle with yourself and trust that with continued practice, forgiveness and letting go will become more natural and liberating.

By cultivating forgiveness and letting go, you reclaim your power, create emotional freedom, and open yourself to a life filled with love, joy, and authenticity.

Embracing the Imperfections Within

Embracing the imperfections within ourselves is a transformative mindset that allows us to let go of the pursuit of perfection and embrace our authentic selves. Perfectionism, with its unrealistic standards and constant self-criticism, can hinder our self-discovery and personal growth. By acknowledging and accepting our imperfections, we create space for self-compassion, growth, and authenticity.

To embrace the imperfections within, consider the following perspectives and practices:

Recognize the inherent human nature of imperfection: Understand that perfection is an illusion and that every human being has flaws, makes mistakes, and faces challenges. Imperfections are not something to be ashamed of but rather an essential part of our shared human experience.

Challenge societal expectations and standards: Society often imposes unrealistic expectations of perfection on us, whether it be in our appearance, achievements, or relationships. Recognize that these standards are arbitrary and subjective. Reframe your mindset to value progress, growth, and authenticity over flawless perfection.

Cultivate self-compassion: Treat yourself with kindness, understanding, and patience. Instead of harshly criticizing yourself for your perceived imperfections, practice self-compassion by offering yourself the same empathy and understanding you would extend to a loved one. Embrace self-compassion as a guiding principle in your self-discovery journey.

Shift the focus from external validation to internal fulfillment: Release the need for external validation and approval. Instead, focus on internal fulfillment and aligning your actions with your values and aspirations. Recognize that true fulfillment comes from living authentically and embracing your unique qualities, strengths, and imperfections.

Embrace vulnerability and take risks: Embracing imperfections requires vulnerability and the willingness to take risks. Understand that growth and self-discovery often occur outside of our comfort zones.

Allow yourself to be vulnerable, make mistakes, and learn from them. Embrace the process of trial and error as a valuable part of your personal growth.

Practice gratitude and self-acceptance: Cultivate gratitude for the journey of self-discovery, including both the successes and the setbacks. Embrace self-acceptance by appreciating and celebrating who you are in this moment, imperfections and all. Embrace a mindset of gratitude and self-acceptance as powerful tools for embracing imperfections.

Surround yourself with supportive and accepting individuals: Surround yourself with people who accept and appreciate you for who you are, including your imperfections. Seek out supportive relationships and communities that foster growth, authenticity, and self-compassion. Engage in conversations that promote vulnerability and acceptance.

Embrace the process of continuous growth: Recognize that self-discovery is an ongoing journey of growth and learning. Embrace the idea that imperfections are opportunities for growth, self-reflection, and self-improvement. View challenges and setbacks as valuable lessons that contribute to your personal development.

By embracing the imperfections within, you liberate yourself from the constraints of perfectionism and create space for self-acceptance, self-compassion, and growth. Embracing imperfections allows you to live authentically, connect with others on a deeper level, and pursue your true passions and aspirations without fear of judgment or failure. Embrace your imperfections as unique facets of your being and celebrate the beauty of your authentic self.

Integrating Shadow Aspects for Wholeness

Integrating shadow aspects is a transformative process that involves bringing awareness, acceptance, and understanding to the parts of ourselves that we have disowned or rejected. These shadow aspects encompass our unacknowledged emotions, desires, traits, and behaviors that we have deemed as negative, unacceptable, or incompatible with our self-image. By embracing and integrating these aspects, we unlock hidden potential, deepen our self-understanding, and achieve a sense of wholeness.

To embark on the journey of integrating shadow aspects, consider the following practices:

Cultivate self-awareness: Develop a deep understanding of your thoughts, emotions, and behaviors. Pay attention to patterns, triggers, and reactions that may indicate the presence of shadow aspects. Self-awareness serves as the foundation for recognizing and integrating these aspects.

Embrace curiosity and non-judgment: Approach your shadow aspects with curiosity and an open mind. Rather than judging or condemning them, seek to understand their origins, motivations, and underlying needs. Adopt an attitude of non-judgment and self-compassion as you explore these aspects of yourself.

Engage in shadow work: Shadow work involves actively exploring and confronting your shadow aspects. This can be done through various practices such as journaling, therapy, meditation, or inner dialogue. Create a safe and non-judgmental space to delve into the deeper layers of your psyche and bring light to the shadows.

Identify and acknowledge your shadow aspects: Reflect on the qualities, emotions, and behaviors that you have denied or suppressed within yourself. These may include anger, jealousy, selfishness, or vulnerability, among others. Be honest and courageous in recognizing these aspects without judgment.

Understand the origins and underlying beliefs: Examine the origins of your shadow aspects. Explore the experiences, conditioning, or societal influences that may have contributed to their development. Identify the underlying beliefs or fears associated with these aspects and question their validity.

Cultivate self-compassion and acceptance: Extend compassion and acceptance to the parts of yourself that you have disowned. Recognize that these aspects are a natural part of being human and that they serve a purpose in your growth and development. Practice self-compassion as you navigate the process of integration.

Seek support and guidance: Engage in conversations with trusted friends, mentors, or professionals who can provide support and guidance on your journey of integrating shadows. Their perspectives and insights can offer valuable insights and help you navigate any challenges that arise.

Embrace the lessons and gifts of shadow aspects: Recognize that integrating shadow aspects brings forth valuable lessons, growth opportunities, and hidden strengths. Embracing these aspects allows you to tap into your full potential and experience a greater sense of wholeness and authenticity.

Practice self-care and self-reflection: Engage in self-care practices that nourish and support your well-being throughout the integration process. Regular self-reflection allows you to monitor your progress, adjust your approach as needed, and honor your evolving understanding of yourself.

Embrace ongoing growth and integration: Integration of shadow aspects is a continuous process that evolves over time. Embrace the ever-unfolding journey of self-discovery and growth. Stay open to new insights, challenges, and opportunities for integration that arise along your path.

By integrating shadow aspects, you move towards a more holistic and authentic expression of yourself. Embracing the totality of your being, including the shadow aspects, allows you to live more fully, embody your true potential, and experience a deeper sense of wholeness and self-acceptance. Engage in the practices of integrating shadows and embrace the transformative power they hold for your personal growth and well-being.

Embracing Change and Adaptability

Change is an inherent part of life, and embracing it is crucial for personal growth and self-discovery. In this chapter, we will explore strategies for embracing change, cultivating adaptability, and navigating transitions with resilience and openness. By developing a mindset that embraces change as an opportunity for growth and transformation, we can thrive in the face of uncertainty and navigate life's transitions with greater ease.

Embrace a growth mindset: Adopt a mindset that sees change as an opportunity for learning and growth. Embrace the belief that you have the capacity to adapt, learn new skills, and overcome challenges. Cultivate a positive attitude towards change, viewing it as a catalyst for personal development and self-discovery.

Cultivate flexibility and adaptability: Develop the ability to adapt to new situations and embrace flexibility. Recognize that rigidity and resistance to change can hinder personal growth. Practice being open to new ideas, perspectives, and experiences. Adaptability allows you to navigate transitions and unexpected changes with greater ease and resilience.

Develop self-awareness: Cultivate self-awareness to recognize your reactions and emotions in the face of change. Understand how you tend to respond to different types of changes and identify any resistance or fears that may arise. Self-awareness enables you to consciously choose your responses and make informed decisions during times of change.

Embrace uncertainty and step outside your comfort zone: Change often brings uncertainty, and embracing it involves stepping outside your comfort zone. Challenge yourself to try new things, take calculated risks, and explore unfamiliar territories. Embracing uncertainty fosters personal growth, expands your horizons, and enhances your adaptability.

Practice resilience and self-care: Build resilience to navigate the challenges that come with change. Develop healthy coping strategies, such as practicing self-care, seeking support from loved ones, and maintaining a balanced lifestyle. Prioritize self-care activities that nurture your physical, emotional, and mental well-being.

Develop problem-solving skills: Enhance your problem-solving skills to effectively navigate the obstacles that may arise during times of change. Approach challenges with a solution-oriented mindset and seek creative and innovative approaches to problem-solving. Embrace a mindset that views obstacles as opportunities for growth and learning.

Emphasize continuous learning and personal development: View change as an opportunity for continuous learning and personal development. Seek out new knowledge, acquire new skills, and engage in personal growth activities. Embracing change with a growth mindset enables you to capitalize on the opportunities that arise and adapt to new circumstances.

Seek support and connection: During times of change, it is essential to seek support from others. Surround yourself with a supportive network of family, friends, mentors, or coaches who can offer guidance, encouragement, and perspective. Share your experiences, fears, and aspirations with trusted individuals who can provide support and understanding.

Practice mindfulness and self-reflection: Cultivate mindfulness and self-reflection to navigate change with greater awareness and presence. Mindfulness allows you to stay grounded in the present moment, reducing anxiety and stress associated with change. Regular self-reflection helps you gain insights, process emotions, and make conscious choices during times of change.

Embrace the opportunities for growth and self-discovery: Finally, recognize that change presents opportunities for personal growth and self-discovery. Embrace the chance to learn more about yourself, explore new possibilities, and redefine your goals and aspirations. View change as a catalyst for positive transformation and embrace the journey of self-discovery that accompanies it.

By embracing change and cultivating adaptability, you open yourself up to a world of possibilities and growth. Through a growth mindset, resilience, self-awareness, and support, you can navigate life's transitions with greater ease and openness. Embrace change as an opportunity for personal growth and self-discovery,

Exploring the Connection Between Fear and Growth

Fear is a powerful emotion that often arises when we encounter the unknown or face challenges in our lives. It can manifest as self-doubt, anxiety, or a reluctance to step outside our comfort zones. While fear can be paralyzing and hinder our growth, it also holds the potential for transformation and personal development.

Understand the nature of fear: Fear is a natural human response designed to protect us from potential harm. It alerts us to potential risks and triggers our fight-or-flight response. Recognizing that fear is a normal part of the human experience can help us approach it with greater understanding and compassion.

Identify your fears: Take the time to identify the specific fears that are holding you back. Is it the fear of failure, rejection, or the unknown? By understanding the root causes of your fears, you can address them more effectively and develop strategies to overcome them.

Reframe fear as an opportunity for growth: Rather than viewing fear as a negative emotion, reframe it as an opportunity for growth. Understand that stepping outside your comfort zone and facing your fears is where real personal development occurs. Embrace fear as a sign that you are stretching yourself and pushing your boundaries.

Cultivate self-compassion and self-belief: Fear often stems from a lack of self-confidence and self-belief. Cultivate self-compassion by being kind and understanding towards yourself. Remind yourself that it is okay to feel fear and that everyone experiences it at some point. Build your self-belief by acknowledging your strengths and past successes, and focus on your potential for growth.

Take small steps and celebrate progress: Overcoming fear does not mean completely eliminating it. Start by taking small steps outside your comfort zone and gradually increase the level of challenge. Celebrate each step you take and acknowledge your courage and progress. Recognize that growth happens incrementally, and every step counts.

Develop a support system: Surround yourself with a supportive network of friends, family, mentors, or like-minded individuals who can encourage and motivate you. Share your fears and aspirations with them, and seek their guidance and support. Having a support system can provide you with the confidence and reassurance to face your fears.

Practice mindfulness and self-reflection: Engage in mindfulness practices to observe and acknowledge your fears without judgment. Mindfulness helps you become more present and aware of your thoughts and emotions, allowing you to respond to fear with greater clarity and intention. Regular self-reflection allows you to gain insights into your fears and develop strategies for overcoming them.

Challenge limiting beliefs: Fear is often fueled by limiting beliefs and negative self-talk. Challenge these beliefs by questioning their validity and replacing them with more empowering and positive beliefs. Cultivate a growth mindset that embraces challenges and views failure as an opportunity for learning and growth.

Seek professional guidance if needed: If your fears are deeply rooted or significantly impacting your life, seeking professional guidance from a therapist or coach can be beneficial. They can provide you with tools, techniques, and support to navigate and overcome your fears.

Embrace discomfort and take action: Ultimately, growth requires embracing discomfort and taking action despite fear. Embrace the idea that growth happens outside your comfort zone. Take calculated risks, pursue your dreams, and trust in your ability to handle challenges along the way. Remember that the most significant growth occurs when you step into the unknown.

By exploring the connection between fear and growth, you can transform fear from a barrier to an opportunity. Embrace fear as a natural part of the growth process and use it as fuel to propel yourself forward. With courage, self-compassion, and a willingness to step outside your comfort zone, you can unlock new levels of self-discovery and personal development.

Finding Strength in Vulnerability

Vulnerability is often misunderstood and associated with weakness or being exposed to potential harm. However, embracing vulnerability can be a tremendous source of strength and personal growth. When we allow ourselves to be vulnerable, we open the door to authentic connections, deep self-expression, and profound transformation.

Embrace authenticity: Vulnerability starts with embracing your authentic self. Be willing to show up as you are, without pretense or masks. Embrace your imperfections and allow yourself to be seen for who you truly are. Authenticity creates a foundation for genuine connections and meaningful relationships.

Cultivate self-acceptance: Practice self-acceptance and self-compassion. Recognize that vulnerability is a part of being human, and it doesn't make you weak or inadequate. Embrace all aspects of yourself, including your strengths and vulnerabilities. Treat yourself with kindness and understanding as you navigate the ups and downs of life.

Trust yourself and others: Vulnerability requires trust, both in yourself and in others. Trust your own instincts and intuition, and have faith in your ability to handle whatever arises. Build trusting relationships with others who demonstrate empathy, respect, and non-judgment. Surround yourself with a supportive network that encourages vulnerability and understands its value.

Practice open communication: Express your thoughts, feelings, and needs openly and honestly. Communicate your vulnerabilities with trusted individuals who can provide a safe space for you to be heard and understood. Effective communication fosters deeper connections and allows for mutual understanding and growth.

Embrace discomfort and take risks: Vulnerability often involves stepping into discomfort and taking emotional risks. It may mean initiating difficult conversations, expressing your true feelings, or pursuing goals that scare you. Embrace the discomfort as a sign of growth and be willing to take calculated risks to expand your horizons.

Learn from setbacks and failures: Vulnerability can involve the risk of failure or rejection. Embrace setbacks as opportunities for learning and growth. Recognize that failure is not a reflection of your worth but a stepping stone towards progress. Embrace the lessons and insights gained from these experiences, and use them to fuel your personal development.

Create a safe and supportive environment: Surround yourself with people who create a safe and supportive environment for vulnerability. Foster relationships where you can share your fears, insecurities, and dreams without judgment. Build a community that encourages vulnerability, empathy, and authentic expression.

Celebrate vulnerability as courage: Shift your perspective on vulnerability and see it as an act of courage. Recognize that it takes strength to be vulnerable, to expose your true self and risk emotional exposure. Celebrate your courage and the growth that comes from embracing vulnerability.

Practice self-care and self-compassion: Engage in self-care practices that nurture your physical, mental, and emotional well-being. Prioritize self-compassion by treating yourself with kindness and understanding, especially during vulnerable moments. Practice self-care rituals that replenish your energy and support your overall well-being.

Reflect and journal: Set aside time for reflection and journaling to explore your vulnerabilities, fears, and growth. Write about your experiences, thoughts, and emotions to gain insights and deepen your self-understanding. Journaling can be a powerful tool for processing vulnerability and uncovering hidden strengths.

By embracing vulnerability, you tap into your authentic self and open the door to personal growth and transformation. It is through vulnerability that we form deeper connections, discover our true strengths, and cultivate a meaningful and fulfilling life. Embrace vulnerability as a source of strength and embark on a journey of self-discovery and personal empowerment.

Cultivating a Supportive Network

Cultivating a supportive network is essential for our personal growth and well-being. Surrounding ourselves with individuals who understand, encourage, and uplift us can provide the necessary support and guidance on our journey of self-discovery. *Here are some strategies for nurturing meaningful relationships and building a supportive network:*

Identify your support system: Reflect on the people in your life who genuinely support and inspire you. These may include close friends, family members, mentors, or members of supportive communities. Identify those individuals who understand and respect your journey of self-discovery and who you can rely on for guidance, encouragement, and constructive feedback.

Seek like-minded individuals: Engage in activities, groups, or communities where you can connect with like-minded individuals who share similar interests, values, or goals. Seek out spaces where you can engage in discussions, share experiences, and learn from one another. These connections can provide a sense of belonging and understanding, as well as opportunities for growth and inspiration.

Be open and vulnerable: In order to foster deeper connections, be open and vulnerable with those you trust. Share your thoughts, feelings, and experiences related to your self-discovery journey. Be willing to listen to others' perspectives and experiences as well. Vulnerability allows for authentic connections to form and creates a safe space for support and understanding.

Practice active listening: Actively listen to others when they share their stories, challenges, or insights. Show genuine interest and empathy in their experiences. By actively listening, you demonstrate that you value and respect their perspectives, strengthening the bond within your supportive network.

Offer support to others: Building a supportive network is a two-way street. Offer your support, encouragement, and assistance to others who are on their own journeys of self-discovery. Be a source of inspiration, guidance, and understanding. By being supportive to others, you create a reciprocal environment where everyone can thrive and grow together.

Communicate your needs: Clearly communicate your needs and boundaries within your relationships. Let others know how they can support you and what kind of support is most beneficial. Effective communication ensures that your relationships are built on mutual understanding and respect.

Celebrate successes together: Celebrate each other's successes and milestones. Acknowledge and celebrate the achievements and growth of those within your supportive network. By celebrating together, you create a positive and uplifting environment that fosters motivation and inspiration.

Seek feedback and guidance: Don't hesitate to seek feedback and guidance from trusted individuals within your network. They can provide valuable insights, perspectives, and constructive criticism to help you navigate challenges and continue your personal growth. Be open to receiving feedback and use it as an opportunity for self-reflection and improvement.

Maintain healthy boundaries: While it is important to be supportive and connected, it is equally important to maintain healthy boundaries within your relationships. Respect each other's personal space, privacy, and individual journeys. Setting and respecting boundaries ensures that your relationships remain balanced and supportive.

Express gratitude and appreciation: Regularly express gratitude and appreciation to those within your supportive network. Let them know how much you value their presence, support, and contributions to your growth. Gratitude strengthens the bonds within your network and creates a positive and uplifting atmosphere.

Remember, building a supportive network takes time and effort. Nurture your relationships, invest in meaningful connections, and be patient with the process. By cultivating a supportive network, you create an empowering and nourishing environment that fuels your personal growth and helps you thrive on your journey of self-discovery.

Transforming Fear into Fuel for Action

Transforming fear into fuel for action is a powerful mindset shift that allows us to overcome the paralyzing effects of fear and use it as a catalyst for personal growth. Here are some practical techniques for transforming fear into motivation and harnessing its energy for positive action:

Recognize and acknowledge fear: The first step in transforming fear is to acknowledge its presence. Recognize that fear is a natural response to the unknown and that it is a part of the human experience. By acknowledging fear, you take away its power to control and limit you.

Reframe fear as an opportunity: Instead of viewing fear as a negative emotion, reframe it as an opportunity for growth and self-discovery. Understand that fear often arises when we are stepping outside of our comfort zones and embarking on new experiences. Embrace fear as a sign that you are stretching yourself and challenging your limits.

Identify the root cause of fear: Take the time to understand the underlying cause of your fear. Is it rooted in past experiences, limiting beliefs, or the fear of failure? By identifying the source of your fear, you can address it directly and develop strategies to overcome it.

Set realistic goals and break them down: Break down your goals into smaller, manageable steps. This approach helps to minimize feelings of overwhelm and makes the path forward less daunting. Focus on taking one small action at a time, gradually building momentum and confidence.

Visualize success and positive outcomes: Visualize yourself successfully navigating through the challenges and achieving your desired outcomes.

By visualizing positive outcomes, you build a sense of confidence and reinforce your belief in your ability to overcome obstacles.

Take calculated risks: Embrace calculated risks as opportunities for growth. Assess the potential risks and rewards of a situation, and if the potential for growth outweighs the potential risks, take the leap. Remember that taking risks is an essential part of personal development and can lead to transformative experiences.

Develop a support system: Surround yourself with a supportive network of individuals who believe in you and encourage your growth. Seek guidance and support from mentors, friends, or professionals who can provide valuable insights and help you navigate challenges.

Take action despite fear: Rather than waiting for fear to dissipate before taking action, take action despite fear. Start with small steps and gradually build up your courage and confidence. Taking action helps to break the cycle of fear and creates momentum towards your goals.

Learn from failures and setbacks: View failures and setbacks as valuable learning opportunities rather than signs of defeat. Embrace a growth mindset and see challenges as stepping stones on your journey of personal growth. Reflect on what you can learn from each experience and use it to improve and adjust your approach.

Practice self-compassion: Be kind and compassionate with yourself throughout the process. Recognize that fear is a natural part of growth, and it is okay to feel scared or uncertain. Treat yourself with kindness, encourage yourself, and celebrate your progress along the way.

By reframing fear as an opportunity for growth, you can transform it into a powerful motivator that propels you forward on your journey of personal development. Embrace fear, take calculated risks, and remember that the most profound growth often happens outside of your comfort zone. With determination, resilience, and a willingness to face your fears, you can harness fear as a driving force for positive action and achieve remarkable personal growth.

Embracing Self-Expression and Authenticity

Embracing self-expression and authenticity is a powerful way to discover and express your true self. When you allow yourself to be authentic and express who you truly are, you create a deep connection with yourself and others. *Here are some key points to consider when it comes to embracing self-expression and authenticity:*

Recognize your unique voice: Each person has a unique voice and perspective. Take the time to discover and understand your own voice. What are your values, passions, and beliefs? What makes you different? Embracing your unique voice allows you to communicate and express yourself authentically.

Share your truth: Authentic self-expression involves sharing your truth and being honest with yourself and others. It requires vulnerability and the courage to speak your mind and share your experiences. When you share your truth, you create opportunities for deep connections and meaningful conversations.

Explore different forms of self-expression: Self-expression can take various forms, such as art, writing, music, dance, or even public speaking. Experiment with different modes of expression to find what resonates with you. Engaging in creative activities allows you to tap into your inner self and express your thoughts and emotions in a unique and authentic way.

Embrace vulnerability: Authentic self-expression often involves being vulnerable. It requires letting go of the fear of judgment or rejection and allowing yourself to be seen and heard. Embrace vulnerability as a path to growth and connection. When you are open and vulnerable, you create space for others to do the same.

Release the need for approval: Authenticity means staying true to yourself, even if it means not seeking validation or approval from others. Let go of the need to please everyone and focus on expressing yourself in a way that feels authentic and aligned with your values. Remember that your worth does not depend on the acceptance or approval of others.

Practice active listening: Authentic self-expression is not just about speaking your truth; it also involves actively listening to others. Cultivate the skill of deep listening, being present, and genuinely understanding others' perspectives. When you create space for others to express themselves authentically, you foster an environment of trust and respect.

Honor your boundaries: Authentic self-expression requires setting and honoring your boundaries. Be aware of what feels right for you and communicate your boundaries to others. Respecting your boundaries allows you to maintain your authenticity and protect your well-being.

Embrace authenticity in all areas of life: Authenticity is not limited to creative expression; it is a way of being in all aspects of life. Bring your authentic self into your relationships, work, and daily interactions. When you show up as your true self, you attract meaningful connections and create a life that aligns with your values and aspirations.

Remember that embracing self-expression and authenticity is a lifelong journey. It requires self-reflection, courage, and a commitment to staying true to yourself. By embracing your unique voice, sharing your truth, and expressing yourself authentically, you invite others to do the same and create a world where everyone feels seen, heard, and valued for who they truly are.

Embracing the shadows is a transformative journey that requires courage, self-compassion, and a willingness to explore the depths of our being. By understanding and integrating our shadows, we gain a deeper understanding of ourselves and experience profound personal growth. This chapter offers insights, practices, and strategies for embracing the shadows and finding wholeness in our self-discovery journey. As we embrace our shadows and step into our authentic selves, we create a life filled with purpose, fulfillment, and authenticity.

5

Navigating Relationships

Navigating relationships is an integral part of our personal growth and well-being. This chapter explores various aspects of relationships and offers guidance on how to cultivate healthy, empowering connections. Here are the key topics covered in this chapter:

Relationships as Mirrors of Self-Reflection

Our relationships are not just external connections; they are also powerful mirrors that reflect aspects of ourselves back to us. These mirrors provide invaluable opportunities for self-reflection, growth, and self-discovery. When we engage with others, we often see parts of ourselves that we may not have been aware of or fully understood. By observing and reflecting on our interactions, we gain insights into our patterns, behaviors, and emotions, leading to a deeper understanding of ourselves.

The Reflective Nature of Relationships: In the context of relationships, the concept of mirroring refers to the way others reflect our own qualities, traits, and unresolved issues. This reflection can manifest in various ways, such as mirroring our strengths, highlighting our insecurities, triggering our emotions, or revealing our unconscious patterns. These reflections are not meant to judge or criticize us but rather to offer opportunities for growth and self-awareness.

Recognizing Patterns and Behaviors: When we pay attention to the patterns and behaviors that emerge in our relationships, we start to see recurring themes that provide valuable insights into ourselves. For example, if we consistently attract partners who are emotionally unavailable, it may indicate a pattern of seeking validation or fear of intimacy. By recognizing these patterns, we can explore the underlying beliefs and experiences that contribute to them, paving the way for personal growth and healthier relationships.

Understanding Triggers and Emotions: Our reactions and emotional responses within relationships can also serve as mirrors, reflecting our inner landscape. When someone's words or actions trigger strong emotional reactions in us, it often reveals unresolved wounds or unhealed aspects within ourselves. These triggers provide opportunities to delve deeper into our emotional wounds, explore their origins, and work towards healing and self-compassion.

Self-Reflection and Growth: Engaging in self-reflection within the context of relationships is a transformative practice. By taking responsibility for our own thoughts, emotions, and actions, we empower ourselves to make conscious choices and break free from unconscious patterns. Self-reflection helps us identify areas for personal growth, gain clarity on our values and needs, and cultivate healthier ways of relating to others.

Compassion and Non-Judgment: When we approach self-reflection with compassion and non-judgment, we create a safe and supportive environment for our personal growth. It is important to remember that the purpose of self-reflection is not to criticize or blame ourselves but rather to understand ourselves more deeply and make positive changes. Cultivating self-compassion allows us to embrace our imperfections and learn from our mistakes, fostering growth and self-acceptance.

Practicing Self-Inquiry: Self-inquiry is a powerful tool for self-reflection in relationships. It involves asking ourselves honest and introspective questions, such as:

What patterns do I notice in my relationships?

How do I contribute to the dynamics in my relationships?

What emotions and reactions are triggered within me in specific situations?

What unresolved issues or wounds might be influencing my behavior?

How can I show up more authentically and consciously in my relationships?

By engaging in self-inquiry, we deepen our understanding of ourselves and develop greater self-awareness, which in turn enhances the quality of our relationships.

Cultivating Mindfulness in Relationships: Mindfulness is a valuable practice for self-reflection within relationships. By being fully present and aware in our interactions, we can observe our thoughts, emotions, and reactions without judgment. Mindfulness allows us to respond consciously rather than react impulsively, fostering healthier and more authentic connections with others.

Seeking Feedback and Support: In the process of self-reflection, seeking feedback from trusted individuals who know us well can provide valuable insights and perspectives. Their observations can help us gain a more objective view of our behaviors, patterns, and blind spots. Additionally, seeking support from therapists or coaches can provide guidance and facilitate deeper self-reflection.

Embracing relationships as mirrors of self-reflection is an empowering approach to personal growth and self-discovery. By recognizing patterns, exploring triggers, and engaging in self-inquiry, we gain valuable insights into ourselves and can make conscious choices for growth and transformation. Cultivating compassion, practicing mindfulness, and seeking support from others enhance our self-reflection journey within relationships. By embracing this process, we deepen our self-awareness, foster healthier connections, and create a more fulfilling and meaningful life.

Recognizing Healthy and Unhealthy Dynamics

In order to navigate relationships effectively, it is essential to distinguish between healthy and unhealthy dynamics. Healthy relationships are built on mutual respect, trust, open communication, and support, while unhealthy dynamics can be characterized by manipulation, control, lack of boundaries, and toxicity. This section explores the key characteristics of healthy relationships and highlights signs of unhealthy dynamics, enabling individuals to cultivate healthier and more fulfilling connections.

Characteristics of Healthy Relationships

Healthy relationships are marked by several key characteristics that contribute to a positive and supportive dynamic. ***These include:***

Mutual Respect: Healthy relationships are founded on a deep respect for one another's boundaries, opinions, and autonomy. There is an acknowledgment and appreciation of each person's individuality and worth.

Trust and Honesty: Trust forms the foundation of healthy relationships. Honesty and transparency are valued, and there is a sense of reliability and dependability in the relationship.

Effective Communication: Open and honest communication is essential in healthy relationships. There is a willingness to listen, express needs and concerns, and engage in constructive dialogue.

Support and Empathy: Healthy relationships are characterized by support, empathy, and understanding. There is a genuine interest in each other's well-being and a willingness to provide emotional support during both good times and challenging moments.

Equality and Balance: Healthy relationships strive for equality, where power and decision-making are shared. Both individuals feel valued and have an equal voice in the relationship.

Signs of Unhealthy Dynamics

Unhealthy dynamics can manifest in various ways, and it is important to recognize the signs to protect one's well-being and maintain healthy boundaries. Some signs of unhealthy dynamics include:

Lack of Respect: In unhealthy relationships, disrespect may be evident through dismissive or belittling behavior, constant criticism, or disregard for boundaries.

Control and Manipulation: Unhealthy dynamics often involve one person exerting control over the other through manipulation, coercion, or attempts to isolate them from friends and family.

Lack of Trust and Honesty: Unhealthy relationships may be characterized by a lack of trust, dishonesty, or frequent betrayal of trust.

Poor Communication: In unhealthy dynamics, communication breakdowns are common. This can include avoiding difficult conversations, passive-aggressive behavior, or an inability to listen and understand each other's perspectives.

Emotional or Physical Abuse: Unhealthy dynamics may involve emotional, verbal, or physical abuse. This can include threats, intimidation, constant criticism, or physical harm.

Imbalanced Power: Unhealthy relationships often exhibit imbalanced power dynamics, with one person exerting control or dominance over the other, leading to feelings of helplessness or disempowerment.

Cultivating Healthy Dynamics

Recognizing and addressing unhealthy dynamics is essential for fostering healthier relationships. ***Here are some strategies for cultivating healthy dynamics:***

Establishing Boundaries: Clearly defining and communicating personal boundaries is crucial in maintaining healthy dynamics. Boundaries protect one's well-being and ensure mutual respect and consideration.

Effective Communication Skills: Developing strong communication skills, such as active listening and assertiveness, enhances healthy dynamics. It allows for open dialogue, understanding, and conflict resolution.

Seeking Support and Professional Help: If unhealthy dynamics persist, seeking support from trusted friends, family, or professionals can provide guidance and assistance in navigating challenges.

Self-Awareness and Personal Growth: Engaging in self-reflection and personal growth practices allows individuals to become more aware of their own behaviors, triggers, and patterns. This self-awareness helps to break unhealthy cycles and cultivate healthier dynamics.

Letting Go of Toxic Relationships: Recognizing when a relationship is consistently harmful or toxic is essential. Letting go of such relationships is an act of self-care and creates space for healthier connections to flourish.

Recognizing the characteristics of healthy relationships and identifying signs of unhealthy dynamics is crucial for navigating relationships effectively. By cultivating healthy dynamics based on respect, trust, effective communication, support, and equality, individuals can foster meaningful and fulfilling connections. Recognizing and addressing unhealthy dynamics empowers individuals to establish boundaries, seek support, and engage in personal growth, leading to healthier and more satisfying relationships.

Setting Boundaries for Healthy Relationships

Setting and communicating boundaries is an essential aspect of maintaining healthy relationships. Boundaries help to establish a sense of personal autonomy, protect individual well-being, and foster mutual respect. This section explores the importance of setting boundaries and provides strategies for effectively enforcing them, as well as addressing boundary violations in a constructive manner.

The Importance of Setting Boundaries

Setting boundaries is crucial for creating a healthy and balanced dynamic in relationships. *Here are some key reasons why boundaries are important:*

Self-Respect and Self-Care: Boundaries reflect a sense of self-respect and self-care. They demonstrate that you value your own needs, emotions, and personal space, and that you are committed to nurturing your own well-being.

Establishing Personal Space: Boundaries help define personal space and individuality within a relationship. They ensure that each person has the freedom to pursue their own interests, engage in self-reflection, and recharge.

Maintaining Healthy Dynamics: Clear boundaries contribute to maintaining healthy dynamics by preventing issues such as codependency, resentment, and imbalance of power. They promote mutual respect, open communication, and a sense of equality.

Strategies for Setting and Enforcing Boundaries

Effectively setting and enforcing boundaries requires self-awareness, assertiveness, and clear communication. *Here are some strategies to consider:*

Self-Reflection: Reflect on your needs, values, and personal limits. Understand what is acceptable and unacceptable to you in different aspects of your relationships.

Communicate Clearly: Clearly express your boundaries to others in a calm and assertive manner. Use "I" statements to communicate your needs and expectations, focusing on how their behavior impacts you.

Consistency: Consistency is key in enforcing boundaries. Be firm in upholding your boundaries and consistently communicate and reinforce them.

Self-Care: Prioritize self-care and ensure that you are meeting your own needs. This reinforces the importance of your boundaries and sets a positive example for others.

Seek Support: Seek support from trusted friends, family, or professionals if you encounter challenges in setting or enforcing boundaries. They can provide guidance, validation, and encouragement.

Addressing Boundary Violations

Despite our efforts, boundary violations may still occur in relationships. Here are strategies for addressing such violations:

Assertive Communication: Clearly and calmly communicate your feelings and concerns to the person who violated your boundaries. Use "I" statements to express the impact of their actions on you and assert your need for respect.

Reassess the Relationship: Evaluate the relationship and assess whether the person is willing to respect your boundaries and make necessary changes. Consider whether the relationship is healthy and aligned with your values and well-being.

Reinforce Boundaries: Reinforce your boundaries by restating them clearly and consistently. Be prepared to take appropriate action if the violations persist.

Seek Mediation or Professional Help: In more challenging cases, seeking mediation or professional help can provide guidance and support in addressing boundary violations and navigating complex relationship dynamics.

Setting and communicating boundaries is an essential aspect of maintaining healthy relationships. Boundaries promote self-respect, personal space, and mutual respect. By reflecting on your needs, communicating clearly, and consistently enforcing boundaries, you establish a foundation of healthy dynamics. Addressing boundary violations through assertive communication and seeking support when needed ensures that your boundaries are respected. Embracing boundaries in relationships fosters healthier connections based on respect, autonomy, and open communication.

Cultivating Empathy and Active Listening

Cultivating empathy and practicing active listening are essential skills for nurturing deeper and more meaningful connections in relationships. This section explores the significance of understanding others' perspectives, developing empathy, and engaging in active listening. By honing these skills, we create a safe and supportive space for authentic communication and foster empathy within our relationships.

The Importance of Understanding Others' Perspectives

Understanding others' perspectives is a key component of empathy and effective communication. It involves recognizing that each person has unique experiences, beliefs, and emotions that shape their worldview. ***Here are some reasons why understanding others' perspectives is important:***

Enhanced Communication: By understanding others' perspectives, we can communicate more effectively and bridge potential gaps in understanding. It promotes empathy and helps create a safe environment for open and honest dialogue.

Strengthened Relationships: Understanding others' perspectives fosters a sense of validation, respect, and mutual understanding. It strengthens the foundation of relationships by acknowledging and appreciating the diversity of experiences and viewpoints.

Conflict Resolution: Understanding others' perspectives facilitates conflict resolution by promoting empathy and allowing for a more comprehensive understanding of the underlying issues. It enables us to find common ground and work towards mutually satisfactory solutions.

Cultivating Empathy

Empathy is the ability to understand and share the feelings of another person. It allows us to connect with others on a deeper level and respond to their experiences with compassion. ***Here are strategies for cultivating empathy:***

Active Curiosity: Approach interactions with genuine curiosity about the other person's experiences and emotions. Ask open-ended questions and listen attentively to their responses.

Practice Perspective-Taking: Put yourself in the other person's shoes and try to understand their thoughts, emotions, and motivations. Consider how their experiences might shape their perspective.

Validate Emotions: Validate the other person's emotions by acknowledging and accepting them without judgment. Show empathy by expressing understanding and support.

Seek Common Ground: Look for shared experiences or values that can create a sense of connection and understanding. Focus on what unites us rather than what divides us.

Active Listening

Active listening is a powerful tool for fostering genuine communication and understanding in relationships. It involves fully engaging with the speaker, both verbally and non-verbally. ***Here are strategies for practicing active listening:***

Give Undivided Attention: Focus solely on the speaker and give them your full attention. Minimize distractions and demonstrate your interest through eye contact, body language, and verbal cues.

Reflect and Clarify: Reflect back what the speaker has said to ensure accurate understanding. Paraphrase their words and ask clarifying questions to deepen your comprehension.

Suspend Judgment: Suspend judgment and remain open-minded during the conversation. Avoid interrupting or imposing your own opinions prematurely.

Show Empathy: Demonstrate empathy through non-verbal cues, such as nodding or facial expressions, to indicate that you understand and validate the speaker's emotions.

Respond Thoughtfully: Respond thoughtfully and considerately after the speaker has finished expressing their thoughts. Offer your perspective, if appropriate, while maintaining a respectful and empathetic tone.

Cultivating empathy and practicing active listening are transformative skills that enhance communication and foster deeper connections in relationships. By understanding others' perspectives, we create a foundation of empathy and respect, allowing for meaningful interactions. Cultivating empathy involves active curiosity, perspective-taking, and validating others' emotions. Active listening requires giving undivided attention, reflecting and clarifying, suspending judgment, showing empathy, and responding thoughtfully. By honing these skills, we create a safe space for open and authentic communication, nurturing healthier and more fulfilling relationships based on understanding and empathy.

Effective Communication Skills

Effective communication is vital for building and maintaining healthy relationships. This section delves into techniques that promote clear, assertive, and respectful communication. It also emphasizes the importance of active communication, which involves both speaking and listening attentively. By honing these skills, we enhance our ability to express ourselves authentically and connect with others on a deeper level.

Expressing Yourself Clearly, Assertively, and Respectfully

Expressing yourself clearly, assertively, and respectfully is crucial for effective communication. It involves conveying your thoughts, feelings, and needs while respecting the perspectives of others. ***Here are some techniques to enhance your communication skills:***

Clarity: Use clear and concise language to express your thoughts and intentions. Avoid ambiguity or vague statements that can lead to misunderstandings.

Assertiveness: Assertiveness involves expressing your needs, opinions, and boundaries in a direct and confident manner. It enables you to communicate your desires and advocate for yourself while considering the feelings and needs of others.

Active Listening: Actively listen to others by paying full attention to what they are saying. Avoid interrupting or formulating responses in your mind while they are speaking. Show genuine interest and validate their perspective.

Respect: Treat others with respect and kindness in your communication. Use polite and courteous language, and avoid demeaning or derogatory remarks. Respectful communication fosters trust and creates a positive atmosphere.

Non-Verbal Cues: Pay attention to your non-verbal cues, such as body language, facial expressions, and tone of voice. Ensure that your non-verbal signals align with your verbal communication to avoid mixed messages.

Active Communication: Speaking and Listening Attentively

Active communication involves both speaking and listening attentively. It enables effective and meaningful exchanges between individuals. **Here are strategies for active communication:**

Speaking Attentively: When speaking, be mindful of your message, tone, and timing. Choose appropriate moments to express yourself, ensuring that you have the listener's attention. Use active and engaging language to capture their interest.

Listening Attentively: Actively listen to the speaker without interrupting or formulating responses prematurely. Give them your undivided attention and show genuine interest in their words. Use non-verbal cues, such as nodding or maintaining eye contact, to demonstrate attentiveness.

Clarification: Seek clarification when needed to ensure mutual understanding. Paraphrase or summarize the speaker's message to confirm your comprehension and show that you are actively engaged in the conversation.

Empathy: Practice empathy while listening to others. Try to understand their emotions, perspectives, and underlying needs. Show empathy through supportive and validating responses.

Mindful Response: Respond mindfully and thoughtfully after the speaker has finished expressing their thoughts. Consider their perspective and choose your words carefully. Respond in a way that promotes understanding, respect, and constructive dialogue.

Effective communication is a cornerstone of healthy relationships. By expressing yourself clearly, assertively, and respectfully, you create an environment of open and honest communication. Active communication, which involves both speaking and listening attentively, deepens connections and fosters mutual understanding. By honing these skills, you can navigate relationships with greater ease and cultivate meaningful connections based on effective and authentic communication.

Resolving Conflict Constructively

Conflict is an inevitable part of any relationship, and how we handle conflicts can greatly impact the health and longevity of those relationships. This section explores strategies for resolving conflicts in a constructive and respectful manner. By employing techniques such as active listening, compromise, and finding win-win solutions, we can navigate conflicts effectively and strengthen our relationships.

Active Listening: Understanding the Perspectives of Others

Active listening is a vital skill when it comes to resolving conflicts. By actively listening to the perspectives of others, we demonstrate respect and create a safe space for open communication. ***Here are some strategies for active listening:***

- Give your full attention to the person speaking, maintaining eye contact and minimizing distractions.
- Avoid interrupting and allow the person to express themselves fully without judgment.
- Paraphrase or summarize their points to ensure accurate understanding and show that you are actively engaged in the conversation.
- Validate their feelings and experiences, acknowledging that their perspective is important and valid.

Finding Common Ground: Seeking Win-Win Solutions

Resolving conflicts involves finding common ground and seeking win-win solutions that address the concerns of all parties involved. ***Here are techniques to facilitate this process:***

- Identify shared goals or interests that can serve as a foundation for finding common ground.
- Brainstorm possible solutions together, encouraging input and ideas from all parties.
- Explore compromises and alternatives that meet the needs and interests of everyone involved.
- Focus on the problem at hand rather than personal attacks or blame.

Communication and Collaboration: Foster Constructive Dialogue

Constructive dialogue is crucial for resolving conflicts in a healthy and respectful manner. *Here are strategies to foster effective communication and collaboration:*

- Use "I" statements to express your thoughts and feelings without blaming or accusing the other person.
- Express yourself assertively but respectfully, focusing on the specific issue or behavior rather than generalizing or making personal attacks.
- Practice active problem-solving by exploring various perspectives and brainstorming solutions together.
- Seek understanding by asking open-ended questions and encouraging the other person to express their thoughts and feelings.
- Maintain a calm and composed demeanor, even when emotions are running high, to create an atmosphere conducive to constructive dialogue.

Seeking Mediation or Professional Help

In some cases, conflicts may be too complex or challenging to resolve without outside assistance. Seeking mediation or professional help, such as couples counseling or conflict resolution specialists, can provide valuable support and guidance in navigating conflicts.

Resolving conflicts constructively is vital for maintaining healthy and harmonious relationships. By actively listening, finding common ground, and fostering constructive dialogue, we can address conflicts with respect and understanding. Remember that conflicts can be opportunities for growth and deeper connection when approached with empathy and a willingness to find mutually beneficial solutions. By employing these strategies, we can navigate conflicts successfully and foster stronger, more resilient relationships.

Embracing Differences and Diversity

In any relationship, it is common to encounter individuals with different perspectives, backgrounds, and experiences. Embracing these differences and recognizing the value of diverse viewpoints is essential for fostering healthy and enriching relationships. This section explores strategies for embracing diversity, fostering inclusivity, and cultivating respect and understanding within relationships.

Embracing Open-Mindedness: Recognizing the Value of Differences

Open-mindedness is a key attitude for embracing diversity within relationships. By acknowledging that different perspectives and experiences enrich our interactions, we can create a more inclusive and respectful environment. *Here are some strategies for embracing open-mindedness:*

- Challenge assumptions and preconceived notions about others based on their background, culture, or beliefs.
- Approach conversations with curiosity and a genuine desire to understand others' viewpoints.
- Cultivate a willingness to learn from others, recognizing that their unique experiences can broaden our own understanding.

Cultivating Empathy and Respect: Valuing Others' Perspectives

Empathy and respect are fundamental in embracing diversity within relationships. By seeking to understand and appreciate others' perspectives, we foster a sense of inclusivity and create space for genuine connection. *Here are strategies for cultivating empathy and respect:*

- Practice active listening and validate others' experiences, even if they differ from your own.
- Put yourself in others' shoes and try to imagine their thoughts, emotions, and motivations.
- Suspend judgment and approach differences with an open heart and a genuine desire to connect.
- Celebrate and value the unique strengths and contributions that diverse individuals bring to the relationship.

Promoting Inclusivity and Equality: Creating a Safe Space

Creating a safe and inclusive space within relationships is crucial for embracing diversity. *Here are strategies for promoting inclusivity and equality:*

- Encourage open and honest communication where all individuals feel heard and respected.
- Foster an environment where individuals feel comfortable expressing their true selves without fear of judgment or discrimination.
- Challenge discriminatory or exclusionary behaviors and language within the relationship.
- Actively seek out diverse perspectives and actively include individuals from different backgrounds in decision-making processes.

Learning from Differences: Growth and Personal Development

Embracing diversity within relationships provides an opportunity for personal growth and learning. By engaging with individuals who have different perspectives, backgrounds, and experiences, we expand our own understanding and challenge our own biases. *Here are strategies for learning from differences:*

- Engage in open and respectful conversations where you can learn from others' viewpoints.
- Educate yourself about different cultures, beliefs, and experiences through reading, documentaries, or participating in cultural events.
- Reflect on your own biases and assumptions, and be open to unlearning and reevaluating your perspectives.

Embracing differences and diversity within relationships is an on-going journey of growth and understanding. By embracing open-mindedness, cultivating empathy and respect, promoting inclusivity and equality, and learning from differences, we create a space where diverse perspectives are valued and celebrated. Remember that embracing diversity enriches our relationships and provides an opportunity for personal development. By incorporating these strategies, we can foster inclusive, respectful, and meaningful connections with others.

The Power of Collaboration and Cooperation

Collaboration and cooperation are essential elements for building strong, harmonious relationships. When individuals come together and work towards shared goals, they create a supportive and enriching environment that promotes mutual growth and success. This section highlights the power of collaboration and cooperation within relation-ships and provides strategies for fostering a culture of teamwork and celebration.

Fostering Mutual Support: Building Each Other Up

Mutual support is the foundation of collaboration and cooperation within relationships. When individuals uplift and encourage one an-other, they create an atmosphere of trust, encouragement, and shared success. *Here are strategies for fostering mutual support:*

- Celebrate each other's achievements and milestones, acknowledging the efforts and contributions of each individual.
- Offer help and assistance when needed, providing support and encouragement in times of challenges or setbacks.
- Practice active listening and empathy, providing a safe space for individuals to share their aspirations, concerns, and ideas.
- Recognize and appreciate the unique strengths and talents that each individual brings to the relationship, encouraging their growth and development.

Working Towards Shared Goals: Collaborating for Success

Working towards shared goals strengthens relationships and creates a sense of purpose and unity. When individuals align their efforts and collaborate effectively, they can achieve more together than they could alone. ***Here are strategies for working towards shared goals:***

- Clearly define and communicate shared goals, ensuring that everyone understands and is committed to them.
- Divide tasks and responsibilities based on individual strengths and interests, promoting a sense of ownership and contribution.
- Foster open and transparent communication, providing regular updates, sharing progress, and addressing any challenges or obstacles that arise.
- Encourage brainstorming and the exchange of ideas, valuing diverse perspectives and fostering creativity and innovation.

Celebrating Achievements: Acknowledging Collective Success

Celebrating achievements within relationships reinforces a sense of accomplishment and strengthens the bond between individuals. By acknowledging and celebrating each other's successes, individuals feel valued and appreciated for their contributions. ***Here are strategies for celebrating achievements:***

- Create opportunities for recognition and appreciation, such as team gatherings, award ceremonies, or heartfelt expressions of gratitude.
- Encourage individuals to share their accomplishments and milestones, allowing others to express their support and congratulations.
- Foster a culture of celebration, where achievements, big or small, are acknowledged and celebrated collectively.
- Use celebrations as a platform for reflection and setting new goals, encouraging continuous growth and improvement.

Collaboration and cooperation are powerful forces that can transform relationships into thriving and fulfilling partnerships. By fostering mutual support, working towards shared goals, and celebrating achievements, individuals create a culture of teamwork and success. Through collaboration and cooperation, relationships become spaces where individuals can grow, learn from one another, and achieve collective greatness. By implementing the strategies outlined in this section, individuals can harness the power of collaboration and cooperation to strengthen their relationships and create a positive and harmonious environment.

Building Supportive Networks

Building and nurturing a supportive network of relationships is essential for personal growth, well-being, and a sense of belonging. These networks provide individuals with emotional support, guidance, and opportunities for collaboration and learning. This section explores strategies for building and nurturing supportive networks that contribute to individual and collective growth.

Seeking Like-Minded Individuals: Finding Your Tribe

Seeking like-minded individuals who share similar values, interests, and aspirations can create a sense of belonging and foster meaningful connections. Here are strategies for finding your tribe:

- Identify your passions, interests, and values, and seek out communities, groups, or organizations that align with them.
- Attend events, workshops, or seminars related to your interests, where you can meet and connect with individuals who share your passions.
- Utilize online platforms and social media to connect with like-minded individuals in virtual communities or interest groups.
- Engage in activities or hobbies that allow you to meet new people with similar interests, such as joining a sports club, book club, or volunteer organization.

Engaging in Shared Interests: Building Common Ground

Engaging in shared interests is a powerful way to connect with others and build supportive networks. By participating in activities or projects that align with your passions, you create opportunities for meaningful connections. Here are strategies for engaging in shared interests:

- Join groups or organizations centered around your interests, such as hobby clubs, professional associations, or community groups.
- Take part in collaborative projects or initiatives that allow you to work alongside others who share a common goal or purpose.
- Attend workshops, seminars, or classes related to your interests, where you can learn, collaborate, and connect with individuals who share your passions.
- Organize or participate in events or gatherings that bring together individuals with similar interests, providing a space for networking and collaboration.

Offering Support to Others: Being a Source of Encouragement

Supporting others is a key element of building a supportive network. By offering encouragement, advice, and assistance to others, you contribute to the growth and well-being of those around you. Here are strategies for offering support to others:

- Actively listen to others, offering a safe space for them to share their thoughts, concerns, and aspirations.
- Provide encouragement and validation, recognizing and acknowledging the strengths and achievements of others.
- Offer assistance or guidance when appropriate, sharing your knowledge, skills, or resources to support others in their endeavors.
- Collaborate on projects or initiatives, fostering a spirit of teamwork and collective growth.

Building and nurturing a supportive network of relationships is a vital component of personal growth and well-being. By seeking like-minded individuals, engaging in shared interests, and offering support to others, individuals create a network that provides emotional support, guidance, and opportunities for collaboration and learning. Through these strategies, individuals can build and maintain meaningful connections that contribute to their personal and collective growth. A supportive network not only enhances individual well-being but also fosters a sense of belonging and community. By implementing the strategies outlined in this section, individuals can build and nurture a supportive network that empowers and uplifts them on their journey of self-discovery and personal growth.

Nurturing Meaningful Connections

Nurturing and deepening relationships is essential for cultivating meaningful connections that stand the test of time. This section provides guidance on nurturing relationships through acts of kindness, expressing gratitude, and showing up authentically.

Acts of Kindness: Small Gestures, Big Impact

Acts of kindness can strengthen relationships and create a positive and supportive atmosphere. ***Here are strategies for incorporating acts of kindness into your relationships:***

- Be attentive to the needs and desires of your loved ones, offering help and support when they need it without expecting anything in return.
- Engage in random acts of kindness, such as sending a thoughtful message, surprising someone with a small gift, or offering assistance when it's least expected.
- Practice active listening and show genuine interest in others' lives, offering a compassionate ear and a safe space for them to share their thoughts and feelings.
- Be mindful of your words and actions, aiming to uplift and inspire rather than criticize or judge.

Expressing Gratitude: Recognizing and Appreciating

Expressing gratitude is a powerful way to nurture relationships and show appreciation for the people in your life. ***Here are strategies for incorporating gratitude into your relationships:***

- Regularly express gratitude to your loved ones, acknowledging their presence, support, and contributions to your life.

- Write heartfelt thank-you notes or letters to express your gratitude and appreciation for specific actions or qualities that you admire in the other person.
- Take the time to reflect on the positive impact the person has had on your life, and share your gratitude with them verbally or through written messages.
- Practice gratitude in your own life, cultivating an attitude of appreciation that extends to your interactions with others.

Showing Up Authentically: Being Present and True to Yourself

Authenticity is a cornerstone of meaningful connections. Showing up authentically allows for genuine and deep connections based on trust and understanding. *Here are strategies for showing up authentically in your relationships:*

- Be true to yourself and honor your values and beliefs, even if they differ from those around you.
- Share your thoughts, feelings, and vulnerabilities openly and honestly, allowing others to see and understand the real you.
- Practice active listening and show genuine interest in others' perspectives and experiences, creating a space for authentic dialogue and connection.
- Respect boundaries and individual autonomy, allowing others to express themselves authentically without judgment or criticism.

Nurturing meaningful connections requires ongoing effort and attention. By incorporating acts of kindness, expressing gratitude, and showing up authentically, individuals can deepen their relationships and create a positive and supportive environment. Acts of kindness not only strengthen bonds but also create a ripple effect of positivity. Expressing gratitude allows individuals to recognize and appreciate the contributions of others. Showing up authentically fosters genuine connections based on trust and understanding. By implementing these strategies, individuals can nurture and sustain meaningful connections that enrich their lives and the lives of those around them.

Cultivating Empowering Relationships

Empowering relationships have the power to uplift, inspire, and support personal growth. This section emphasizes the importance of seeking out relationships that encourage self-expression, provide a safe space for vulnerability and authenticity, and support individual development.

Supportive of Personal Growth

Seek relationships with individuals who support your personal growth and encourage you to pursue your passions, goals, and aspirations.

Surround yourself with people who believe in your potential and provide constructive feedback and guidance to help you reach your full potential.

Engage in open and honest conversations with your loved ones about personal growth, sharing your goals and aspirations, and asking for their support and encouragement.

Encourage and support the personal growth of others by offering words of affirmation, providing resources or opportunities for learning and development, and celebrating their achievements.

Create a supportive and growth-oriented community by actively seeking out like-minded individuals who share similar values and aspirations. Attend networking events, join clubs or organizations, or participate in online communities where you can connect with others who are on a similar path of personal growth.

Engage in meaningful conversations and collaborations with individuals who inspire and challenge you. Surround yourself with people who are committed to their own personal growth and are willing to support and uplift you on your journey as well.

Be open to receiving constructive feedback and guidance from others. Recognize that feedback is an opportunity for growth and improvement, and embrace it with an open mind and a willingness to learn. Seek out mentors or coaches who can provide valuable insights and guidance based on their own experiences and expertise.

At the same time, remember to be discerning in the relationships you cultivate. Surround yourself with individuals who genuinely believe in your potential and support your growth, rather than those who may undermine your aspirations or hold you back.

Encourage and support the personal growth of others as well. Offer words of affirmation, provide resources or recommendations for books, courses, or workshops that have helped you in your own journey, and celebrate the achievements and milestones of those around you. By fostering a culture of growth and support, you create an environment where everyone can thrive and reach their full potential.

Remember that personal growth is not a solitary journey. It is greatly enhanced by the connections and relationships we cultivate along the way. Surrounding yourself with individuals who support your personal growth and encourage you to pursue your passions and aspirations can be a powerful catalyst for your own transformation and success.

Encouraging Self-Expression

Seek relationships where you can freely express your thoughts, feelings, and ideas without fear of judgment or rejection.

Surround yourself with individuals who listen attentively, show empathy, and validate your experiences, allowing you to express yourself authentically.

Create an environment of mutual respect and acceptance, where everyone feels safe to share their perspectives, even if they differ from one another.

Encourage self-expression in others by actively listening, showing curiosity about their thoughts and experiences, and offering support and encouragement for their unique viewpoints.

Embrace different forms of self-expression, such as writing, art, music, or any creative outlet that resonates with you. Allow yourself the freedom to explore and express your innermost thoughts, emotions, and desires through these mediums.

Practice self-reflection and introspection as a means of understanding and expressing your true self. Set aside dedicated time for introspective activities such as journaling, meditation, or engaging in solitary pursuits that allow you to connect with your inner voice.

Take risks and step outside of your comfort zone when it comes to self-expression. Challenge yourself to express your opinions, share your talents, and showcase your unique perspective. Embrace vulnerability and trust that by expressing yourself authentically, you are inviting deeper connections and meaningful interactions.

Remember that self-expression is a continuous journey of self-discovery. Your authentic voice and self-expression may evolve and change over time, and that's perfectly natural. Embrace the process of self-exploration and give yourself permission to grow and adapt as you discover new aspects of yourself.

Celebrate and honor your own self-expression. Recognize the courage it takes to share your true self with the world. Acknowledge and appreciate the value and impact of your unique voice. By honoring your own self-expression, you inspire others to do the same.

Finally, be patient and compassionate with yourself as you navigate the path of self-expression. It may take time to fully embrace and express your authentic self. Embrace the imperfections and embrace the journey of self-expression as a continuous process of growth and self-discovery.

By encouraging self-expression, both in yourself and others, you create a supportive and empowering environment where everyone feels seen, heard, and valued. Embracing self-expression allows you to connect more deeply with your own truth and authenticity, fostering personal growth, and nurturing genuine connections with others.

Providing a Safe Space for Vulnerability and Authenticity

Cultivate relationships where vulnerability is embraced and supported, allowing for deeper connections and emotional intimacy.

Share your vulnerabilities with trusted individuals, knowing that they will hold space for you without judgment or criticism.

Encourage others to be authentic and vulnerable by modeling it yourself and creating a safe and non-judgmental environment for them to express their true selves.

Practice active listening and empathy when someone shares their vulnerabilities, providing a compassionate and supportive presence.

Be gentle with yourself and honor your own vulnerability. Allow yourself to be authentic and open, even when it feels uncomfortable or challenging.

Create rituals or practices that promote vulnerability and authenticity, such as journaling, meditation, or engaging in creative expression. These activities can help you connect with your emotions and express your true self.

Recognize that vulnerability is a strength, not a weakness. It takes courage to be vulnerable and share your authentic self with others.

Set boundaries to protect your vulnerability. Choose to share your vulnerabilities with those who have earned your trust and have proven themselves to be safe and supportive.

Celebrate and honor the vulnerability and authenticity of others. Acknowledge their courage and create a space where they feel valued and appreciated for being their true selves.

Embrace the growth and connection that comes from being vulnerable and authentic. Recognize that by allowing yourself to be seen and known, you create opportunities for deeper connections, understanding, and personal growth.

In creating a safe space for vulnerability and authenticity, you create an environment where individuals feel accepted, heard, and understood. This fosters deeper connections, emotional healing, and a sense of belonging. By embracing vulnerability and authenticity, you invite others to do the same, creating a community that supports and celebrates each other's true selves.

Fostering Mutual Growth and Development

Seek relationships that promote mutual growth and development, where both parties are invested in each other's well-being and success.

Engage in open and honest communication about goals, aspirations, and areas for growth, and actively support each other in achieving them.

Collaborate on shared projects or pursuits, leveraging each other's strengths and skills for collective growth and success.

Celebrate each other's achievements and milestones, fostering a sense of shared accomplishment and encouragement.

Create a safe and supportive space for vulnerability and exploration, where both individuals can freely express their thoughts, emotions, and fears without judgment.

Encourage each other to step out of comfort zones and take on new challenges, pushing each other to reach new heights and discover untapped potentials.

Practice active listening and empathy, seeking to understand each other's perspectives and experiences. Offer constructive feedback and guidance when needed, fostering a culture of continuous learning and improvement.

Embrace the concept of lifelong learning together, exploring new ideas, skills, and experiences side by side. Attend workshops, seminars, or courses together to expand your knowledge and deepen your connection.

Celebrate the uniqueness of each other's journeys and respect the individual paths of growth and development. Encourage autonomy and personal agency while maintaining a strong foundation of support and collaboration.

By fostering relationships that promote mutual growth and development, you create an environment where both individuals can thrive and evolve. Together, you can inspire each other to reach new levels of personal and professional success while cultivating a deep sense of connection and shared purpose.

Conclusion

Cultivating empowering relationships is essential for personal growth and well-being. By seeking out relationships that support personal growth, encourage self-expression, and provide a safe space for vulnerability and authenticity, individuals can thrive and be inspired to reach their full potential. Supporting the personal growth of others and fostering mutual growth and development in relationships creates a positive and empowering environment. By implementing these strategies, individuals can cultivate empowering relationships that uplift, inspire, and support their journey of self-discovery and personal development.

Identifying Toxic Relationships and Letting Go

Toxic relationships can have a detrimental impact on our personal growth and overall well-being. This section focuses on identifying the signs of toxic relationships and provides guidance on letting go of unhealthy connections for the sake of our emotional and mental health.

Recognizing Signs of Toxic Relationships

Pay attention to consistent patterns of disrespect, manipulation, or control in the relationship. These behaviors can include verbal or emotional abuse, gaslighting, or constant criticism.

Notice if the relationship is characterized by a lack of trust, constant conflict, or an imbalance of power where one person dominates and disregards the needs and boundaries of the other.

Be aware of situations where your values, beliefs, and personal boundaries are consistently disregarded or invalidated.

Take note of any relationships that drain your energy, leaving you feeling depleted, anxious, or emotionally overwhelmed.

Pay attention to any signs of isolation or separation from friends and family due to the influence or demands of the other person.

Notice if the relationship causes you to compromise your own values, goals, or dreams in order to please or appease the other person.

Be mindful of any instances of physical aggression or violence, as these are clear indicators of a toxic and potentially dangerous relationship.

Trust your intuition and gut feelings. If something feels off or you have a constant sense of unease in the relationship, it may be a sign that it is toxic.

Recognize if the relationship lacks mutual respect, support, and reciprocity. A healthy relationship should be built on a foundation of equality, trust, and shared values.

If you find yourself constantly making excuses for the other person's behavior or constantly feeling the need to defend them, it may be a sign that the relationship is toxic.

Acknowledge if the relationship hinders your personal growth, self-esteem, or overall well-being. A healthy relationship should uplift and empower you, rather than diminish your sense of self-worth.

Remember that no one deserves to be in a toxic relationship. If you recognize these signs in your relationship, it may be necessary to seek support and consider taking steps to remove yourself from the toxic dynamic.

It is important to prioritize your own well-being and surround yourself with healthy, supportive relationships that nurture your growth and happiness.

Assessing the Impact on Well-being

Reflect on how the relationship affects your overall well-being, including your emotional, mental, and physical health.

Consider if the relationship supports your personal growth and goals, or if it holds you back and prevents you from reaching your full potential.

Evaluate whether the relationship contributes positively to your self-esteem and self-worth, or if it consistently undermines your confidence and self-belief.

Take stock of the level of happiness and fulfillment you experience in the relationship. Consider if it brings you joy, satisfaction, and a sense of emotional safety, or if it consistently brings you pain, stress, and feelings of insecurity.

Reflect on how the relationship affects your overall well-being, including your emotional, mental, and physical health. Assess if being in this relationship brings you more positive emotions such as happiness, love, and contentment, or if it frequently leads to negative emotions like stress, sadness, or anxiety. Consider how the relationship impacts your mental health, such as whether it supports your emotional well-being and provides a healthy space for communication and conflict resolution. Evaluate if being in the relationship contributes to a sense of stability and balance in your life, or if it consistently causes emotional turmoil or disrupts your overall well-being.

Consider if the relationship supports your personal growth and goals, or if it holds you back and prevents you from reaching your full potential. Reflect on whether the relationship encourages your personal development, respects your ambitions, and supports your individuality. Assess if your partner or the relationship as a whole motivates you to pursue your passions, learn new things, and become the best version of yourself. Evaluate if being in this relationship allows you to maintain a healthy balance between your personal goals and the needs of the partnership.

Evaluate whether the relationship contributes positively to your self-esteem and self-worth, or if it consistently undermines your confidence and self-belief. Consider if your partner respects and values you for who you are, and if they provide a supportive and nurturing environment for your self-esteem to thrive. Assess if the relationship fosters a sense of acceptance, appreciation, and validation of your worth, or if it frequently involves criticism, manipulation, or emotional abuse that erodes your self-confidence.

Take stock of the level of happiness and fulfillment you experience in the relationship. Consider if it brings you joy, satisfaction, and a sense of emotional safety. Assess if the relationship allows for open communication, trust, and mutual respect. Reflect on whether your needs for intimacy, connection, and companionship are met in the relationship, or if you consistently feel unfulfilled, neglected, or lonely. Consider if the relationship enhances your overall quality of life and contributes to your overall happiness and well-being.

It is important to approach this assessment with honesty and self-awareness. Sometimes, difficult decisions may need to be made if the relationship consistently has a negative impact on your well-being. Remember that prioritizing your own well-being and happiness is essential for leading a fulfilling and healthy life.

Letting Go of Toxic Relationships

Recognize that letting go of a toxic relationship is an act of self-care and self-preservation. Understand that it is okay to prioritize your emotional and mental well-being.

Seek support from trusted friends, family, or professionals who can provide guidance, validation, and encouragement throughout the process of letting go.

Set clear boundaries with the toxic individual and communicate your decision to end or distance yourself from the relationship, if necessary.

Practice self-compassion and forgiveness, both towards yourself and the toxic person, as you navigate the process of letting go. Understand that it may take time to heal and recover from the effects of the toxic relationship.

Engage in self-care activities and surround yourself with positive influences that support your healing and personal growth.

Focus on rebuilding and nurturing healthy relationships that uplift and empower you. Prioritize spending time with people who genuinely care about your well-being and support your personal growth.

Cultivate self-awareness and reflect on the patterns and dynamics that led to the toxic relationship. Use this insight to set healthy boundaries and establish red flags to watch out for in future relationships.

Practice self-reflection and work on building a strong sense of self-worth and self-esteem. Recognize that you deserve healthy and fulfilling relationships.

Consider seeking therapy or counseling to process your emotions, gain clarity, and develop coping strategies for moving forward.

Embrace the opportunity for personal growth and transformation that comes with letting go of toxic relationships. Use this experience as a catalyst for self-discovery and a chance to redefine your values, priorities, and boundaries.

Remember that letting go is a process and may involve moments of grief, doubt, and vulnerability. Give yourself permission to feel and honor your emotions as you heal and move forward.

Celebrate your strength and resilience in choosing to let go of toxic relationships. Acknowledge the courage it takes to prioritize your well-being and create a healthier, more fulfilling life.

As you let go of toxic relationships, focus on cultivating self-love, self-compassion, and self-care. Engage in activities that bring you joy, nurture your well-being, and support your personal growth.

Surround yourself with a supportive community of like-minded individuals who understand and validate your experiences. Connect with others who have gone through similar journeys and find solace in sharing your stories and supporting one another.

Ultimately, letting go of toxic relationships allows you to reclaim your power, create healthier boundaries, and foster a positive environment for personal growth and happiness. It opens up space for new opportunities, meaningful connections, and a renewed sense of self. Trust that by letting go, you are creating the space to invite healthier, more fulfilling relationships into your life.

Identifying toxic relationships and letting go of unhealthy connections is crucial for our emotional and mental well-being. By recognizing the signs of toxicity, assessing the impact on our overall well-being, and making the decision to let go, we create space for healing, growth, and the cultivation of healthy relationships. Seeking support, setting boundaries, and practicing self-compassion are essential during this process. Remember that letting go of toxic relationships is an act of self-care and a step towards creating a more positive and nurturing environment for personal growth and well-being.

Developing Self-Awareness within Relationships

Developing self-awareness is essential for navigating relationships effectively. This section explores how cultivating self-awareness allows us to understand our own needs, triggers, and patterns, enhancing our ability to engage in healthy and fulfilling connections.

Understanding Our Needs

Take time for self-reflection and identify your emotional, physical, and psychological needs within relationships. Consider what brings you joy, fulfillment, and a sense of security.

Recognize that your needs may evolve over time, and it's important to regularly check in with yourself to understand and communicate your changing needs to your partner or loved ones.

Be honest with yourself about any unmet needs in your relationships. This awareness allows you to address them constructively and seek support if necessary.

Communicate your needs clearly and assertively with your partner or loved ones. Use "I" statements to express how certain behaviors or situations make you feel and what you need from them. Remember that effective communication is essential for building healthy and fulfilling relationships.

Practice self-care and self-compassion as you navigate your needs. Prioritize activities and practices that nourish and fulfill you. This can include setting boundaries, engaging in activities that bring you joy, and taking time for self-reflection and self-care.

Seek support from trusted friends, family members, or professionals if you find it challenging to identify or communicate your needs. Therapy, counseling, or support groups can provide a safe and supportive space for exploring and understanding your needs in a non-judgmental environment.

Be open to compromise and finding win-win solutions in your relationships. Understand that meeting your needs may require negotiation and collaboration with your partner or loved ones. Strive for mutual understanding and finding a balance that honors both your needs and the needs of others involved.

Remember that honoring your needs is not selfish but essential for your overall well-being. Taking care of yourself allows you to show up fully in your relationships and contribute positively to the lives of others. Embracing your needs contributes to a healthier and more fulfilling dynamic within your relationships.

Ultimately, understanding and honoring your needs is a lifelong journey. It requires self-awareness, open communication, and a willingness to prioritize your well-being. By nurturing and fulfilling your needs, you create a solid foundation for healthy and meaningful relationships in your life.

Exploring Triggers and Patterns

Reflect on your emotional triggers—the situations or behaviors that evoke strong emotional reactions within you. Understand the underlying reasons for these triggers, which may be rooted in past experiences or unresolved wounds.

Notice any patterns that arise in your relationships, such as recurring conflicts or dynamics. Consider how these patterns may be influenced by your own thoughts, beliefs, or behaviors.

Take responsibility for your reactions and behaviors within relationships. By recognizing your triggers and patterns, you can respond consciously rather than reactively, fostering healthier interactions.

Engage in self-reflection and introspection to gain a deeper understanding of your triggers and patterns. This may involve journaling, therapy, or other practices that help you explore your emotions, thoughts, and experiences.

Develop self-awareness around your triggers by paying attention to the specific situations or behaviors that elicit a strong emotional response. Take note of the emotions that arise and how they manifest in your body.

Explore the underlying reasons for your triggers. Consider whether they are connected to past traumas, unmet needs, or core beliefs about yourself and the world. Be gentle with yourself as you uncover these deeper layers, and seek support if needed.

Recognize the patterns that show up in your relationships. Notice if there are common themes or dynamics that arise, such as a tendency to seek validation, avoid conflict, or people-please. Reflect on how these patterns may be contributing to your experiences in relationships.

Take responsibility for your reactions and behaviors within relationships. Recognize that while you may not have control over others' actions, you have agency over your own responses. Practice self-compassion and empathy as you navigate challenging interactions.

Consider how your triggers and patterns may be influencing your relationships. Are there ways in which your reactions may be escalating conflicts or perpetuating unhealthy dynamics? Explore alternative ways of responding that align with your values and promote healthier connections.

Seek support from trusted individuals or professionals who can provide guidance and insights as you navigate your triggers and patterns. Therapy, coaching, or support groups can offer valuable perspectives and tools for healing and growth.

Engaging in this process of exploring triggers and patterns requires patience, self-compassion, and a willingness to face discomfort. It is an ongoing journey of self-discovery and personal growth. By developing awareness and understanding around your triggers and patterns, you can cultivate healthier relationships, break free from limiting patterns, and create greater emotional well-being and fulfillment.

Cultivating Self-Reflection and Mindfulness

Practice self-reflection regularly to deepen your understanding of yourself and your relationship dynamics. Set aside dedicated time to introspect and journal about your thoughts, feelings, and experiences within your relationships.

Cultivate mindfulness by bringing present-moment awareness to your interactions. Notice your thoughts, emotions, and physical sensations during conversations or conflicts. This heightened awareness enables you to respond authentically and with greater clarity.

By cultivating self-reflection and mindfulness, you gain valuable insights into your patterns, triggers, and needs. Take time to observe your reactions and responses in various relationship scenarios. Notice any recurring patterns or limiting beliefs that may be influencing your interactions.

Engage in journaling as a powerful tool for self-reflection. Write about your experiences, emotions, and reflections related to your relationships. Explore your values, desires, and boundaries to gain clarity on what you truly want and need in your connections with others.

Developing mindfulness is essential for cultivating authentic and present-moment awareness in your relationships. Practice active listening and being fully present during conversations. Notice your body language, tone of voice, and nonverbal cues. By being fully engaged in the present moment, you can deepen your connection and understanding of others.

Additionally, practicing self-compassion and non-judgment during self-reflection and mindfulness is crucial. Be gentle with yourself as you explore and uncover aspects of yourself that may be challenging or uncomfortable. Embrace the opportunity for growth and learning that self-reflection brings.

Regularly integrating self-reflection and mindfulness into your daily life strengthens your self-awareness and allows you to navigate your relationships with greater authenticity and empathy. As you deepen your understanding of yourself, you can foster healthier and more fulfilling connections with others.

Seeking Feedback and Self-Assessment

Seek feedback from trusted individuals who can provide insights and perspectives on your behavior and impact within relationships. Be open to receiving constructive criticism and use it as an opportunity for growth.

Engage in self-assessment exercises, such as journaling or introspection, to gain a comprehensive view of yourself within relationships. Ask yourself reflective questions and explore areas where you can improve or make adjustments.

Identify patterns or behaviors that may be hindering your personal growth and relationships. Take responsibility for your actions and behaviors, and be willing to make changes where necessary.

Develop self-awareness by paying attention to your thoughts, emotions, and reactions in different situations. Notice any patterns or triggers that arise and explore their underlying causes. This self-awareness will help you understand yourself better and make conscious choices in your interactions with others.

Seek feedback from trusted individuals who can provide honest and constructive insights. These can be friends, family members, mentors, or even professionals such as therapists or coaches. Create a safe and supportive space for open and honest communication, and be receptive to the feedback you receive.

Consider the feedback you receive with an open mind and without defensiveness. Reflect on the validity of the feedback and how it aligns with your own self-assessment. Use this feedback as a valuable tool for self-improvement and growth.

Continuously evaluate your actions and behaviors, and be willing to make changes when necessary. This may involve setting goals, creating action plans, and seeking additional support or resources to help you in your journey of self-improvement.

Regularly assess your progress and celebrate your achievements along the way. Acknowledge the growth you have made and the positive impact it has had on your relationships. Recognize that personal growth is an ongoing process and that there will always be room for further improvement.

Incorporate self-reflection practices into your routine, such as journaling, meditation, or mindfulness exercises. These practices can help you deepen your self-awareness, gain clarity, and make conscious choices aligned with your values and aspirations.

Remember that seeking feedback and engaging in self-assessment is not about seeking perfection or validation from others. It is about self-growth, self-improvement, and fostering healthier and more fulfilling relationships. Embrace the process with curiosity, openness, and a commitment to personal growth.

Practicing Self-Compassion

Be compassionate towards yourself as you navigate the complexities of relationships. Acknowledge that self-awareness is a continuous journey, and it's normal to have moments of confusion or uncertainty.

Embrace self-compassion by treating yourself with kindness, understanding, and forgiveness. Offer yourself the same empathy and support you would extend to a loved one facing similar challenges.

Practice self-care to nurture your well-being and recharge emotionally. Engage in activities that bring you joy, reduce stress, and promote self-reflection.

Prioritize self-care by setting aside dedicated time for self-care activities, such as meditation, exercise, journaling, or engaging in hobbies that bring you fulfillment.

Cultivate self-compassionate self-talk by challenging self-criticism and negative self-judgment. Replace self-critical thoughts with kind and encouraging words, acknowledging that you are doing your best in every moment.

Develop a support system by surrounding yourself with positive and understanding individuals who uplift and validate your experiences. Seek out relationships that promote growth, empathy, and acceptance.

Set healthy boundaries to protect your emotional well-being. Learn to say no to activities or commitments that do not align with your values or deplete your energy. Prioritize your own needs and make self-care a non-negotiable part of your daily life.

Celebrate your successes and milestones, no matter how small they may seem. Acknowledge your growth, progress, and achievements along the journey of self-discovery. Take pride in your efforts and give yourself credit for the steps you have taken.

Remember that self-compassion is an ongoing practice. Be patient and gentle with yourself as you navigate the complexities of relationships and self-awareness. Embrace the journey with kindness, understanding, and a genuine desire to nurture your own well-being.

Through practicing self-compassion, you cultivate a strong foundation of self-love and acceptance. This foundation allows you to navigate the challenges of relationships with greater resilience, empathy, and authenticity. It empowers you to honor your own needs and emotions, while also fostering healthy and fulfilling connections with others.

Developing self-awareness within relationships is a transformative process that allows us to understand our needs, triggers, and patterns. By cultivating self-awareness, we gain insights into our behaviors and reactions, empowering us to engage in healthier and more fulfilling connections. Through self-reflection, mindfulness, seeking feedback, and practicing self-compassion, we deepen our understanding of ourselves and enhance our ability to navigate relationships with authenticity, empathy, and growth. Remember that self-awareness is an ongoing journey, and as we continue to explore and understand ourselves, we foster stronger, more harmonious relationships.

Honoring Individual Autonomy and Independence

Honoring individual autonomy and independence is vital for maintaining healthy and fulfilling relationships. This section emphasizes the importance of recognizing and respecting each other's unique identities, needs, and desires, fostering an environment of mutual independence and self-expression.

Embracing Self-Identity

Acknowledge and celebrate your own unique identity within the context of your relationships. Recognize that you are an individual with your own interests, values, and aspirations.

Encourage and support your partner or loved ones in cultivating their own sense of self. Respect their individuality and provide space for them to pursue their passions and personal growth.

Understand that your self-identity is not fixed or static. It is a fluid and evolving aspect of who you are. Embrace the process of self-discovery and allow yourself the freedom to explore different facets of your identity.

Take time for self-reflection and introspection. Engage in activities that bring you joy and allow you to connect with your authentic self. Explore your interests, hobbies, and passions, and let them shape your self-identity.

Be open to growth and change. Embrace new experiences and challenges that push you outside of your comfort zone. Allow yourself to evolve and adapt as you discover new aspects of your identity.

Embrace self-compassion and self-acceptance. Recognize that your self-identity may include both strengths and areas for growth. Embrace your imperfections and treat yourself with kindness and understanding.

Seek support and guidance when needed. Surround yourself with a supportive community of friends, mentors, or professionals who can provide guidance and encouragement as you navigate your self-identity journey.

Remember that self-identity is not defined by external validation or comparison to others. It is an internal process of self-awareness and self-acceptance. Embrace who you are authentically and trust in your own unique path.

By embracing your self-identity, you can cultivate a sense of empowerment, authenticity, and fulfillment in your relationships and in all areas of your life. Embrace the journey of self-discovery and let your true self shine.

Establishing Boundaries

Communicate and establish clear boundaries that honor your individual needs and values. Discuss and negotiate boundaries with your partner or loved ones to ensure that both parties feel respected and valued.

Respect the boundaries set by others. Understand that boundaries are essential for maintaining a healthy balance of independence and to prevent feelings of suffocation or resentment.

Recognize that setting boundaries is not a selfish act but a necessary step towards self-care and self-preservation. It allows you to prioritize your well-being and protect your energy from being depleted or compromised.

Take time to reflect on your own needs, values, and limits. Identify areas where you feel overwhelmed, drained, or taken advantage of. Use this self-awareness to establish clear and assertive boundaries that align with your values and promote your overall well-being.

Communicate your boundaries openly and assertively, expressing your needs and expectations in a respectful manner. Clearly communicate your limits and what is and isn't acceptable to you. Be firm in your boundaries and hold yourself accountable to enforcing them.

Be prepared for potential resistance or pushback from others, as they may be accustomed to your previous behavior or may not fully understand the importance of boundaries. Stay committed to your boundaries and reinforce them consistently. Remember, it is not your responsibility to please everyone at the expense of your own well-being.

Regularly reassess and adjust your boundaries as needed. As you grow and evolve, your boundaries may shift and change. Be flexible and willing to adapt to new circumstances and personal growth.

Respect the boundaries of others and be mindful of their needs and limitations. Just as you expect others to honor your boundaries, extend the same courtesy to them. Practice active listening and empathy when someone communicates their boundaries to you.

Remember that setting and maintaining boundaries is a continuous process. It requires ongoing self-reflection, self-advocacy, and effective communication. By establishing and respecting boundaries, you create a healthier and more fulfilling environment that fosters mutual respect, understanding, and personal growth.

Nurturing Personal Growth

Encourage personal growth and self-development within yourself and your relationships. Support each other's goals and aspirations, providing space for individual exploration and learning.

Foster a growth mindset by embracing challenges and encouraging each other to step outside of comfort zones. Celebrate personal achievements and growth, both individually and as a couple or group.

Create an environment of continuous learning and self-improvement. Engage in activities such as reading books, attending workshops, or pursuing new hobbies that stimulate personal growth. Encourage each other to set goals and take steps towards achieving them.

Practice open and honest communication, creating a safe space for sharing thoughts, feelings, and ideas. Engage in active listening, seeking to understand each other's perspectives and experiences. Provide support and constructive feedback to help each other grow and overcome obstacles.

Embrace self-reflection as a tool for personal growth. Encourage regular introspection and journaling to gain insight into thoughts, emotions, and patterns of behavior. Reflect on past experiences and identify areas for improvement or further exploration.

Embrace diversity and different perspectives. Engage in discussions and activities that challenge preconceived notions and broaden understanding. Embrace the opportunity to learn from each other's unique backgrounds, experiences, and viewpoints.

Practice self-care as an essential component of personal growth. Prioritize physical, mental, and emotional well-being. Engage in activities that promote relaxation, self-reflection, and self-nurturing. This includes practicing mindfulness, engaging in regular exercise, getting adequate rest, and engaging in activities that bring joy and fulfillment.

Lastly, be patient and compassionate with yourself and others as personal growth is a gradual process. Celebrate progress and milestones along the way, acknowledging that growth takes time and effort.

Embrace the journey of personal growth with an open heart and a commitment to lifelong learning and self-discovery.

Cultivating Trust and Security

Build trust and security within your relationships by honoring commitments, being reliable, and respecting each other's boundaries and privacy.

Foster open and honest communication, creating an environment where individuals feel safe to express their thoughts, feelings, and desires without fear of judgment or rejection.

Create a foundation of trust by being trustworthy yourself. Act with integrity and follow through on your words and promises. This cultivates a sense of security and reliability in your relationships.

Respect the boundaries and privacy of others. Recognize that each person has their own comfort levels and limits. Seek consent and ask for permission before sharing personal information or engaging in activities that may affect others.

Practice active listening and empathy in your interactions. Validate the feelings and experiences of others and make an effort to understand their perspective. This creates an environment of mutual understanding and support.

Be transparent and honest in your communication. Avoid deceit or manipulation, as this erodes trust and can damage relationships. Instead, strive for openness and authenticity in your interactions.

When conflicts or disagreements arise, approach them with respect and a willingness to find common ground. Seek to understand the underlying needs and interests of all parties involved. Engage in constructive dialogue to find mutually beneficial solutions.

Celebrate and honor the uniqueness of each individual. Embrace diversity and create an inclusive space where everyone feels valued and accepted for who they are. Foster an atmosphere of respect, kindness, and acceptance.

Regularly express gratitude and appreciation for the people in your life. Acknowledge their contributions and let them know they are valued. This strengthens the bonds of trust and deepens the sense of security in your relationships.

Remember that building trust and security is an ongoing process. It requires consistent effort, communication, and a willingness to work through challenges together. By cultivating trust and security in your relationships, you create a foundation for deeper connection, intimacy, and fulfillment.

Balancing Togetherness and Independence

Find a healthy balance between togetherness and independence. Recognize that spending quality time together is important, but also allow for individual space and activities that nourish your personal well-being.

Foster a sense of interdependence, where each individual's independence enhances and strengthens the relationship rather than diminishing it.

Understand that healthy relationships require both togetherness and independence. While it is natural to want to spend time with your partner or loved ones, it is equally important to maintain your own sense of self and pursue activities that bring you joy and fulfillment.

Communicate openly and honestly with your partner about your needs for personal space and independence. Discuss and establish boundaries that respect each other's individuality and allow for time alone or engaging in separate hobbies and interests. This will help maintain a healthy balance and prevent feelings of suffocation or dependency.

Nurture your own passions, hobbies, and self-care practices. Dedicate time to activities that bring you joy and help you grow as an individual. This will not only enrich your own life but also contribute positively to the relationship as you bring your own unique experiences and perspectives to it.

Recognize that being independent does not mean neglecting the relationship or distancing yourself emotionally. It means honoring and valuing your own needs while also nurturing the connection with your partner. Foster a sense of interdependence, where you and your partner support each other's personal growth and encourage individual pursuits.

Practice active listening and empathy in your relationships. When spending time together, be fully present and engaged, and strive to understand and appreciate each other's perspectives. Create a safe and supportive environment where both partners feel comfortable expressing their needs and desires.

Remember that finding a balance between togetherness and independence is an ongoing process. It requires ongoing communication, self-awareness, and adjustment. Be open to revisiting and renegotiating boundaries as your needs and circumstances change over time.

By balancing togetherness and independence, you create a foundation for a healthy and fulfilling relationship. You honor your own individuality while also nurturing the bond with your partner. This balance allows for personal growth, mutual respect, and a deepening connection based on trust, love, and understanding.

Honoring individual autonomy and independence is essential for maintaining healthy and fulfilling relationships. By embracing and respecting each other's unique identities, establishing clear boundaries, nurturing personal growth, cultivating trust and security, and finding a healthy balance between togetherness and independence, we create an environment where individuals can thrive and relationships can flourish. Remember that honoring individual autonomy does not diminish the connection within relationships but instead allows for a deeper sense of self and a stronger foundation for mutual support and growth.

Balancing Giving and Receiving in Relationships

Maintaining a healthy balance of giving and receiving is crucial for nurturing harmonious and fulfilling relationships. This section explores strategies for fostering reciprocity, avoiding codependency, and cultivating a mutually supportive dynamic.

Understanding Giving and Receiving

Recognize that relationships thrive on a reciprocal exchange of love, support, and care. Both giving and receiving are important components of a balanced and healthy relationship.

Reflect on your own patterns of giving and receiving. Are you comfortable with receiving from others, or do you tend to take on the role of the perpetual giver? Examine any underlying beliefs or fears that may hinder your ability to receive.

Understand that giving and receiving are interconnected and necessary for the well-being of both individuals and relationships. It is essential to create a harmonious balance between the two.

Take time to reflect on your own patterns and beliefs surrounding giving and receiving. Are you comfortable with receiving from others, or do you struggle with accepting help, support, or compliments? Explore any underlying beliefs or fears that may be influencing your ability to receive. Often, these beliefs stem from feelings of unworthiness, a fear of vulnerability, or a sense of self-reliance.

Recognize the importance of receiving graciously. Allow yourself to be open and receptive to the love, care, and support offered by others. Understand that receiving is not a sign of weakness, but rather a demonstration of trust and a willingness to be vulnerable. It allows others to contribute to your well-being and strengthens the bond within relationships.

Practice gratitude for both giving and receiving. Acknowledge the joy and fulfillment that comes from giving to others, but also appreciate the value and impact of receiving from others. By expressing gratitude, you cultivate a deeper sense of appreciation for the interconnectedness and reciprocity of relationships.

Communicate your needs and boundaries with clarity and assertiveness. Learn to ask for help when needed and to accept it when offered. Understand that allowing others to give to you can be a gift in itself, as it provides them with the opportunity to contribute and feel valued.

Embrace vulnerability and trust in the process of giving and receiving. Understand that it requires courage to be open and vulnerable with others, both in giving and receiving. By embracing vulnerability, you create a safe space for authentic connections and meaningful relationships to flourish.

Remember that giving and receiving are not transactions, but rather expressions of love, care, and connection. Embrace the joy of giving selflessly and without expecting anything in return. Similarly, allow yourself to receive without guilt or obligation, knowing that it enriches both you and the giver.

By understanding the dynamics of giving and receiving and cultivating a balanced approach, you foster healthier relationships, deeper connections, and a greater sense of fulfillment in your interactions with others. Embrace the beauty of both giving and receiving, and honor the reciprocal nature of love and support within your relationships.

Communicating Needs and Expectations

Openly communicate your needs, desires, and expectations to your partner or loved ones. Clearly express what you require in terms of support, affection, and assistance, as well as what you are willing and able to give.

Encourage open and honest communication from the other person as well. Create a safe space where both parties can express their needs and expectations without judgment or fear of rejection.

This open communication allows for a deeper understanding and connection between individuals, fostering healthy and fulfilling relationships. By expressing your needs and expectations, you provide others with the opportunity to meet them, creating a mutually satisfying dynamic.

When communicating your needs and expectations, be specific and assertive, using "I" statements to express how you feel and what you require. Avoid blaming or criticizing the other person, as this can create defensiveness and hinder effective communication. Instead, focus on expressing your needs and desires in a constructive and respectful manner.

Active listening is an essential component of effective communication. Give your full attention to the other person when they are expressing their needs and expectations. Seek clarification if necessary, and validate their feelings and concerns. This demonstrates empathy and shows that you value their perspective.

It is important to note that communication is a two-way street. Encourage the other person to express their needs and expectations as well. Create a safe and non-judgmental space for them to share their thoughts and feelings. Listen attentively and validate their experiences, just as you would expect them to do for you.

As you engage in this open and honest communication, remember that compromise and negotiation may be necessary. Finding common ground and mutually agreeable solutions is key to maintaining harmony and understanding in relationships. Be willing to be flexible and seek win-win outcomes whenever possible.

Regular check-ins and ongoing communication are essential to ensure that both parties' needs and expectations are being met. Relationships evolve over time, and individual needs may change. Therefore, it is important to keep the lines of communication open and revisit discussions about needs and expectations periodically.

By openly communicating your needs and expectations and encouraging the same from others, you create an environment of trust, understanding, and respect. This fosters healthier, more fulfilling relationships where both parties feel heard, supported, and valued. Effective communication is a cornerstone of strong relationships and paves the way for greater intimacy, connection, and mutual growth.

Establishing Healthy Boundaries

Set and maintain healthy boundaries to ensure a balanced give-and-take dynamic. Boundaries help prevent codependency and establish clear guidelines for how much you are willing to give and receive in a relationship.

Respect the boundaries set by others and avoid overstepping them. Allow individuals the space to give and receive according to their comfort level.

Communicate your boundaries openly and assertively, expressing your needs, limits, and expectations clearly. Be honest with yourself and others about what feels comfortable and what doesn't. Remember that setting boundaries is not about being selfish, but about taking care of your own well-being and maintaining healthy relationships.

Be aware of red flags or situations that may require stricter boundaries. Trust your intuition and listen to any feelings of discomfort or unease. It is important to prioritize your emotional and physical safety.

Practice self-care as a way to honor and reinforce your boundaries. Take time for yourself, engage in activities that bring you joy and relaxation, and prioritize your well-being. Self-care is not selfish, but a necessary practice for maintaining your own mental, emotional, and physical health.

Be prepared for resistance or pushback when establishing boundaries, especially if you have previously been more accommodating or if the relationship dynamics are shifting. Stay firm and confident in your boundaries, and remember that you have the right to set limits that protect your well-being.

Reevaluate your boundaries periodically and adjust them as needed. As you grow and evolve, your boundaries may change. Regularly check in with yourself and assess if your boundaries still align with your needs and values.

Remember that establishing boundaries is an ongoing process and requires practice. It may feel uncomfortable or challenging at times, but it is a vital part of creating healthy relationships and maintaining your own well-being. Be patient with yourself and others as you navigate this journey of boundary-setting.

By establishing and maintaining healthy boundaries, you create a foundation of respect, trust, and mutual understanding in your relationships. You empower yourself to prioritize your needs and protect your well-being. Boundaries contribute to healthier and more fulfilling connections, allowing for greater authenticity, harmony, and emotional balance in your life.

Practicing Reciprocity

Reciprocity is about creating a balanced exchange of giving and receiving in relationships. It involves a genuine desire to support and uplift one another, fostering a sense of mutual care and growth. *Here are some ways to practice reciprocity in your relationships:*

- *Active Listening:* Be present and attentive when others are expressing themselves. Listen with empathy and seek to understand their perspective without judgment. Show that you value their thoughts and feelings by providing a safe space for open communication.
- *Offering Support:* Be proactive in offering support to your loved ones. Whether it's lending a listening ear, providing practical help, or offering emotional support, be willing to step in and assist when needed. Show genuine concern and a willingness to go the extra mile for their well-being.
- *Expressing Gratitude:* Take time to express your gratitude and appreciation for the contributions and support you receive from others. Acknowledge and recognize the efforts and kindness

shown to you. This simple act of gratitude can strengthen the bond and inspire continued acts of reciprocity.

- *Setting Boundaries:* While it's important to be giving, it's equally important to maintain healthy boundaries. Recognize and communicate your own needs and limits, ensuring that you take care of your well-being. By setting boundaries, you create a balance that allows for healthy reciprocity without feeling overwhelmed or depleted.

- *Receiving with Grace:* Practice openness to receiving support and assistance from others. Allow yourself to be vulnerable and accept help when it is offered. Remember that reciprocity involves both giving and receiving, and by graciously accepting support, you give others the opportunity to experience the joy of giving.

- *Continuous Communication:* Engage in open and honest communication with your loved ones to ensure that the exchange of support and care remains reciprocal. Regularly check in with each other, sharing your needs, desires, and concerns. This ongoing dialogue helps maintain a healthy balance and strengthens the foundation of your relationships.

- *Mutual Growth and Development:* Encourage and support each other's personal growth and development. Celebrate each other's achievements and be a source of encouragement and inspiration. Create an environment where both individuals can thrive and reach their full potential.

By practicing reciprocity, you foster a culture of mutual care, respect, and support within your relationships. This not only enhances the well-being of all individuals involved but also strengthens the bonds and creates a foundation of trust and love. Embrace the power of reciprocity and experience the transformative impact it can have on your connections with others.

Avoiding Codependency

Be mindful of codependent patterns in relationships, where one person excessively relies on the other for their emotional well-being or neglects their own needs in favor of meeting the needs of the other.

Cultivate a sense of independence and self-sufficiency within yourself and encourage the same in your partner or loved ones. Each individual should have their own interests, goals, and support systems outside of the relationship.

Maintain healthy boundaries by recognizing and honoring your own needs, desires, and limits. Be assertive in expressing your thoughts and feelings, and be receptive to the boundaries set by others. Respect the autonomy and individuality of yourself and others.

Develop self-awareness and self-care practices that promote your emotional well-being and fulfillment. Engage in activities that bring you joy, cultivate a strong support network, and prioritize self-care rituals that nourish your mind, body, and spirit.

Seek therapy or counseling if you notice recurring patterns of codependency in your relationships. A professional can provide guidance and tools to help you navigate and heal from codependent behaviors. Engage in self-reflection and explore the underlying beliefs and traumas that contribute to codependent tendencies.

Practice healthy communication skills that encourage open and honest dialogue. Express your needs, feelings, and concerns assertively and respectfully, and listen actively to the perspectives and needs of others. Strive for mutual understanding and compromise in your relationships.

Develop a strong sense of self-worth and self-love. Recognize that you are deserving of healthy, balanced, and mutually supportive relationships. Prioritize your own well-being and happiness, and let go of the need to constantly seek validation or approval from others.

Remember that you are responsible for your own happiness and fulfillment. Avoid placing the burden of your emotional well-being solely on others. Take ownership of your emotions, and explore healthy coping mechanisms and self-soothing techniques that promote your emotional resilience and independence.

By cultivating healthy boundaries, fostering independence, practicing self-care, and engaging in open and honest communication, you can avoid codependency and create relationships that are balanced, fulfilling, and supportive of individual growth and well-being.

Balancing giving and receiving is essential for maintaining healthy and fulfilling relationships. By understanding the importance of reciprocity, communicating needs and expectations, establishing healthy boundaries, practicing reciprocity, and avoiding codependency, we create an environment of balance and mutual support. Remember that a balanced give-and-take dynamic allows relationships to flourish and grow, nurturing both individuals involved. Strive for a harmonious equilibrium where both giving and receiving are valued and celebrated, creating a foundation of trust, understanding, and mutual well-being.

By exploring these topics and applying the principles and strategies presented, you can navigate relationships with greater awareness, empathy, and intentionality. Cultivating healthy and empowering connections contributes to your personal growth, happiness, and overall well-being.

6

Reclaiming Personal Power

Examining Self-Limiting Beliefs and Conditioning

Self-limiting beliefs and conditioning can significantly impact our personal power and hold us back from reaching our full potential. These beliefs are often ingrained in us through societal norms, past experiences, and the messages we receive from others. They create a framework that shapes how we see ourselves and what we believe we are capable of achieving.

In this section, we encourage readers to examine their self-limiting beliefs and conditioning. This involves taking a close look at the thoughts and beliefs that may be holding them back from pursuing their dreams, taking risks, or stepping into their power. By becoming aware of these beliefs, individuals can begin to challenge and question their validity.

It is essential to understand that these self-limiting beliefs are not necessarily based on reality but are often rooted in fear, insecurity, or a lack of confidence. By recognizing this, individuals can start to separate themselves from these beliefs and understand that they do not define their true potential.

- To challenge self-limiting beliefs and conditioning, individuals can ask themselves probing questions such as:

- What beliefs do I hold about myself that may be limiting my personal power?
- Where did these beliefs come from, and are they based on objective evidence or subjective perceptions?
- How have these beliefs influenced my choices, actions, and decisions in the past?
- What would be possible for me if I let go of these self-limiting beliefs?
- What evidence do I have that contradicts these beliefs?

Through self-reflection and introspection, individuals can begin to identify the specific beliefs that are holding them back. Once these beliefs are identified, they can be challenged by gathering evidence to counteract them. This evidence may come from past accomplishments, positive feedback from others, or examples of individuals who have overcome similar challenges.

It is also helpful to surround oneself with supportive and empowering influences. Engaging with individuals who believe in our potential and challenge our self-limiting beliefs can provide a fresh perspective and encouragement to break free from old patterns.

By examining and challenging self-limiting beliefs and conditioning, individuals can open themselves up to new possibilities and unlock their full potential. This process requires courage, self-awareness, and a commitment to personal growth. As individuals become more conscious of their beliefs and actively work to reframe them, they can reclaim their personal power and create a life aligned with their true desires and aspirations.

Challenging Negative Self-Talk

Negative self-talk can have a profound impact on our sense of personal power and self-esteem. It is the internal dialogue that reinforces self-doubt, criticizes our abilities, and creates a negative perception of ourselves. Challenging and reframing negative self-talk is crucial for reclaiming our personal power and fostering self-empowerment and self-confidence.

In this section, we explore the power of our inner dialogue and offer techniques to challenge and reframe negative self-talk. By becoming aware of our negative self-talk patterns, we can interrupt and transform them into more positive and empowering thoughts.

One effective technique for challenging negative self-talk is to identify and question the validity of our self-critical thoughts. We can ask ourselves:

- Is there any evidence to support this negative thought?
- Would I say the same thing to a friend in a similar situation?
- What alternative, more empowering thought could replace this negative thought?

By questioning the basis of our negative self-talk, we can gain a more balanced perspective and challenge the accuracy of our self-criticisms.

Another technique is to reframe negative self-talk by replacing it with more positive and affirming statements. This involves consciously replacing negative thoughts with empowering ones. For example, if the negative thought is "I always mess things up," we can reframe it to "I am capable of learning from my mistakes and improving with each experience." This shift in self-talk can promote self-compassion and foster a more positive self-perception.

Additionally, cultivating self-compassion is crucial in challenging negative self-talk. Being kind and understanding towards ourselves allows us to acknowledge our imperfections and mistakes without harsh self-judgment. Instead of berating ourselves for perceived failures, we can offer ourselves support, encouragement, and understanding.

Practicing mindfulness can also help in challenging negative self-talk. By observing our thoughts without judgment, we can create distance from them and recognize that they are not necessarily true or reflective of our capabilities. Mindfulness allows us to be present in the moment and let go of negative self-talk patterns.

It is important to remember that challenging negative self-talk is an ongoing process that requires patience and self-compassion. It may take time to rewire deeply ingrained patterns, but with consistent effort and practice, we can shift our internal dialogue towards self-empowerment and self-confidence.

By challenging and reframing negative self-talk, we can reclaim our personal power, enhance our self-esteem, and cultivate a more positive and empowering mindset. This shift in self-talk can have a profound impact on our overall well-being and our ability to pursue our goals and dreams with confidence and resilience.

Cultivating Self-Confidence and Self-Efficacy

Cultivating self-confidence and self-efficacy is crucial for reclaiming our personal power and pursuing our goals with determination and resilience. Self-confidence is the belief in our own abilities, while self-efficacy refers to our belief in our ability to achieve specific tasks or goals. In this section, we delve into strategies for cultivating self-confidence and self-efficacy, recognizing our strengths, and developing a belief in our ability to accomplish our goals and overcome challenges.

Identify and celebrate your strengths: Take time to reflect on your unique qualities, skills, and accomplishments. Recognize your strengths and acknowledge the value they bring to your life and the lives of others. Celebrate your achievements, no matter how small they may seem, and use them as evidence of your capabilities.

Set realistic and achievable goals: Break down your larger goals into smaller, more manageable steps. By setting achievable goals, you build a track record of success, which boosts your self-confidence and reinforces your belief in your ability to accomplish what you set out to do.

Challenge yourself: Step out of your comfort zone and embrace new experiences and opportunities. Pushing yourself beyond your perceived limits allows you to discover your hidden strengths and capabilities. Each time you take on a new challenge and overcome it, your self-confidence grows.

Practice self-compassion: Treat yourself with kindness, understanding, and acceptance. Embrace the reality that making mistakes and facing setbacks is a natural part of growth and learning. Instead of berating yourself for perceived failures, offer yourself compassion and learn from the experience.

Surround yourself with positive influences: Surround yourself with supportive and encouraging individuals who believe in your abilities and uplift you. Seek out mentors, friends, or role models who inspire you and provide guidance and support on your journey towards self-confidence and self-efficacy.

Visualize success: Visualize yourself accomplishing your goals and experiencing success. Create vivid mental images of yourself confidently overcoming challenges and achieving what you desire. Visualization helps rewire your subconscious mind and instills a sense of belief and confidence in your abilities.

Practice self-care: Take care of your physical, emotional, and mental well-being. Engage in activities that bring you joy, reduce stress, and recharge your energy. When you prioritize self-care, you boost your self-esteem and create a strong foundation for cultivating self-confidence and self-efficacy.

Keep a record of achievements: Maintain a journal or list of your achievements, both big and small. Refer to this list when you need a reminder of your capabilities and progress. Seeing tangible evidence of your past successes reinforces your belief in your abilities and boosts your self-confidence.

Surround yourself with positive affirmations: Use positive affirmations to reinforce positive beliefs about yourself and your abilities. Repeat affirmations such as "I am capable," "I believe in myself," or "I have what it takes to succeed" regularly. Over time, these affirmations become ingrained in your mindset and contribute to cultivating self-confidence and self-efficacy.

Seek feedback and learn from it: Be open to receiving feedback from others, as it provides valuable insights into your strengths and areas for improvement. Embrace constructive criticism as an opportunity for growth and learning. Actively seek feedback from trusted individuals and use it to refine your skills and enhance your self-efficacy.

By implementing these strategies, you can cultivate self-confidence and self-efficacy, which are essential for reclaiming your personal power and pursuing your goals with determination, resilience, and belief in your abilities. Remember, building self-confidence is a continuous journey, and it requires practice, self-reflection, and patience. With time and effort, you can develop a strong sense of self-assurance and empower yourself to achieve the life you desire.

Embracing Failure and Learning from Setbacks

Embracing failure and learning from setbacks is crucial for reclaiming our personal power and achieving personal growth and success. In this section, we explore the importance of viewing failure as a valuable learning experience and reframing setbacks as opportunities for growth and resilience.

Shift your mindset: Embrace a growth mindset that sees failure as a stepping stone to success. Understand that failure is not a reflection of your worth or ability, but rather a necessary part of the learning process. See setbacks as opportunities for growth, learning, and self-improvement.

Learn from mistakes: Take the time to reflect on the lessons learned from your failures and setbacks. Analyze what went wrong, identify areas for improvement, and develop strategies for moving forward. Use failure as an opportunity to gain valuable insights and adjust your approach.

Cultivate resilience: Build resilience by developing the ability to bounce back from failure and setbacks. Recognize that setbacks are temporary and that you have the inner strength to overcome them. Focus on developing coping mechanisms, practicing self-care, and seeking support from others when needed.

Normalize failure: Understand that failure is a common experience shared by everyone. Many successful individuals have faced numerous failures on their path to success. Normalize failure as a natural part of the journey and recognize that it does not define your worth or potential.

Reframe failure as feedback: Instead of viewing failure as a personal defeat, reframe it as feedback that helps you refine your approach and make better choices in the future. Embrace failure as an opportunity to learn, grow, and adapt.

Take calculated risks: Push yourself outside your comfort zone and take calculated risks. Embracing failure means being willing to try new things, even if there is a chance of setbacks. Recognize that taking risks is necessary for personal growth and achieving your goals.

Practice self-compassion: Be kind to yourself when facing failure or setbacks. Treat yourself with the same compassion and understanding you would offer a friend. Practice self-compassion by acknowledging your efforts, accepting imperfections, and offering yourself encouragement and support.

Celebrate progress: Focus on the progress you have made rather than dwelling on failures. Acknowledge and celebrate the small victories along the way. Recognize that each step forward, no matter how small, is a testament to your resilience and determination.

Seek support: Surround yourself with a supportive network of friends, family, or mentors who can offer guidance and encouragement during challenging times. Seek their support when facing failure or setbacks, as their perspective and insights can help you navigate through difficult moments.

Keep your goals in perspective: Remind yourself of your long-term goals and the bigger picture. Understand that setbacks are often temporary roadblocks that can be overcome with perseverance and determination. Stay focused on your vision and continue to take steps towards your goals, even in the face of failure.

By embracing failure as a valuable learning experience, reframing setbacks, and using them as stepping stones towards personal empowerment, you can reclaim your personal power and cultivate resilience, growth, and success. Remember, failure is not the end but an opportunity for growth and self-improvement. With each setback, you become stronger, wiser, and more equipped to overcome future challenges.

Taking Responsibility for Personal Choices and Actions

Taking responsibility for our personal choices and actions is a fundamental aspect of reclaiming our personal power. It empowers us to be the drivers of our own lives and create the outcomes we desire. In this section, we delve into the importance of personal responsibility and provide strategies for embracing it:

Reflect on your choices: Take the time to reflect on the choices you have made in the past and their consequences. Recognize that you have the power to make conscious decisions that align with your values, goals, and well-being.

Accept accountability: Accepting accountability means acknowledging that you are responsible for the choices you make and the actions you take. Avoid blaming external circumstances or other people for the outcomes in your life. Instead, focus on what you can control and take ownership of your role in shaping your reality.

Evaluate your values: Clarify your personal values and ensure that your choices and actions align with them. When you make decisions that are in line with your values, you empower yourself to live authentically and create a life that is meaningful to you.

Practice self-reflection: Engage in regular self-reflection to assess your choices and actions. Ask yourself whether your decisions are serving your growth, happiness, and overall well-being. Be honest with yourself and make adjustments as necessary.

Learn from mistakes: When you make mistakes or encounter challenges, view them as opportunities for growth and learning. Instead of avoiding responsibility or dwelling in self-blame, use setbacks as lessons to inform future choices and actions.

Make conscious choices: Develop the habit of making conscious choices by considering the potential outcomes and impacts of your decisions. Take into account both short-term and long-term consequences, and evaluate whether a particular choice aligns with your values and goals.

Set goals and take action: Set clear goals for yourself and take consistent action towards achieving them. Break your goals down into manageable steps and hold yourself accountable for making progress. By taking action aligned with your goals, you actively create the life you desire.

Seek feedback: Be open to feedback from trusted individuals who can offer constructive insights and different perspectives. Consider their input when evaluating your choices and actions. Incorporate feedback into your growth journey and use it to make informed decisions.

Practice self-compassion: While taking responsibility is important, it's equally vital to practice self-compassion. Treat yourself with kindness and understanding, acknowledging that mistakes and missteps are part of being human. Learn from them, forgive yourself, and use the lessons to fuel your personal growth.

Stay committed to personal growth: Embrace personal growth as a lifelong journey. Continuously seek opportunities for learning and self-improvement. Be open to new experiences, perspectives, and challenges, as they provide fertile ground for expanding your personal power.

By taking responsibility for your personal choices and actions, you reclaim your power to shape your life. Remember that you have the ability to make conscious decisions, learn from mistakes, and create the life you desire. Embrace personal responsibility as a catalyst for growth and transformation, and let it guide you towards a more empowered and fulfilling life.

Cultivating Resilience and Adaptability

Cultivating resilience and adaptability is crucial for reclaiming personal power in the face of challenges and change. Resilience allows us to bounce back from adversity, while adaptability enables us to navigate through life's uncertainties and embrace new opportunities. In this section, we explore strategies for building resilience and embracing adaptability:

Develop a growth mindset: Adopt a growth mindset, which is the belief that our abilities and intelligence can be developed through effort and learning. Embrace challenges as opportunities for growth and see setbacks as temporary setbacks rather than permanent failures. Cultivate a positive attitude towards learning and personal development.

Build a support network: Surround yourself with a supportive network of friends, family, mentors, or support groups. These individuals can provide emotional support, encouragement, and guidance during challenging times. Lean on them for strength and perspective when facing difficulties.

Practice self-care: Prioritize self-care to nurture your physical, emotional, and mental well-being. Engage in activities that recharge and rejuvenate you, such as exercise, meditation, spending time in nature, or engaging in hobbies. Taking care of yourself strengthens your resilience and ability to adapt.

Foster optimism: Cultivate an optimistic outlook by focusing on the positive aspects of situations and looking for opportunities for growth and learning. Train yourself to reframe challenges as opportunities and setbacks as stepping stones to success. Positive thinking can enhance your resilience and adaptive capacity.

Develop problem-solving skills: Enhance your problem-solving skills to effectively navigate challenges. Break problems down into manageable steps, explore different solutions, and seek alternative perspectives. Approach problems with a proactive mindset, taking action to address them rather than becoming overwhelmed or avoiding them.

Practice flexibility: Embrace flexibility in your thoughts and actions. Be open to new ideas, perspectives, and approaches. Recognize that change is a constant in life and be willing to adapt your plans and strategies when necessary. Flexibility allows you to navigate uncertainties and seize new opportunities.

Cultivate emotional intelligence: Develop emotional intelligence by enhancing your self-awareness, empathy, and emotional regulation skills. Understand and manage your own emotions, as well as empathize with others. Emotional intelligence helps you navigate interpersonal challenges and adapt to different situations effectively.

Learn from setbacks: View setbacks as learning opportunities rather than failures. Reflect on what went wrong and identify lessons that can be applied in the future. Use setbacks as stepping stones for personal growth and resilience. Embrace a mindset of continuous learning and improvement.

Seek challenges and take calculated risks: Step out of your comfort zone and seek challenges that stretch your abilities. Take calculated risks and embrace new experiences that promote personal growth and build resilience. By challenging yourself, you expand your capabilities and develop confidence in your ability to adapt to different situations.

Cultivate gratitude and mindfulness: Practice gratitude by focusing on the positive aspects of your life and expressing appreciation for the things you have. Embrace mindfulness by staying present and fully engaged in the present moment. These practices enhance resilience by fostering a sense of perspective, gratitude, and inner strength.

By cultivating resilience and adaptability, you reclaim personal power by developing the ability to navigate challenges and embrace change with confidence and determination. Remember that resilience is a skill that can be developed and strengthened over time. Embrace the journey of growth, stay open to new experiences, and approach challenges with a resilient mindset.

Setting Meaningful Goals and Taking Action

Setting meaningful goals and taking action is essential for reclaiming personal power and creating a fulfilling life. ***Here are steps to guide you in this process:***

Reflect on your values and passions: Start by reflecting on what truly matters to you and what brings you joy and fulfillment. Consider your values, interests, and aspirations. This self-reflection will help you identify goals that align with your authentic self.

Set SMART goals: Create goals that are Specific, Measurable, Achievable, Relevant, and Time-bound (SMART). Be clear about what you want to achieve, define measurable milestones, ensure the goals are realistic and aligned with your values, and set a timeline for completion.

Break down your goals into actionable steps: Break down each goal into smaller, actionable steps. This helps you create a clear roadmap and prevents overwhelm. Assign deadlines to each step to maintain momentum and track progress.

Create an action plan: Develop a detailed action plan that outlines the specific tasks, resources, and timelines required to achieve each goal. This plan will serve as a guide and keep you focused and organized.

Take consistent action: Taking consistent action is key to achieving your goals. Prioritize tasks, manage your time effectively, and commit to taking small, consistent steps towards your goals. Celebrate each milestone achieved, which will fuel your motivation and determination.

Stay committed and resilient: Challenges and obstacles may arise along the way. Stay committed to your goals and maintain a resilient mindset. Embrace setbacks as learning opportunities and adjust your approach if needed. Perseverance and resilience will help you overcome obstacles and keep moving forward.

Seek support and accountability: Share your goals with trusted friends, family members, or a mentor who can offer support and hold you accountable. Regularly update them on your progress and seek their guidance when needed. Having support and accountability can boost your motivation and help you stay on track.

Review and adjust your goals: Regularly review your goals and assess your progress. Reflect on what's working well and what needs adjustment. Adjust your goals or action plan if necessary to stay aligned with your evolving aspirations and circumstances.

Celebrate achievements: Celebrate your achievements along the way, no matter how small they may seem. Acknowledge your progress and the effort you've put into reaching your goals. Celebrating milestones will boost your confidence and motivation to keep moving forward.

Stay adaptable and open to growth: Be open to adjusting your goals as you grow and evolve. Your aspirations may change over time, and that's okay. Embrace new opportunities and be willing to explore different paths that align with your evolving vision of a fulfilling life.

By setting meaningful goals and taking consistent action, you reclaim personal power and create a life that aligns with your values and aspirations. Stay committed, resilient, and adaptable on your journey, and remember to celebrate your progress along the way. Your dedication and perseverance will lead you towards personal empowerment and the fulfillment of your dreams.

Overcoming Procrastination and Perfectionism

Overcoming procrastination and perfectionism is crucial for reclaiming personal power and making progress towards your goals. ***Here are some techniques to help you overcome these tendencies:***

Recognize the underlying causes: Procrastination and perfectionism often have deeper underlying causes such as fear of failure, fear of judgment, or a need for control. Take time to reflect on the reasons behind your tendencies and identify any limiting beliefs or fears that may be contributing to them.

Break tasks into smaller steps: Procrastination often stems from feeling overwhelmed by the magnitude of a task. Break your tasks into smaller, more manageable steps. This will make them less intimidating and easier to approach, increasing your motivation to take action.

Set realistic deadlines: Establish realistic deadlines for your tasks and hold yourself accountable to them. Break down your tasks and allocate specific time slots in your schedule to work on them. This creates a sense of urgency and helps you stay focused and productive.

Use the 5-minute rule: When you find yourself procrastinating, commit to working on the task for just five minutes. Often, getting started is the most challenging part. Once you begin, you may find that the momentum builds, and it becomes easier to continue.

Challenge perfectionistic tendencies: Perfectionism can lead to paralysis and a fear of making mistakes. Challenge perfectionistic tendencies by embracing a mindset of progress over perfection. Focus on taking consistent action and learning from mistakes rather than aiming for flawless outcomes.

Practice self-compassion: Be kind to yourself and practice self-compassion. Recognize that everyone makes mistakes and that progress is more important than perfection. Treat yourself with understanding and forgiveness when things don't go as planned.

Set realistic standards: Perfectionism often stems from setting unrealistically high standards for yourself. Set realistic and achievable standards that still push you to grow and improve but also allow for mistakes and learning opportunities along the way.

Seek support and accountability: Share your goals and deadlines with someone you trust, such as a friend, family member, or mentor. Having someone to hold you accountable can provide motivation and encouragement to overcome procrastination and perfectionism.

Focus on the process, not just the outcome: Shift your focus from solely fixating on the end result to appreciating and enjoying the process.

Embrace the learning and growth that comes from taking action and making progress, regardless of the final outcome.

Celebrate small victories: Acknowledge and celebrate your achievements, no matter how small they may seem. Recognize the effort and progress you make along the way, as this will reinforce positive behavior and motivate you to continue taking action.

By implementing these strategies, you can overcome procrastination and perfectionism, reclaim your personal power, and make significant progress towards your goals. Remember, it's about progress, not perfection. Embrace the journey and celebrate your growth and accomplishments along the way.

Developing Assertiveness and Advocacy Skills

Developing assertiveness and advocacy skills is essential for reclaiming personal power and effectively expressing ourselves. Here are some key strategies and techniques to help you develop these skills:

Self-awareness: Start by developing self-awareness and understanding your own needs, values, and boundaries. Take time to reflect on what is important to you and what you want to advocate for.

Effective communication: Learn and practice effective communication skills. This includes being clear and concise in expressing your thoughts and feelings, actively listening to others, and using assertive body language and tone of voice.

Use "I" statements: When expressing your needs or concerns, use "I" statements to assert yourself without sounding accusatory or confrontational. For example, say, "I feel..." or "I need..." instead of pointing fingers or using blaming language.

Set clear boundaries: Assertiveness involves setting and enforcing boundaries that protect your well-being and values. Clearly communicate your boundaries to others, and be firm in upholding them. Remember, it is okay to say "no" when necessary.

Practice assertive body language: Adopt confident and assertive body language, such as maintaining eye contact, standing or sitting upright, and using appropriate gestures. This nonverbal communication can reinforce your assertiveness and convey your message effectively.

Active listening: Actively listen to others by giving them your full attention and showing genuine interest in their perspective. This not only demonstrates respect but also helps you understand their needs and concerns better, enabling you to respond assertively.

Conflict resolution: Develop skills in constructive conflict resolution. This involves finding win-win solutions, seeking compromises, and being open to understanding different viewpoints. Focus on finding common ground and maintaining respectful communication during conflicts.

Practice assertiveness in small steps: Begin by practicing assertiveness in low-stakes situations. Start with expressing your opinions or preferences with friends or colleagues. As you gain confidence, gradually apply assertiveness skills to more challenging situations.

Seek support and feedback: Seek support from trusted individuals who can provide guidance and feedback on your assertiveness and advocacy skills. This can be through role-playing scenarios or discussing real-life situations to gain insight and refine your approach.

Stay true to your values: Advocacy involves standing up for what you believe in and advocating for the rights and well-being of yourself and others. Stay true to your values and use your assertiveness skills to address issues and promote positive change.

Remember that developing assertiveness and advocacy skills takes practice and patience. Start with small steps, and gradually build your confidence and assertiveness over time. As you become more comfortable expressing yourself and advocating for your needs, you will reclaim your personal power and create more fulfilling relationships and experiences.

Practicing Self-Care and Prioritizing Well-Being

Practicing self-care and prioritizing well-being is crucial for reclaiming personal power and living a fulfilling life. *Here are some key strategies to help you incorporate self-care and prioritize your well-being:*

Self-awareness: Start by developing self-awareness and understanding your own needs, both physically and emotionally. Take time to reflect on what activities, practices, and habits contribute to your well-being and make you feel nourished and energized.

Establish healthy boundaries: Set clear boundaries to protect your time, energy, and emotional well-being. Learn to say "no" when necessary and prioritize activities that align with your values and bring you joy and fulfillment.

Prioritize self-care activities: Make self-care a priority by scheduling regular time for activities that rejuvenate and nurture you. This can include activities such as exercise, meditation, spending time in nature, engaging in hobbies, practicing mindfulness, or connecting with loved ones.

Physical well-being: Take care of your physical health by adopting healthy habits such as regular exercise, balanced nutrition, sufficient sleep, and managing stress. Prioritize activities that promote physical well-being and support your overall vitality.

Emotional well-being: Cultivate emotional well-being by nurturing your emotions and expressing them in healthy ways. This can include journaling, seeking support from trusted friends or therapists, practicing self-compassion, and engaging in activities that bring you joy and fulfillment.

Set realistic goals: Set realistic and achievable goals that support your well-being. Break them down into smaller, manageable steps to avoid overwhelm and increase your sense of accomplishment.

Practice self-compassion: Be kind and compassionate towards yourself. Treat yourself with the same care and understanding you would offer to a loved one. Embrace imperfections and let go of self-judgment and self-criticism.

Connect with others: Cultivate meaningful connections with supportive individuals who uplift and inspire you. Surround yourself with people who appreciate and respect your well-being and provide a positive and nurturing environment.

Manage stress: Develop healthy coping mechanisms to manage stress effectively. This can include relaxation techniques, such as deep breathing exercises, meditation, or engaging in activities that promote relaxation and stress reduction.

Regular self-reflection: Take time for self-reflection to assess your well-being and make necessary adjustments. Check in with yourself regularly and evaluate if your current lifestyle and choices align with your overall well-being and personal empowerment.

Remember that self-care is not selfish; it is necessary for your overall well-being and personal empowerment. By prioritizing self-care and making choices that support your well-being, you reclaim your personal power and create a foundation for a fulfilling and balanced life.

Cultivating a Positive Mindset

Cultivating a positive mindset is a powerful way to reclaim personal power and navigate life's challenges with resilience and optimism. Here are some strategies to help you cultivate a positive mindset:

Practice gratitude: Cultivate a daily gratitude practice by acknowledging and appreciating the positive aspects of your life. This can involve keeping a gratitude journal, expressing gratitude to others, or simply reflecting on what you are grateful for.

Positive self-talk: Pay attention to your inner dialogue and replace negative self-talk with positive and empowering affirmations. Challenge negative thoughts and replace them with positive and realistic perspectives.

Reframe challenges: View challenges as opportunities for growth and learning. Instead of dwelling on setbacks, focus on the lessons and opportunities they provide. Look for the silver lining in difficult situations and find ways to turn them into positive experiences.

Surround yourself with positivity: Surround yourself with positive influences, whether it's through supportive relationships, uplifting books and media, or engaging in activities that bring you joy and inspiration. Minimize exposure to negative influences that can dampen your positivity.

Practice mindfulness: Cultivate mindfulness by staying present in the moment and observing your thoughts and emotions without judgment. This helps you become aware of negative thought patterns and enables you to consciously choose more positive and empowering thoughts.

Visualize success: Use visualization techniques to imagine yourself achieving your goals and experiencing success. Visualize the positive outcomes you desire and create a vivid mental image of yourself thriving.

Celebrate progress: Acknowledge and celebrate your achievements, no matter how small. Recognize your progress and give yourself credit for the steps you have taken towards your goals. Celebrating milestones boosts confidence and reinforces a positive mindset.

Seek inspiration: Surround yourself with sources of inspiration, whether it's through books, podcasts, motivational speakers, or role models who inspire you. Engage with content that uplifts and motivates you to maintain a positive mindset.

Practice self-care: Prioritize self-care activities that nourish your mind, body, and spirit. Taking care of yourself physically, emotionally, and mentally enhances your overall well-being and contributes to a positive mindset.

Cultivate resilience: Build resilience by viewing setbacks and failures as opportunities for growth. Develop a mindset that sees challenges as temporary and believes in your ability to overcome them. Focus on solutions and keep moving forward.

Remember that cultivating a positive mindset is a practice that requires consistent effort and self-awareness. By consciously choosing positive thoughts and perspectives, you reclaim your personal power and create a positive foundation for personal growth and empowerment.

Embracing Personal Strengths and Unique Gifts

Embracing our personal strengths and unique gifts is a powerful way to reclaim our personal power and create a meaningful impact in our lives and the lives of others. ***Here are some techniques to help you embrace your personal strengths and unique gifts:***

Self-reflection: Take time for self-reflection and introspection. Explore your values, passions, and interests. Identify the activities that bring you joy and energize you. Reflect on past experiences where you felt fulfilled and accomplished. This self-awareness will help you uncover your personal strengths and unique gifts.

Identify your strengths: Pay attention to the things that you excel at and that come naturally to you. Identify your key strengths, such as problem-solving, creativity, leadership, empathy, or perseverance. Consider seeking feedback from trusted individuals who can provide insight into your strengths.

Celebrate your accomplishments: Acknowledge and celebrate your past accomplishments and successes. Reflect on the skills and qualities that contributed to those achievements. Recognize the unique strengths and gifts you demonstrated during those moments.

Embrace your uniqueness: Embrace the qualities that make you unique. Understand that your individuality and perspective bring value to the world. Embrace your quirks, talents, and passions, and see them as sources of strength and differentiation.

Seek new experiences: Step out of your comfort zone and explore new experiences that allow you to discover and develop your strengths. Engage in activities that challenge you and provide opportunities for growth. Embracing new experiences expands your horizons and helps you uncover hidden strengths and gifts.

Surround yourself with support: Surround yourself with supportive and encouraging individuals who recognize and appreciate your strengths and unique gifts. Seek out mentors, coaches, or like-minded peers who can help you nurture and develop your talents. Their support and guidance can bolster your self-belief and confidence.

Leverage your strengths: Identify ways to leverage your strengths and unique gifts in various areas of your life. Look for opportunities to apply your strengths at work, in personal projects, or in volunteer activities. When you align your strengths with your pursuits, you'll experience a sense of fulfillment and accomplishment.

Continuous learning and growth: Commit to continuous learning and personal growth. Seek opportunities for further developing your strengths and expanding your knowledge in areas that align with your unique gifts. This ongoing process of self-improvement enhances your personal power and effectiveness.

Share your gifts with others: Use your strengths and unique gifts to make a positive impact on others. Find ways to contribute to your community, help others, or share your knowledge and talents. By sharing your gifts, you not only uplift others but also experience a sense of purpose and fulfillment.

Remember that embracing your personal strengths and unique gifts is a lifelong journey. It requires self-discovery, self-acceptance, and a willingness to continuously grow and evolve. By recognizing and leveraging your strengths, you reclaim your personal power and create a meaningful and fulfilling life that aligns with your true self.

Embodying Self-Compassion and Self-Love

Embodying self-compassion and self-love is a transformative practice that supports our personal power and well-being. ***Here are some practices to nurture self-compassion and embrace self-love:***

Cultivate self-awareness: Start by cultivating awareness of your inner dialogue and self-judgment. Notice when you are being self-critical or harsh towards yourself. Be mindful of the thoughts and beliefs that undermine your self-worth. Developing self-awareness is the first step towards cultivating self-compassion.

Practice self-kindness: Treat yourself with kindness and understanding, just as you would treat a dear friend. Offer yourself words of encouragement, support, and comfort. Replace self-criticism with self-compassion by acknowledging that everyone makes mistakes and experiences challenges. Embrace your humanness and be gentle with yourself.

Develop self-acceptance: Embrace all aspects of yourself, including your perceived flaws and imperfections. Practice radical self-acceptance by recognizing that you are worthy and deserving of love and compassion, just as you are. Let go of the need for perfection and embrace your uniqueness.

Practice self-care: Prioritize self-care activities that nourish your mind, body, and soul. Engage in activities that bring you joy, relaxation, and rejuvenation. Take time to rest, engage in hobbies, practice mindfulness, exercise, and nourish your body with healthy food. Self-care is an essential aspect of self-love and self-compassion.

Set healthy boundaries: Establish clear boundaries to protect your well-being and honor your needs. Learn to say no to activities or relationships that drain your energy or compromise your values. Setting boundaries is an act of self-care and self-respect, allowing you to prioritize your own needs and maintain healthy relationships.

Celebrate your accomplishments: Acknowledge and celebrate your achievements, big or small. Recognize your progress and the efforts you have made towards personal growth. Take pride in your accomplishments and use them as reminders of your capabilities and worthiness.

Practice self-forgiveness: Release yourself from past mistakes or regrets by practicing self-forgiveness. Recognize that everyone makes mistakes and that they do not define your worth. Learn from your past experiences and choose to grow and evolve.

Surround yourself with positivity: Surround yourself with positive influences, supportive individuals, and environments that uplift and inspire you. Minimize exposure to negativity, comparison, and toxic relationships. Create a positive support network that reinforces your self-compassion and self-love.

Practice gratitude: Cultivate a practice of gratitude to shift your focus towards appreciation and abundance. Regularly express gratitude for the blessings and qualities you possess. Recognize the strengths and gifts within yourself and express gratitude for them.

Seek support: If you find it challenging to cultivate self-compassion and self-love on your own, consider seeking support from a therapist, counselor, or support group. They can provide guidance, tools, and a safe space for exploration and growth.

Remember that embodying self-compassion and self-love is an on-going practice. Be patient and kind with yourself as you cultivate these qualities. With time and commitment, you will develop a deep sense of self-compassion and self-love, unlocking your personal power and living a more fulfilling and authentic life.

Embracing Growth Mindset and Lifelong Learning

Embracing a growth mindset and committing to lifelong learning are transformative practices that empower personal growth and development. ***Here are some strategies for embracing a growth mindset and cultivating a commitment to lifelong learning:***

Embrace the belief in growth: Adopt the belief that your abilities, intelligence, and talents can be developed through effort, practice, and learning. Embrace the idea that challenges and setbacks are opportunities for growth, and failures are stepping stones to success. Emphasize progress and improvement rather than focusing solely on outcomes.

Cultivate curiosity and open-mindedness: Maintain a sense of curiosity and a willingness to explore new ideas, perspectives, and experiences. Approach learning with an open mind, seeking out diverse viewpoints and challenging your own assumptions. Stay curious about the world around you and engage in lifelong learning as a continuous process of discovery.

Embrace challenges as learning opportunities: Rather than shying away from challenges, embrace them as opportunities for growth. Step out of your comfort zone and take on new challenges that push your boundaries and expand your skills. Embrace the mindset that the greatest growth often occurs outside of your comfort zone.

Persist in the face of setbacks: View setbacks and failures as valuable learning experiences rather than signs of defeat. Maintain resilience and perseverance in the face of obstacles, knowing that they provide opportunities for learning and improvement. Reframe setbacks as stepping stones on your journey toward personal growth and success.

Seek feedback and learn from others: Be open to receiving feedback from others and use it as an opportunity for growth. Surround yourself with mentors, coaches, or trusted individuals who can provide constructive feedback and guidance. Actively seek opportunities to learn from others' experiences and perspectives, recognizing that everyone has something to teach.

Set learning goals: Set specific learning goals that align with your interests, passions, and areas for growth. Break these goals down into actionable steps and create a plan for achieving them. Regularly assess your progress, celebrate milestones, and adjust your goals as needed. This proactive approach to learning helps you stay focused and motivated.

Engage in diverse learning experiences: Explore a wide range of learning experiences, including formal education, online courses, workshops, seminars, books, podcasts, and immersive experiences. Embrace different learning modalities and seek out opportunities to apply what you've learned in practical settings. Embrace a growth mindset that values continuous learning and improvement.

Reflect on your learning journey: Regularly take time to reflect on your learning journey and the progress you have made. Celebrate your achievements and acknowledge the growth and development you have experienced. Reflect on the lessons learned from both successes and failures and apply them to future endeavors.

Foster a supportive learning environment: Surround yourself with individuals who share your commitment to growth and learning. Engage in communities or groups that foster a culture of learning and support. Share your knowledge and experiences with others, creating a collaborative and inspiring environment that fuels collective growth.

Embrace self-directed learning: Take ownership of your learning journey by identifying areas of interest and pursuing knowledge independently. Develop self-discipline and self-motivation to engage in self-directed learning. Leverage technology and resources available to you to access information and learning opportunities.

By embracing a growth mindset and committing to lifelong learning, you empower yourself to continuously grow, evolve, and reach your full potential. Embrace challenges, seek out new experiences, and approach learning with curiosity and open-mindedness. Through lifelong learning, you will discover new possibilities, expand your capabilities, and reclaim your personal power.

Stepping into Leadership and Influence

Stepping into leadership and influence is a powerful way to reclaim personal power and make a positive impact on the world around us. **Here are some key aspects to consider when stepping into leadership:**

Define your values and vision: Clarify your values and identify what matters most to you. Develop a clear vision of the kind of impact you want to make and the values you want to uphold as a leader. This foundation will guide your actions and decisions.

Lead by example: Leadership is not just about holding a position or title; it's about setting an example through your actions. Demonstrate integrity, authenticity, and ethical behavior. Be a role model for the qualities and values you want to see in others.

Develop effective communication skills: Effective leaders are skilled communicators. Hone your communication skills, both verbal and nonverbal, to effectively convey your ideas, inspire others, and build strong relationships. Listen actively and empathetically, and foster open and transparent communication within your team or community.

Foster collaboration and teamwork: Effective leaders understand the value of collaboration and teamwork. Create an environment that encourages collaboration, where diverse perspectives are valued, and everyone has the opportunity to contribute. Foster a sense of belonging and create opportunities for growth and development within your team or community.

Cultivate emotional intelligence: Emotional intelligence is crucial for effective leadership. Develop self-awareness, empathy, and the ability to understand and manage your emotions and those of others. Cultivate strong interpersonal skills and build meaningful connections with others.

Empower and inspire others: Great leaders empower others to reach their full potential. Delegate responsibilities, provide guidance and support, and create opportunities for growth and development. Inspire and motivate others through your words and actions, encouraging them to take ownership of their roles and contribute their unique talents.

Embrace continuous learning and personal growth: Leadership is a journey of continuous learning and personal growth. Stay open to feedback, seek opportunities for learning and development, and continuously strive to improve your leadership skills. Embrace a growth mindset and be willing to adapt and evolve as a leader.

Foster a positive and inclusive culture: Create a culture that values diversity, inclusivity, and a positive mindset. Promote a safe and inclusive environment where everyone feels respected, valued, and empowered to contribute. Foster a culture of learning, innovation, and continuous improvement.

Embrace challenges and take calculated risks: Leaders face challenges and uncertainties. Embrace challenges as opportunities for growth and learning. Be willing to take calculated risks and make difficult decisions when necessary. Show resilience and adaptability in the face of adversity.

Serve others and make a positive impact: Leadership is ultimately about serving others and making a positive impact on individuals, communities, or organizations. Consider the needs and aspirations of those you lead and work towards creating positive change and improving the lives of others.

By stepping into leadership and influence, you reclaim your personal power and create a ripple effect of positive change. Lead by example, cultivate effective communication, foster collaboration, and empower others to reach their full potential. Embrace continuous learning, personal growth, and a positive mindset. Through your leadership, you can make a meaningful difference in the lives of others and contribute to a better world.

Reclaiming personal power is a transformative journey that involves examining and challenging self-limiting beliefs, cultivating self-confidence, embracing failure, taking responsibility for our choices, developing resilience, setting meaningful goals, practicing self-care, and embodying self-compassion and self-love. By embracing personal strengths, adopting a growth mindset, and stepping into leadership and influence, we unlock our true potential and create a life of empowerment, fulfillment, and impact.

7

Integrating Mind, Body, and Spirit

The Mind-Body-Spirit Connection

The mind, body, and spirit are intricately connected, forming a dynamic triad that profoundly influences our overall well-being and personal growth. Understanding and nurturing this connection is essential for achieving greater balance, harmony, and wholeness in our lives.

The mind encompasses our thoughts, beliefs, perceptions, and consciousness. It is the seat of our intellect and cognitive functions, shaping our understanding of the world and ourselves. The body represents our physical form, with its intricate systems, organs, and senses that allow us to navigate and experience the world. The spirit encompasses our essence, our deeper sense of self, and our connection to something greater than ourselves, whether we call it the universe, higher power, or divine presence. It is the source of our intuition, inner wisdom, and innate knowing.

While modern society often emphasizes the separation of these aspects of our being, a holistic perspective recognizes their profound interconnectedness. When one aspect is neglected or imbalanced, it reverberates through the others, impacting our overall well-being and quality of life. Conversely, when we actively cultivate and nurture the mind-body-spirit connection, we experience a sense of harmony and alignment that supports our personal growth and transformation.

Cultivating this connection begins with mindfulness and present moment awareness. Mindfulness involves intentionally paying attention to the present moment, without judgment or attachment. By bringing our awareness to the here and now, we can fully experience and engage with our thoughts, emotions, sensations, and the world around us. This practice helps to quiet the mind's constant chatter and brings us into a state of presence, where we can access deeper levels of awareness and connect with our inner selves.

Meditation and breathwork practices are powerful tools for deepening our connection to the mind, body, and spirit. Through meditation, we enter a state of focused attention and inner stillness, allowing us to cultivate inner peace, clarity, and insight. Breathwork practices, such as deep belly breathing or pranayama techniques, help to regulate our breath and activate the body's relaxation response, promoting physical and mental well-being. These practices enhance our self-awareness, reduce stress, and create a space for self-reflection and inner growth.

Nurturing our physical well-being is another integral aspect of the mind-body-spirit connection. Our bodies are a vessel through which we experience life and express ourselves. Honoring our bodies through proper nutrition, regular exercise, restful sleep, and self-care practices supports our overall health and vitality. When we prioritize our physical well-being, we create a solid foundation for personal growth and empowerment.

The body also holds its own wisdom and intuition. By tuning into bodily sensations and listening to its signals, we can gain valuable insights and guidance. This requires cultivating body awareness, which involves paying attention to sensations, emotions, and the energy flowing through our bodies. Through practices like body scans, yoga, or somatic experiencing, we can deepen our connection with our bodies and access the valuable information they provide.

Movement and embodiment practices are another powerful means of connecting with our bodies and expressing ourselves fully. Engaging in activities such as yoga, dance, tai chi, or any form of mindful movement allows us to synchronize our movements with our breath, release tension, and connect with our physicality. These practices help us develop a deeper sense of body awareness, improve flexibility and strength, and foster a sense of embodied presence.

The mind-body-spirit connection also encompasses the power of our thoughts and beliefs. Visualization and affirmations are techniques that harness the power of our minds to shape our reality. By visualizing our goals, desires, and intentions, and repeating positive affirmations, we program our subconscious mind and align our energy with what we wish to manifest. These practices help us cultivate a positive mindset, enhance our self-confidence, and create a sense of alignment between our inner world and outer experiences.

Nature and the elements offer profound opportunities for connection and grounding. Spending time in nature, whether it's walking in the woods, sitting by the ocean, or tending to a garden, helps us reconnect with the natural rhythms of life. Nature reminds us of our interdependence with all living beings and nurtures our sense of awe, gratitude, and connection to something greater than ourselves. Similarly, connecting with the elements, such as through fire ceremonies, water rituals, or earth-based practices, allows us to tap into the primal forces and wisdom present in the natural world.

Creating sacred spaces and engaging in rituals further deepen our connection to the spiritual aspect of our being. Sacred spaces can be physical areas in our homes or natural settings where we can retreat, reflect, and connect with our spirituality. Engaging in rituals, whether it's lighting candles, practicing mindfulness, or performing ceremonial acts, helps us honor our connection to the divine and create a sense of sacredness in our daily lives. These practices provide a sense of solace, reverence, and connection to the greater mysteries of life.

Exploring and nurturing our spiritual beliefs and practices is deeply personal and can take many forms. It may involve engaging with organized religions, following spiritual traditions, or cultivating a personal spirituality that aligns with our values and beliefs. This exploration invites us to question, seek, and connect with our own understanding of the divine and the greater purpose of our existence.

Embracing stillness and silence is an essential practice for inner reflection and self-discovery. In a world filled with noise and distractions, carving out time for stillness and silence allows us to listen to our inner voice, access our intuition, and gain clarity. Whether through meditation, contemplation, or simply taking quiet walks in nature, these moments of stillness provide a sacred space for introspection and self-awareness.

Engaging in creative expression and artistic outlets is another powerful way to connect with our inner selves and the divine. Through art, music, writing, or any form of creative expression, we tap into our innate creativity and connect with the deeper aspects of our being. These activities allow us to express ourselves authentically, explore our emotions, and tap into the collective consciousness.

Cultivating a balanced lifestyle is crucial for nurturing the mind-body-spirit connection. It involves consciously integrating self-care, work, relationships, leisure, and personal growth into our daily lives. Finding a harmonious rhythm that supports our overall well-being allows us to thrive and maintain a sense of balance and fulfillment.

Embracing joy, playfulness, and fun is a reminder to not take life too seriously and to embrace the joyous moments that bring us alive. Engaging in activities that bring us pleasure, laughter, and a sense of lightness uplifts our spirits and connects us with the inherent joy within us.

Finally, creating a personal self-care and spiritual practice is a way of honoring our own needs and nurturing our inner selves. This involves consciously setting aside time for self-care activities that replenish our energy, such as taking baths, journaling, practicing gratitude, or engaging in hobbies we enjoy. It also involves establishing a regular spiritual practice that supports our connection to the divine and deepens our sense of purpose and meaning.

Integrating the mind, body, and spirit is a lifelong journey of self-discovery, growth, and transformation. By recognizing and nurturing this interconnectedness, we unlock our innate personal power and create a foundation for living a balanced, fulfilled, and purposeful life. As we cultivate the mind-body-spirit connection, we awaken to the infinite possibilities within ourselves and become co-creators of our own reality.

Cultivating Mindfulness and Present Moment Awareness

In our fast-paced and often chaotic lives, cultivating mindfulness and present moment awareness is a transformative practice that allows us to experience greater presence, clarity, and connection. Mindfulness involves intentionally paying attention to the present moment, with an attitude of openness, curiosity, and non-judgment. By directing our awareness to the here and now, we can tap into a deeper sense of presence and engage fully with our inner and outer experiences.

One of the most widely practiced methods of cultivating mindfulness is through meditation. Meditation is a practice of training the mind to focus and redirect its attention. By dedicating time to sit in stillness and observe the breath, sensations, or thoughts without getting caught up in them, we develop the ability to be fully present. Regular meditation practice enhances our self-awareness, cultivates inner calmness, and strengthens our ability to stay present in our daily lives.

Breathing exercises are another effective tool for cultivating mindfulness. The breath serves as an anchor to the present moment, as it is always with us. By bringing conscious awareness to our breath, we can ground ourselves in the present and regulate our nervous system. Simple techniques, such as deep belly breathing or box breathing, help to calm the mind, reduce stress, and bring us into a state of greater presence and relaxation.

In addition to formal meditation and breathwork, we can bring mindfulness into our everyday activities. This involves consciously engaging with our senses and fully experiencing each moment. For example, while eating, we can savor the flavors, textures, and smells of our food, paying attention to each bite. While walking, we can feel the sensation of our feet touching the ground, listen to the sounds around us, and notice the sights along our path. By engaging our senses, we bring our attention back to the present moment and cultivate a deeper appreciation for the richness of our experiences.

Another aspect of cultivating mindfulness is developing non-judgmental awareness. This involves observing our thoughts, emotions, and sensations without attaching labels or evaluating them as good or bad. Instead, we cultivate an attitude of curiosity and acceptance, allowing whatever arises in our awareness to be as it is. This practice helps us let go of judgment and resistance, allowing us to meet each moment with openness and compassion.

Mindfulness not only enhances our connection to the present moment, but it also deepens our connection to ourselves and others. By being fully present with ourselves, we become more attuned to our thoughts, emotions, and physical sensations. This self-awareness allows us to respond to our own needs and desires with greater clarity and compassion. It also enhances our ability to listen deeply and empathetically to others, fostering more meaningful and authentic connections in our relationships.

Practicing mindfulness and present moment awareness is a journey that requires regular commitment and gentle persistence. It is not about achieving a state of perfection or constantly being in a state of presence, but rather about bringing an attitude of mindful awareness to our experiences as they unfold. By consistently nurturing this practice, we gradually expand our capacity for presence and cultivate a deeper sense of connection to ourselves, others, and the world around us.

As we cultivate mindfulness and present moment awareness, we unlock the transformative power of the present moment. We become more attuned to the beauty and richness of life, finding joy and fulfill-ment in each unfolding moment. Through the practice of mindfulness, we reclaim our power to fully engage with our experiences, cultivate inner peace, and live with a greater sense of purpose and authenticity.

Exploring Meditation and Breathwork Practices: Nurturing Relax-ation, Clarity, and Inner Peace

Meditation and breathwork practices are powerful tools for nurtur-ing relaxation, clarity, and inner peace in our lives. They offer profound benefits for the mind, body, and spirit, helping us cultivate a deeper sense of self-awareness and connection to the present moment. In this section, we will explore different meditation techniques and breathwork practices, providing guidance on how to incorporate them into our daily lives.

Meditation is a practice of intentionally directing our attention and bringing a sense of focused awareness to our present experience. There are various meditation techniques to explore, each with its own focus and approach. One commonly practiced technique is mindfulness meditation, which involves paying non-judgmental attention to the sen-sations of the breath, the body, or the sounds in the environment. This practice helps to calm the mind, increase self-awareness, and cultivate a sense of inner stillness and presence.

Another meditation technique is loving-kindness meditation, also known as Metta meditation. This practice involves directing well-wishes and compassion towards ourselves and others. By cultivating feelings of love, kindness, and goodwill, we enhance our connection to others and nurture a sense of empathy and understanding.

Visualization meditation is another powerful technique that involves using the imagination to create and focus on positive mental images. By visualizing ourselves in a peaceful or desired state, we can enhance our sense of relaxation, confidence, and clarity. This practice can be especially helpful in reducing stress and anxiety, as well as manifesting our goals and aspirations.

Breathwork practices, on the other hand, focus specifically on the breath as a means of calming the mind, energizing the body, and cultivating inner awareness. One such practice is deep belly breathing, also known as diaphragmatic breathing. This technique involves breathing deeply into the lower abdomen, allowing the breath to fully expand the belly. Deep belly breathing helps to activate the relaxation response, slow down the heart rate, and bring a sense of calmness and centeredness.

Another breathwork practice is alternate nostril breathing, also known as Nadi Shodhana. This technique involves using the fingers to alternate the airflow through each nostril while breathing. Alternate nostril breathing helps balance the left and right hemispheres of the brain, harmonizes the energy flow in the body, and promotes mental clarity and focus.

Incorporating meditation and breathwork practices into our daily lives can be a transformative journey. It is important to create a quiet and comfortable space where we can engage in these practices without distractions. Starting with just a few minutes a day and gradually increasing the duration can help us establish a regular practice and experience the benefits more fully.

Consistency and gentle persistence are key in meditation and breathwork. It is natural for the mind to wander or for challenges to arise as we engage in these practices. However, by gently redirecting our focus back to the breath or the chosen object of meditation, we cultivate resilience and deepen our ability to stay present.

The benefits of meditation and breathwork extend beyond the practice itself. As we incorporate these practices into our daily lives, we begin to experience a greater sense of calmness, clarity, and inner peace. We become more attuned to our own thoughts, emotions, and bodily sensations, allowing us to respond to life's challenges with greater wisdom and equanimity.

Meditation and breathwork also have profound effects on our physical health. They can help lower blood pressure, reduce stress and anxiety, improve sleep quality, and enhance overall well-being. These practices support the mind-body connection, promoting holistic health and harmony.

In conclusion, exploring meditation and breathwork practices opens the door to a deeper connection with ourselves and the present moment. By nurturing relaxation, clarity, and inner peace, we embark on a journey of self-discovery and personal growth. As we incorporate these practices into our daily lives, we unlock the transformative power of stillness, breath, and focused awareness, bringing greater balance, harmony, and well-being to our mind, body, and spirit.

Nurturing Physical Well-Being and Health

Physical well-being is a crucial aspect of our overall well-being and personal power. When we take care of our bodies, we enhance our energy, vitality, and resilience, allowing us to fully engage with life and pursue our passions. In this section, we will explore the importance of nurturing our bodies through proper nutrition, regular exercise, restful sleep, and self-care practices that support our physical well-being and vitality.

Proper nutrition is the foundation of physical health. Fueling our bodies with nutritious and balanced meals provides the essential nutrients, vitamins, and minerals needed for optimal functioning. It is important to prioritize whole, unprocessed foods, such as fruits, vegetables, whole grains, lean proteins, and healthy fats. By choosing nourishing foods, we support our immune system, enhance our energy levels, and promote overall well-being.

Hydration is also vital for our physical well-being. Drinking an adequate amount of water throughout the day helps maintain proper bodily functions, supports digestion, regulates body temperature, and promotes healthy skin. It is recommended to drink at least 8 cups (64 ounces) of water daily, but individual needs may vary depending on factors such as activity level, climate, and overall health.

Regular exercise is essential for maintaining a strong and healthy body. Engaging in physical activity not only improves cardiovascular health, strength, and flexibility but also releases endorphins, which uplift mood and reduce stress. Finding activities that we enjoy, whether it's walking, jogging, dancing, yoga, or any other form of exercise, allows us to incorporate movement into our daily lives and experience the benefits of an active lifestyle.

Restful sleep is crucial for our physical and mental well-being. During sleep, our bodies repair and regenerate, and our minds process information and emotions. Establishing a consistent sleep routine, creating a comfortable sleep environment, and practicing relaxation techniques before bed can improve the quality and duration of our sleep. Aim for 7-9 hours of uninterrupted sleep each night to support optimal functioning and overall health.

Self-care practices play a significant role in nurturing our physical well-being. Taking time for ourselves, engaging in activities that bring us joy and relaxation, and prioritizing self-care rituals are essential for replenishing our energy and reducing stress. This can include practices such as taking soothing baths, practicing mindfulness or meditation, engaging in hobbies or creative outlets, or simply dedicating quiet time for reflection and rejuvenation.

Listening to our bodies and honoring their wisdom and intuition is crucial in nurturing our physical well-being. Each person's body has unique needs and signals. Tuning in and being mindful of how we feel physically, emotionally, and mentally allows us to respond to our bodies' cues and make choices that support our overall health and vitality. This may involve adjusting our diet, modifying our exercise routine, or seeking professional healthcare guidance when needed.

Incorporating these practices into our daily lives requires commitment and consistency. Making small, sustainable changes gradually and building healthy habits over time is key. It's important to approach our physical well-being with self-compassion and avoid comparing ourselves to others. Each person's journey towards optimal health is unique, and what works for one may not work for another. It's about finding what feels nourishing and sustainable for us individually.

By nurturing our physical well-being and health, we enhance our personal power and create a solid foundation for overall well-being. When we prioritize self-care, exercise regularly, fuel our bodies with nutritious foods, and prioritize restful sleep, we support our bodies' natural ability to thrive. This, in turn, empowers us to live life fully, engage in meaningful activities, and pursue our goals and dreams with vitality and enthusiasm.

In conclusion, nurturing our physical well-being and health is an essential aspect of holistic self-care. By focusing on proper nutrition, regular exercise, restful sleep, and self-care practices, we cultivate vitality, enhance our energy levels, and support our overall well-being. Prioritizing our physical health allows us to reclaim our personal power and live a vibrant and fulfilling life.

Honoring the Body's Wisdom and Intuition

Our bodies are remarkable sources of wisdom and intuition. They carry valuable information and provide subtle cues that guide us towards optimal well-being and personal empowerment. In this section, we explore the importance of listening to our bodies, honoring their signals and needs, and developing a deeper connection with our intuitive guidance. By engaging in embodiment practices and self-reflection, we can tap into the inherent wisdom of our bodies and enhance our personal power.

Listening to our bodies is a practice of attunement and self-awareness. Our bodies communicate with us through sensations, emotions, and physical cues, offering valuable insights into our overall well-being. By cultivating mindfulness and paying attention to our bodily sensations, we can become more attuned to the messages our bodies are conveying. This involves pausing, taking a moment to scan our bodies, and noticing any areas of tension, discomfort, or ease. It's about developing a compassionate and curious relationship with our bodies, rather than dismissing or disregarding their signals.

Honoring our body's needs involves responding to its messages with care and respect. This means nourishing ourselves with healthy foods, engaging in regular physical activity, prioritizing rest and relaxation, and attending to any discomfort or pain in a timely manner. It also means setting boundaries and saying no when our bodies need rest, space, or protection. Honoring our body's needs requires us to prioritize self-care and make choices that support our overall well-being, even if they go against societal expectations or external pressures.

Embodiment practices play a significant role in deepening our connection with our bodies and accessing our intuitive guidance. These practices, such as yoga, Tai Chi, dance, or somatic movement, encourage us to fully inhabit and explore our physical selves. Through conscious movement, we can tap into the wisdom stored in our bodies, release tension, and cultivate a sense of presence and groundedness. Embodiment practices also allow us to access our intuitive knowing by creating a space for nonverbal communication and subtle body sensations to arise.

Self-reflection is an integral part of cultivating a deeper connection with our bodies and intuition. Taking time for introspection and journaling can help us explore the messages and insights that arise from within. By reflecting on our physical sensations, emotions, and intuitive nudges, we can gain clarity and deepen our understanding of ourselves. This practice of self-inquiry allows us to align our actions and choices with our inner wisdom, leading to greater authenticity and personal empowerment.

Trusting and following our intuition is an essential aspect of honoring our body's wisdom. Intuition is our inner knowing, a deep-seated sense of what feels right and aligned for us. It often arises as a subtle feeling, a gut instinct, or an inner voice that guides us towards the choices and paths that serve our highest good. By cultivating mindfulness, self-awareness, and a sense of trust in ourselves, we can tap into our intuitive guidance and make decisions that are in alignment with our authentic selves.

Incorporating practices that support our mind-body connection and intuitive guidance requires patience, consistency, and an open mind-set. It's important to approach this journey with self-compassion and curiosity, recognizing that it is a process of deepening our relationship with ourselves. Engaging in practices such as meditation, body scans, breathwork, or intuitive movement can help us access the wisdom that resides within us and strengthen our intuitive connection.

By honoring the wisdom and intuition of our bodies, we tap into a powerful source of personal guidance and empowerment. Listening to our bodies, responding to their needs, engaging in embodiment practices, and trusting our intuition allow us to make choices that align with our authentic selves and lead to greater well-being and fulfillment. As we develop a deeper connection with our bodies, we reclaim our personal power and embark on a journey of self-discovery and growth.

Exploring Movement and Embodiment Practices

Movement and embodiment practices offer us a profound opportunity to connect with our bodies, express ourselves authentically, and cultivate holistic well-being. In this section, we explore various modalities of movement, such as yoga, dance, and mindful movement, that promote body awareness, self-expression, and a deep sense of connection.

Our bodies are designed to move, and movement is an essential aspect of our physical and emotional well-being. Engaging in intentional and conscious movement practices allows us to tap into the wisdom and intelligence of our bodies, facilitating a greater understanding of ourselves and the world around us. These practices not only benefit our physical health but also provide a means for self-expression, stress relief, and personal growth.

Yoga is a widely recognized movement practice that combines physical postures, breathwork, and mindfulness. Through yoga, we cultivate body awareness, strength, flexibility, and balance. The practice invites us to tune into the sensations of our bodies, connect with our breath, and cultivate present moment awerness. Yoga offers a holistic approach to movement, promoting physical well-being, mental clarity, and emotional stability.

Dance is a vibrant and expressive form of movement that allows us to embody our emotions, tell stories, and connect with our creativity. It is a powerful means of self-expression and can be practiced in various styles, such as contemporary, ballet, hip-hop, or improvisational dance. Dancing encourages us to move with fluidity, grace, and authenticity, fostering a deep connection with our bodies and emotions.

Mindful movement practices, such as Tai Chi or Qigong, focus on slow, deliberate movements combined with breath awareness. These practices promote relaxation, balance, and the cultivation of vital energy (Qi). Mindful movement allows us to synchronize our breath with our movements, fostering a sense of harmony and deepening our mind-body connection.

Incorporating movement and embodiment practices into our lives offers numerous benefits. Firstly, these practices enhance body awareness, allowing us to become more attuned to the sensations, needs, and limitations of our bodies. This heightened awareness can lead to improved posture, alignment, and physical well-being. Additionally, engaging in movement practices supports stress reduction, as physical activity stimulates the release of endorphins, our body's natural feel-good hormones.

Movement and embodiment practices also serve as a powerful outlet for self-expression and emotional release. They provide a safe space to explore and express our emotions, freeing us from the constraints of words and allowing our bodies to communicate our inner experiences. Whether it's through dynamic, energetic movements or gentle, flowing motions, movement practices enable us to connect with our emotions and release any stagnant energy within us.

Moreover, these practices foster a deeper connection with our authentic selves. As we move and express ourselves, we tap into our innate creativity and individuality, allowing us to shine our unique light in the world. Movement becomes a form of self-discovery and self-acceptance, where we can embrace our bodies, celebrate our strengths, and cultivate a positive body image.

Engaging in movement and embodiment practices encourages us to be present in the moment. As we focus our attention on the physical sensations, rhythms, and qualities of our movements, we enter a state of flow, where time seems to disappear, and we are fully immersed in the experience. This state of presence cultivates mindfulness, reducing stress and enhancing our overall well-being.

To incorporate movement and embodiment practices into our lives, it's important to find activities that resonate with us personally. Whether it's joining a yoga class, attending a dance workshop, or practicing mindful movement at home, the key is to choose activities that bring us joy, inspire us, and align with our individual preferences and interests.

By embracing movement and embodiment practices, we embrace the innate wisdom and vitality of our bodies. We create a sacred space where self-expression, self-discovery, and self-acceptance can flourish. Through mindful movement, we reclaim our personal power, enhance our well-being, and cultivate a deeper connection with ourselves and the world around us.

Harnessing the Power of Visualization and Affirmations

Visualization and affirmations are powerful techniques that allow us to tap into the creative power of our minds and shape our reality. By consciously directing our thoughts and beliefs, we can enhance our mindset, manifest our desires, and align with our highest potential.

In this section, we explore how to effectively utilize visualization techniques and affirmations to create positive change in our lives.

Visualization is the practice of creating vivid mental images of the experiences, outcomes, or circumstances we desire. By visualizing ourselves already achieving or experiencing what we desire, we engage our imagination and subconscious mind in a way that activates our inner resources and motivates us to take aligned actions.

To begin the practice of visualization, find a quiet and comfortable space where you can relax and focus your attention. Close your eyes and take a few deep breaths to center yourself. Start by clearly identifying what you want to visualize—a specific goal, a desired outcome, or an experience you wish to manifest.

As you visualize, engage all your senses to make the experience more vivid and real. See the images in your mind's eye, feel the sensations in your body, hear the sounds, and even imagine the smells and tastes associated with your desired experience. Make it as detailed and vibrant as possible.

Immerse yourself fully in this mental image, allowing yourself to feel the emotions and excitement that come with the achievement of your desired outcome. Embrace the joy, confidence, and gratitude as if it has already happened. Hold this visualization for a few minutes, soaking in the positive energy and allowing it to permeate your being.

Consistency is key in the practice of visualization. Set aside dedicated time each day to visualize your desired outcomes. Create a routine that works for you, whether it's in the morning, before bed, or during a quiet moment in the day. The more frequently and vividly you visualize, the more you align your mind, energy, and actions with the realization of your desires.

Affirmations are positive statements that reinforce empowering beliefs and intentions. They are powerful tools for reprogramming our subconscious mind and shifting our thought patterns from limitation to possibility. By consciously choosing affirmations that support our goals and desires, we can cultivate a mindset of abundance, confidence, and success.

To create effective affirmations, start by identifying the areas of your life where you desire positive change or growth. Craft affirmations that reflect your desired reality and state them in the present tense, as if they are already true. For example, if you want to cultivate self-confidence, your affirmation could be: "I am confident and capable in all areas of my life."

Repeat your affirmations regularly, ideally multiple times a day. Say them out loud with conviction, write them down in a journal, or create visual reminders that you can see throughout the day. As you repeat your affirmations, allow yourself to truly embody the belief and intention behind them. Feel the truth of the statements and let them sink into your subconscious mind.

It's important to note that visualization and affirmations work best when coupled with inspired action. While these practices help shift your mindset and align your energy, it's essential to take practical steps towards your goals. Use the clarity and motivation you gain from visualization and affirmations to create a plan and take consistent, aligned action towards manifesting your desires.

Harnessing the power of visualization and affirmations requires patience, consistency, and a willingness to believe in the possibilities that lie within you. As you persistently engage in these practices, you will begin to notice subtle shifts in your mindset, attitude, and actions. You will develop a deep sense of alignment with your desires, and opportunities will arise to support your journey.

Remember, the power to create the life you desire lies within you. Visualization and affirmations are tools that can amplify your personal power and guide you towards the manifestation of your dreams. Embrace these practices with an open heart and an unwavering belief in your own potential, and watch as your reality transforms in remarkable ways.

Connecting with Nature and the Elements

Nature is a remarkable source of inspiration, healing, and connection. In this section, we delve into the importance of connecting with nature and the elements, and explore various ways to deepen our relationship with the natural world.

Spending time outdoors is a simple yet effective way to connect with nature. Take regular walks in the park, hike in the mountains, or simply sit under a tree and observe the beauty around you. Allow yourself to be fully present in the natural environment, immersing your senses in the sights, sounds, smells, and sensations of the natural world. The gentle breeze, the rustling leaves, and the vibrant colors can have a calming and rejuvenating effect on your mind, body, and spirit.

Engaging in nature-based rituals is another way to foster a deeper connection with the natural world. Create rituals that honor the cycles of nature, such as celebrating the changing seasons, the solstices, or the full moon. This can involve gathering natural objects, lighting candles, or performing simple ceremonies to express gratitude, set intentions, or seek guidance. These rituals can serve as reminders of our interconnectedness with the Earth and help us cultivate a sense of harmony and reverence.

Developing a deeper reverence for the natural world and its elements involves recognizing and appreciating the inherent wisdom and beauty present in nature. Take time to observe and learn from the elements—earth, air, fire, water, and spirit—and their qualities. Reflect on the grounding and stability of the earth, the flow and adaptability of water, the transformative power of fire, the expansive energy of air, and the interconnectedness of all things through spirit. By embracing the teachings of the elements, we can gain a deeper understanding of ourselves and our place in the world.

Nature also provides opportunities for self-reflection and inner exploration. Find a quiet spot in nature where you can sit in stillness and silence. Allow yourself to disconnect from distractions and simply be present in the moment. Observe the rhythms of nature and notice how they mirror the rhythms within yourself. Through this practice, you can gain insights, clarity, and a deeper connection to your own inner wisdom.

Engaging in activities that foster a sense of connection with nature is another way to deepen your relationship with the natural world. Gardening, for example, allows you to co-create with the Earth, nurturing plants and witnessing their growth. Outdoor activities such as swimming, surfing, or hiking can provide a sense of adventure and physical engagement with the elements. Engaging in conservation efforts and supporting environmental causes can also be a powerful way to give back and protect the natural world.

By connecting with nature and the elements, we tap into a wellspring of healing, inspiration, and guidance. We recognize that we are part of a larger web of life and that our well-being is intricately connected to the well-being of the Earth. As we cultivate a deeper reverence for nature, we develop a greater sense of responsibility to protect and preserve it for future generations.

Take the time to immerse yourself in nature, to honor its beauty and wisdom, and to listen to its whispers. In doing so, you will not only nourish your own soul but also contribute to the collective healing and transformation of our planet.

Cultivating Sacred Spaces and Rituals

Sacred spaces and rituals provide a sacred container for spiritual connection, self-reflection, and personal growth. In this section, we explore the significance of creating sacred spaces and engaging in rituals, and how they can be integrated into our daily lives to foster grounding, centering, and a deep honoring of our spiritual essence.

Creating a sacred space is an intentional act of setting aside a physical area or creating an energetic atmosphere that is dedicated to spiritual practice and connection. It can be a small altar adorned with meaningful objects, a quiet corner with cushions for meditation, or an entire room dedicated to spiritual activities. The key is to infuse this space with objects, symbols, and elements that hold personal significance and evoke a sense of sacredness. This might include candles, crystals, sacred texts, incense, or artwork. By consciously designating a space as sacred, we create a tangible reminder of our commitment to spiritual growth and self-care.

Engaging in rituals within our sacred spaces is a powerful way to honor our spiritual essence and cultivate a deeper connection to the divine. Rituals can take various forms and can be tailored to suit our individual preferences and beliefs. They may involve lighting candles and offering prayers, performing ceremonial rituals, or engaging in sacred practices such as chanting, drumming, or visualization. The intention behind these rituals is to create a focused and intentional space for spiritual connection, inner reflection, and personal transformation.

Incorporating rituals into our daily lives can provide a sense of rhythm, meaning, and grounding. They serve as anchors that remind us to pause, connect with our inner selves, and honor the sacredness of each moment. Rituals can be as simple as a morning gratitude practice, a daily meditation, or a bedtime ritual for releasing the day's energy. The key is to approach these rituals with intention and presence, allowing them to become transformative moments of connection and self-awareness.

Sacred spaces and rituals can also be shared with others, creating a sense of community and collective spiritual connection. Gathering with like-minded individuals for group rituals, ceremonies, or spiritual circles can amplify the energy and deepen the sense of connection to something greater than ourselves. It is through these shared experiences that we can support each other's spiritual journeys, share wisdom, and create a space of mutual support and understanding.

Beyond physical spaces and structured rituals, it is important to remember that sacredness can be found in the ordinary moments of life. We can infuse our daily activities with mindfulness and reverence, recognizing the divinity in the simplest of actions. Whether it is sipping a cup of tea with awareness, taking a walk in nature with gratitude, or engaging in acts of kindness and compassion, these moments can become sacred rituals that connect us to our spiritual essence.

Cultivating sacred spaces and rituals is an ongoing practice that requires intention, presence, and a willingness to explore and honor our spiritual nature. By creating sacred spaces, engaging in rituals, and infusing our daily lives with a sense of reverence, we invite the sacred to permeate our existence, fostering a deeper connection to ourselves, others, and the divine. In these moments, we discover that the sacred is not separate from us but an inherent part of who we are.

Exploring Spiritual Beliefs and Practices

Spirituality is a deeply personal and multifaceted aspect of human experience. It encompasses our beliefs, values, and practices that relate to our connection with the divine or higher power, as well as our understanding of the meaning and purpose of life. This section encourages individuals to embark on a journey of self-exploration, inviting them to explore different spiritual beliefs and practices and cultivate their own unique relationship with the divine.

Spirituality is not confined to any specific religious tradition or set of beliefs. It embraces a wide range of perspectives and paths, honoring the diversity of human experiences and the richness of cultural and religious traditions. Each individual's spiritual journey is unique, influenced by their upbringing, personal experiences, and the deep longings of their soul.

To begin exploring spirituality, it is important to create a space for self-reflection and introspection. This can involve setting aside dedicated time for contemplation, journaling, or engaging in activities that promote inner stillness and introspection. By turning our attention inward, we can connect with our innermost desires, questions, and curiosities about the nature of existence and our place in the larger scheme of things.

As we embark on this journey, we are invited to explore different spiritual beliefs and traditions. This may involve reading sacred texts, studying the teachings of spiritual leaders and philosophers, or engaging in dialogue with individuals from diverse backgrounds. By expanding our awareness of different spiritual perspectives, we open ourselves to new insights and possibilities, allowing us to connect with aspects of spirituality that resonate with our own unique understanding and yearnings.

In addition to intellectual exploration, personal experiences and practices play a vital role in deepening our spirituality. Engaging in spiritual practices such as prayer, meditation, contemplation, or ritual can foster a sense of connection and transcendence. These practices provide a space for communion with the divine, inner transformation, and the cultivation of virtues such as compassion, gratitude, and forgiveness.

It is essential to approach our exploration of spirituality with an open mind and heart, embracing a sense of curiosity and reverence. As we delve into different spiritual beliefs and practices, we may encounter ideas and experiences that challenge our existing beliefs or expand our understanding of the divine. It is important to approach these encounters with humility and a willingness to learn and grow.

Ultimately, the purpose of exploring spiritual beliefs and practices is not to find definitive answers or adhere to a prescribed set of beliefs. Rather, it is about nurturing a personal relationship with the divine or higher power that resonates with our own inner truth and brings meaning and purpose to our lives. This relationship is a deeply intimate and ongoing journey, shaped by our ongoing exploration, self-reflection, and lived experiences.

As we explore spirituality, it is important to remember that our journey is unique and deeply personal. There is no right or wrong way to connect with the divine or higher power. The key is to approach our exploration with authenticity, integrity, and an open heart, allowing our own inner wisdom to guide us on this profound and transformative path.

In embracing the exploration of spiritual beliefs and practices, we open ourselves to a world of wonder, interconnectedness, and infinite possibilities. Through this exploration, we can cultivate a deeper sense of purpose, inner peace, and a profound connection with the divine that enriches every aspect of our lives.

Embracing Stillness and Silence for Inner Reflection

In our fast-paced and noise-filled world, stillness and silence can be powerful antidotes that allow us to reconnect with ourselves on a deeper level. This section highlights the value of embracing stillness and silence as essential practices for inner reflection, self-awareness, and cultivating a sense of inner peace. It explores the benefits of creating moments of stillness and silence in our lives and offers techniques for incorporating these practices into our daily routines.

In the midst of our busy lives, it can be easy to get caught up in the constant stream of thoughts, distractions, and external stimuli. We may find ourselves overwhelmed, disconnected from our inner selves, and longing for a sense of peace and clarity. Embracing stillness and silence provides an opportunity to pause, to step away from the noise and busyness, and to turn our attention inward.

When we intentionally create space for stillness and silence, we invite the opportunity for deep self-reflection and introspection. In this quietude, we can listen to the whispers of our inner wisdom, uncover hidden truths, and gain insight into our thoughts, emotions, and desires. Stillness and silence provide a sacred space for us to explore the depths of our being, to reconnect with our true selves, and to gain a clearer understanding of our values, needs, and aspirations.

One way to cultivate stillness and silence is through the practice of meditation. Meditation involves deliberately focusing our attention and quieting the mind, allowing us to become fully present in the current moment. By sitting in silence and observing our thoughts without judgment, we develop a heightened sense of self-awareness and cultivate a deeper connection with our inner selves. Meditation can be practiced in various forms, such as mindfulness meditation, loving-kindness meditation, or guided visualization, each offering unique benefits and approaches to stilling the mind.

In addition to formal meditation practices, we can incorporate moments of stillness and silence into our daily lives. This can be as simple as taking short breaks throughout the day to pause, close our eyes, and focus on our breath. It can also involve finding quiet spaces in nature, such as a peaceful garden or a tranquil forest, where we can sit in stillness and attune ourselves to the natural rhythms of the world around us. Engaging in activities that promote silence, such as reading, journaling, or engaging in creative pursuits, can also provide opportunities for inner reflection and stillness.

Creating a regular practice of stillness and silence requires intention and commitment. It may initially feel challenging to quiet the mind and let go of external distractions. However, with persistence and patience, we can gradually cultivate the ability to embrace stillness and silence as a nourishing and transformative practice. As we make space for stillness and silence in our lives, we allow ourselves to access deeper levels of self-awareness, tap into our intuition, and cultivate a sense of inner peace that extends beyond the moments of silence into all aspects of our lives.

Embracing stillness and silence for inner reflection is not about escaping from the world or withdrawing from our responsibilities. Rather, it is a practice of creating moments of presence and deep listening amidst the demands of daily life. In these moments, we cultivate a sense of groundedness, clarity, and connection with our authentic selves. We become more attuned to our needs, values, and the subtle messages that arise from within. This self-awareness and inner peace then ripple outwards, positively impacting our relationships, our work, and our interactions with the world.

In our journey of embracing stillness and silence, it is important to approach the practice with gentleness and compassion. There may be times when we encounter resistance, restlessness, or a flurry of thoughts. Rather than judging ourselves or becoming discouraged, we can simply observe these experiences with non-judgmental awareness and return to the stillness and silence with patience and kindness.

By embracing stillness and silence, we create a sacred space within ourselves for deep reflection, self-discovery, and inner transformation. We tap into the wellspring of wisdom that resides within us, accessing a source of guidance, peace, and clarity. Through the regular practice of stillness and silence, we cultivate a greater sense of self-awareness, deepen our connection with our authentic selves, and navigate life's challenges with grace and resilience.

Engaging in Creative Expression and Artistic Outlets

Creative expression serves as a profound channel for self-discovery, self-expression, and personal transformation. This section explores the importance of engaging in artistic outlets and encourages individuals to explore various forms of creative expression that resonate with their unique interests and talents. By tapping into their innate creativity, individuals can access a deeper level of self-awareness and authenticity, fostering personal growth and empowerment.

Creativity is an inherent aspect of the human experience. It allows us to explore, experiment, and communicate in ways that transcend traditional methods of expression. Engaging in artistic outlets, whether it be writing, painting, music, dance, photography, or any other form of creative expression, offers a gateway to unlocking our inner worlds and giving voice to our thoughts, emotions, and perspectives.

One of the remarkable aspects of creative expression is its ability to bypass the constraints of language and logic. It enables us to access parts of ourselves that may be hidden or dormant, allowing for a deeper exploration of our subconscious mind and inner landscapes. Through the act of creating, we can access our intuition, tap into our deepest emotions, and connect with our authentic selves.

Writing, for example, can be a powerful form of self-expression and self-discovery. Journaling allows us to explore our thoughts and feelings, unravel complex emotions, and gain insights into our experiences. It provides a safe space for us to freely express ourselves without judgment or limitation. Writing poetry or stories allows us to tap into our imagination, giving shape and form to our innermost desires, dreams, and aspirations. The written word can become a bridge between our internal world and the external reality, offering a means of communication and connection.

Visual arts, such as painting, drawing, or sculpting, offer another avenue for creative expression. Through colors, shapes, and textures, we can externalize our internal experiences, thoughts, and emotions. Artistic expression allows us to communicate in a non-verbal language, tapping into our subconscious and allowing our intuition to guide the creative process. As we engage with the materials and immerse ourselves in the act of creation, we are invited to let go of expectations and embrace the process itself, cultivating a sense of freedom and spontaneity.

Music and dance are forms of creative expression that engage not only our minds but also our bodies. They offer a means of channeling emotions, connecting with our physicality, and experiencing a sense of flow and liberation. Playing an instrument, singing, or moving to the rhythm of music allows us to tap into our emotions, express ourselves authentically, and connect with others on a deep level. These forms of creative expression can be deeply therapeutic, providing a means of catharsis, self-discovery, and connection with our own inner rhythm.

Engaging in creative expression and artistic outlets not only fosters self-discovery and self-expression but also cultivates a sense of joy, playfulness, and fulfillment. It provides a space for experimentation, taking risks, and embracing the process rather than focusing solely on the end result. Through the act of creating, we give ourselves permission to explore new possibilities, challenge societal norms, and embrace our uniqueness.

It is important to note that creative expression does not require any formal training or expertise. It is a deeply personal journey that is accessible to everyone. The focus should not be on creating "masterpieces" but on the process of self-exploration, self-expression, and personal growth. By allowing ourselves to engage in creative expression without judgment or self-criticism, we create a nurturing space for our authentic selves to emerge and flourish.

Incorporating creative expression into our lives can be as simple as setting aside regular time for creative activities, creating a dedicated space for artistic pursuits, or joining a community of like-minded individuals who share similar interests. The key is to prioritize and honor our innate need for self-expression and to give ourselves permission to create without fear of judgment or comparison.

Engaging in creative expression and artistic outlets is a powerful way to tap into our inner wisdom, explore our authentic selves, and cultivate personal growth and empowerment. It allows us to transcend limitations, connect with our intuition, and embrace our unique voices. By embracing the power of creative expression, we can embark on a transformative journey of self-discovery, self-expression, and personal fulfillment.

Cultivating a Balanced Lifestyle

A balanced lifestyle is crucial for overall well-being and personal empowerment. It involves consciously attending to and nurturing various aspects of our lives, including our physical, mental, emotional, and spiritual well-being. This section explores strategies for creating and maintaining a balanced lifestyle that honors our diverse needs and allows us to thrive in all areas of life.

One of the foundational elements of a balanced lifestyle is self-care. Self-care encompasses activities and practices that support our well-being and nourish our mind, body, and spirit. It involves prioritizing activities that replenish our energy, bring us joy, and promote a sense of inner peace. This may include engaging in activities such as meditation, exercise, spending time in nature, practicing hobbies, or connecting with loved ones. By consciously carving out time for self-care and honoring our individual needs, we can replenish our energy reserves and enhance our overall well-being.

Effective time management is another essential aspect of a balanced lifestyle. Time is a precious resource, and how we choose to allocate it greatly impacts our overall sense of balance and fulfillment. By prioritizing our activities, setting clear goals, and practicing effective time management techniques, we can create a sense of structure and ensure that our time is spent in alignment with our values and priorities. This may involve creating daily or weekly schedules, breaking tasks into manageable chunks, and learning to say no to commitments that do not align with our goals and values.

Setting boundaries is crucial in maintaining a balanced lifestyle. Boundaries define what is acceptable and what is not in terms of our time, energy, and relationships. They serve as a means of protecting our well-being and ensuring that we have the necessary resources to fulfill our own needs. Setting boundaries involves learning to say no when necessary, clearly communicating our limits and expectations, and advocating for our own well-being. By setting and honoring our boundaries, we create a space that allows us to maintain a sense of balance and prevent the depletion of our resources.

Emotional well-being is an integral part of a balanced lifestyle. It involves recognizing, acknowledging, and processing our emotions in healthy and constructive ways. This may include engaging in practices such as journaling, therapy, or seeking support from loved ones. Cultivating emotional intelligence and resilience allows us to navigate challenges and setbacks more effectively, fostering a greater sense of balance and well-being.

In addition to these aspects, cultivating a balanced lifestyle involves nurturing our spiritual well-being. This may include exploring and deepening our spiritual beliefs and practices, connecting with a higher power or divine presence, or engaging in activities that bring us a sense of meaning and purpose. Connecting with our spirituality provides a source of guidance, comfort, and inspiration, contributing to a greater sense of balance and wholeness in our lives.

A balanced lifestyle is not about achieving perfection or juggling an equal distribution of time and energy in all areas of life. Instead, it is about consciously assessing and responding to our individual needs and priorities in a way that honors our overall well-being. It requires self-awareness, self-compassion, and a willingness to make adjustments and recalibrate when necessary. By nurturing a balanced lifestyle, we create the foundation for personal empowerment, resilience, and a more fulfilling and harmonious life.

Embracing Joy, Playfulness, and Fun

Joy, playfulness, and fun are essential ingredients for a fulfilling and balanced life. They bring a sense of lightness, spontaneity, and wonder that can uplift our spirits and enhance our overall well-being. This section encourages individuals to embrace and prioritize joy, playfulness, and fun as integral aspects of their lives, fostering a deeper sense of happiness, creativity, and spiritual growth.

Finding joy in the simple pleasures of life is a powerful practice. It involves being fully present and savoring the small moments of beauty and happiness that surround us. It could be as simple as enjoying a cup of tea, taking a leisurely walk in nature, or spending quality time with loved ones. By cultivating an attitude of gratitude and awareness, we open ourselves up to experiencing more joy and appreciation for the blessings that exist in our daily lives.

Playfulness invites us to reconnect with our inner child and approach life with a sense of curiosity and wonder. Engaging in playful activities stimulates our creativity, reduces stress, and encourages a lighthearted perspective. It could involve playing games, engaging in hobbies, exploring new interests, or simply allowing ourselves to be silly and spontaneous. By embracing playfulness, we tap into our natural sense of joy and invite more lightness and laughter into our lives.

Fun is a vital component of a balanced and fulfilling life. It is about intentionally engaging in activities that bring us pleasure and excitement. Fun can be different for each individual, depending on their interests and preferences. It could involve pursuing hobbies, attending social events, traveling, or engaging in adventurous activities. By actively seeking out and prioritizing fun, we infuse our lives with positive energy, create lasting memories, and nourish our spirits.

Cultivating a sense of joy, playfulness, and fun also contributes to our spiritual growth. It allows us to let go of seriousness and connect with the inherent joy and creativity of our souls. When we engage in activities that bring us joy, we align ourselves with our true essence and tap into our innate spiritual power. Joy and playfulness provide a gateway to experiencing a deeper connection with ourselves, others, and the world around us.

Incorporating joy, playfulness, and fun into our daily lives requires intention and a willingness to prioritize these experiences. It may involve carving out dedicated time for activities that bring us joy, seeking out new adventures and experiences, and letting go of self-imposed limitations or expectations. By giving ourselves permission to embrace joy, playfulness, and fun, we enhance our overall well-being, nurture our spirits, and create a life that is more vibrant, fulfilling, and spiritually enriching.

Remember, life is meant to be enjoyed, and by embracing joy, playfulness, and fun, we infuse each day with a sense of delight and wonder. So let go of seriousness, embrace your inner child, and allow yourself to experience the joy and magic that life has to offer.

Creating a Personal Self-Care and Spiritual Practice

Self-care and spirituality are deeply intertwined aspects of our lives that contribute to our overall well-being and personal growth. This section invites individuals to create their own personalized self-care and spiritual practices, providing guidance on exploring various techniques and rituals that align with their unique needs, values, and beliefs. By dedicating time and attention to these practices, individuals can cultivate a deeper connection with themselves, nurture their well-being, and foster a sense of harmony and fulfillment in their lives.

To create a personal self-care and spiritual practice, it is important to approach it with openness, curiosity, and a willingness to explore different modalities. Here are some suggestions to guide you in this process:

Reflect on your needs and values: Take time to reflect on what aspects of your well-being are important to you. Consider your physical, mental, emotional, and spiritual needs. Identify the values and beliefs that are meaningful to you and serve as a guiding compass for your practice.

Explore various techniques and rituals: There are countless techniques and rituals that can be incorporated into a self-care and spiritual practice. Some examples include meditation, journaling, prayer, affirmations, energy healing, visualization, gratitude practices, and connecting with nature. Research and experiment with different modalities to discover what resonates with you.

Start with small steps: Begin by incorporating one or two practices into your daily routine. This could be as simple as setting aside a few minutes each day for meditation, writing in a gratitude journal, or engaging in a mindful walk in nature. Consistency is key, so start with manageable commitments and gradually expand your practice as you feel comfortable.

Listen to your intuition: As you explore different practices, pay attention to how they make you feel. Listen to your intuition and trust your inner guidance to lead you towards the practices that nourish and resonate with your authentic self. Your intuition will help you find the practices that support your growth and well-being.

Create sacred space: Designate a physical space in your home or outdoors where you can engage in your self-care and spiritual practices. This space can be adorned with objects that hold personal significance, such as candles, crystals, sacred symbols, or artwork. Creating a sacred space helps to cultivate a sense of reverence and tranquility, and it serves as a reminder to prioritize your practice.

Establish a routine: Consistency is key in developing a self-care and spiritual practice. Establish a routine that works for you, whether it's dedicating a specific time each day or setting aside certain days of the week for your practice. By committing to regular practice, you create a container for self-reflection, growth, and connection.

Adapt and evolve: As you embark on your self-care and spiritual journey, be open to adapting and evolving your practice over time. Your needs and interests may change, and new techniques or rituals may resonate with you as you progress on your path. Allow your practice to evolve with you and be receptive to new insights and experiences along the way.

Remember, your self-care and spiritual practice is unique to you. There is no right or wrong way to approach it. What matters is that you create a practice that supports your well-being, nurtures your connection with yourself and the divine, and brings you a sense of joy, peace, and fulfillment. Embrace the process, trust yourself, and honor the sacredness of your journey.

8

Embracing the Journey

Reflecting on the Progress Made So Far

Reflecting on the Progress Made So Far is an important aspect of personal growth and development. It allows individuals to pause, look back, and acknowledge the milestones they have reached along their journey. This section encourages individuals to take time for self-reflection and celebrate their achievements, no matter how big or small.

By reflecting on the progress made, individuals can gain a deeper understanding of their growth, recognize the challenges they have overcome, and appreciate the lessons learned along the way. This process helps to cultivate a sense of fulfillment, boosting self-confidence and motivation to continue moving forward.

In this section, individuals are guided to engage in self-reflection exercises, such as journaling or creating a progress log, to document their accomplishments and experiences. They are encouraged to celebrate their achievements and give themselves credit for their hard work and dedication.

By acknowledging and celebrating their progress, individuals reinforce a positive mindset and cultivate a sense of gratitude for their personal growth journey. This self-acknowledgment provides the motivation and inspiration needed to continue on the path of self-discovery and empowerment.

Ultimately, reflecting on the progress made so far is a reminder that personal growth is a continuous process. It allows individuals to recognize how far they have come and encourages them to keep pushing forward, embracing new challenges and opportunities for growth. By celebrating achievements and acknowledging the progress made, individuals can fuel their motivation, build resilience, and continue their journey of self-discovery and empowerment with renewed vigor and determination.

Celebrating Milestones and Achievements

Celebrating Milestones and Achievements is a powerful practice that nourishes personal growth and enhances self-worth. This section emphasizes the importance of acknowledging and appreciating the milestones and achievements individuals have accomplished on their journey of personal development.

By celebrating milestones, individuals create opportunities to reflect on their progress, recognize their efforts, and honor the growth they have experienced. This process helps to cultivate a sense of accomplishment and boosts self-confidence, reinforcing the belief in one's abilities and potential.

In this section, individuals are encouraged to identify their milestones and achievements, both big and small, and find meaningful ways to celebrate them. This can include organizing a personal celebration, sharing the accomplishment with loved ones, or rewarding oneself with a meaningful treat or experience.

By celebrating milestones, individuals reinforce positive emotions and create positive associations with their growth journey. This strengthens their motivation and commitment to continue striving for personal excellence.

Furthermore, celebrating achievements provides an opportunity for reflection and gratitude. It allows individuals to appreciate the challenges they have overcome, the lessons they have learned, and the personal growth they have experienced. This gratitude and reflection further fuel their motivation to keep pushing forward and embracing new challenges.

Celebrating milestones and achievements also serves as a reminder that personal growth is not a linear process. It is important to recognize and celebrate progress, even if there are setbacks or moments of uncertainty along the way. By honoring achievements, individuals cultivate resilience, optimism, and a sense of fulfillment.

Ultimately, celebrating milestones and achievements is an empowering practice that nourishes self-worth, strengthens motivation, and fosters a positive mindset. By recognizing and appreciating personal growth, individuals are inspired to continue their journey of self-improvement and strive for personal excellence with renewed enthusiasm and determination.

Embracing the Concept of Lifelong Learning

Embracing the concept of lifelong learning is a transformative mindset that propels personal growth and development. In this section, individuals are encouraged to adopt a learning mentality and recognize that learning is not confined to formal education or a specific phase of life. Instead, it is a lifelong journey that extends across all areas of life.

By embracing lifelong learning, individuals open themselves up to new experiences, knowledge, and perspectives. They understand that every interaction, challenge, and opportunity is an opportunity to learn and grow. This mindset fosters curiosity, adaptability, and a sense of continuous improvement.

Lifelong learning encompasses various aspects, including acquiring new knowledge, developing new skills, and expanding one's understanding of the world. It involves seeking out opportunities for personal and professional development, such as attending workshops, taking online courses, reading books, engaging in meaningful conversations, and exploring new interests.

This section encourages individuals to actively pursue learning opportunities and engage in self-directed learning. It emphasizes the importance of curiosity and self-motivation in seeking out new knowledge and experiences. By doing so, individuals can broaden their horizons, challenge their existing beliefs and assumptions, and develop a deeper understanding of themselves and the world around them.

Embracing lifelong learning also involves cultivating a growth mindset, which is the belief that abilities and intelligence can be developed through dedication and effort. This mindset encourages individuals to embrace challenges, persist in the face of setbacks, and view failures as opportunities for learning and growth.

Lifelong learning goes beyond the acquisition of information; it is about the application and integration of knowledge into everyday life. Individuals are encouraged to reflect on their learning experiences and find ways to incorporate their newfound knowledge and skills into their personal and professional pursuits.

By embracing the concept of lifelong learning, individuals foster personal evolution, adaptability, and resilience. They become more agile in navigating a rapidly changing world and are better equipped to seize opportunities for growth and success.

Ultimately, embracing lifelong learning is an empowering mindset that supports personal development, expands possibilities, and enhances one's ability to thrive in an ever-evolving world. By remaining open, curious, and committed to learning, individuals can unlock their full potential and lead fulfilling and meaningful lives.

Continuing Self-Exploration and Growth

Continuing self-exploration and growth is a transformative journey that unfolds throughout our lives. In this section, individuals are encouraged to embark on an ongoing process of self-reflection, self-inquiry, and self-discovery, nurturing personal growth and transformation.

Self-exploration involves delving into the depths of our being to gain a deeper understanding of ourselves. It requires a willingness to explore our thoughts, emotions, beliefs, values, and motivations. By engaging in self-reflection, individuals can become more aware of their patterns, behaviors, and the impact they have on their lives and relationships.

Through self-inquiry, individuals can ask themselves profound questions that invite introspection and exploration of their authentic selves. This process helps uncover deeper truths, desires, and aspirations, allowing individuals to align their actions and choices with their core values and purpose.

Self-discovery is about uncovering hidden aspects of ourselves and embracing our unique identity. It involves exploring our passions, interests, talents, and strengths, and recognizing the innate qualities that make us who we are. By embracing self-discovery, individuals can cultivate a deeper sense of self-acceptance and authenticity.

The journey of self-exploration and growth is not a linear path, but rather an ongoing process that unfolds over time. It requires a commitment to self-awareness, a willingness to confront and embrace our vulnerabilities, and a curiosity to explore new possibilities and potentials.

This section encourages individuals to engage in practices that facilitate self-exploration and growth. It may involve journaling, meditation, mindfulness practices, therapy, engaging in meaningful conversations, seeking feedback from others, and exploring various modalities of self-discovery, such as personality assessments or creative expression.

By engaging in ongoing self-exploration and growth, individuals deepen their understanding of themselves, their relationships, and their place in the world. They become more attuned to their needs, desires, and values, allowing them to make choices that align with their authentic selves.

Continued self-exploration and growth also foster personal development and transformation. It allows individuals to transcend limitations, break free from self-imposed barriers, and tap into their fullest potential. It empowers individuals to evolve, adapt, and navigate life's challenges with greater resilience and clarity.

Ultimately, the journey of self-exploration and growth is a life-long commitment to personal development and self-actualization. By embracing this process, individuals can cultivate a deep sense of self-awareness, fulfillment, and purpose, leading to a more meaningful and fulfilling life.

Embracing Change and Embracing Uncertainty

Embracing change and navigating uncertainty are essential skills for personal growth and resilience. In this section, individuals are guided on strategies for embracing change and navigating uncertain situations with resilience and adaptability.

Change is a constant in life, and learning to embrace it allows individuals to thrive in an ever-evolving world. By acknowledging that change is a natural part of the human experience, individuals can shift their mindset and perspective to see change as an opportunity for growth and transformation.

One strategy for embracing change is cultivating a mindset of openness and curiosity. Instead of resisting or fearing change, individuals can approach it with a sense of adventure and a willingness to explore new possibilities. This mindset allows individuals to adapt more readily to changing circumstances and seize opportunities that arise.

Another strategy is practicing flexibility and adaptability. This involves being willing to let go of old patterns, beliefs, and attachments that no longer serve us. By embracing flexibility, individuals can navigate transitions with greater ease and grace, adjusting their course when necessary.

Building resilience is also crucial in embracing change and uncertainty. Resilience is the ability to bounce back from setbacks and challenges. By developing resilience, individuals can navigate through uncertainty with confidence and bounce back from adversity with strength and determination. This can be cultivated through practices such as self-care, mindfulness, seeking support, and reframing challenges as opportunities for growth.

Embracing change also requires individuals to embrace the unknown. Uncertainty can be uncomfortable and unsettling, but it is also a fertile ground for personal growth and new possibilities. By developing a sense of trust in oneself and the unfolding of life, individuals can lean into uncertainty with courage and curiosity. This allows them to remain open to new experiences and opportunities that may arise.

Practicing self-compassion is essential when navigating change and uncertainty. It involves being kind to oneself, acknowledging the challenges and difficulties that may arise, and offering oneself support and understanding. By practicing self-compassion, individuals can navigate through uncertainty with greater self-acceptance and resilience.

Lastly, seeking support from others can be instrumental in embracing change and navigating uncertainty. Connecting with a supportive community, seeking guidance from mentors or coaches, or engaging in meaningful conversations with loved ones can provide valuable insights, perspectives, and encouragement during times of change and uncertainty.

By embracing change and navigating uncertainty with resilience and adaptability, individuals can cultivate a greater sense of empowerment and personal growth. They can develop the skills and mindset needed to thrive in a rapidly changing world and embrace the unknown as an opportunity for self-discovery and transformation.

Nurturing Resilience in Times of Challenge

Resilience is a valuable trait that empowers individuals to navigate challenges and bounce back from adversity. In this section, techniques for nurturing resilience are explored, enabling individuals to develop the skills and mindset needed to navigate difficult times with strength and perseverance.

One key aspect of nurturing resilience is cultivating a positive mind-set. This involves consciously choosing to focus on the positive aspects of a situation, reframing challenges as opportunities for growth, and cultivating optimism. By adopting a positive mindset, individuals can maintain a sense of hope and possibility even in the face of adversity.

Practicing self-care is another crucial element in nurturing resilience. Taking care of one's physical, mental, and emotional well-being is essential during challenging times. Engaging in activities that promote relaxation, self-reflection, and self-compassion can help individuals recharge and build their resilience. This may include activities such as exercise, mindfulness practices, journaling, or engaging in hobbies that bring joy and fulfillment.

Seeking support is also instrumental in nurturing resilience. Connecting with others who can provide emotional support, guidance, and encouragement can make a significant difference in navigating challenging times. This may involve reaching out to trusted friends, family members, or seeking professional support from therapists, counselors, or support groups. Sharing experiences and feelings with others can help individuals gain perspective, receive validation, and find practical solutions to their challenges.

Developing effective coping strategies is another aspect of nurturing resilience. Coping strategies can include problem-solving skills, stress management techniques, and emotional regulation strategies. By developing a repertoire of coping strategies, individuals can better navigate and manage stressors and challenges that arise.

Building resilience also involves practicing self-compassion. It is essential to treat oneself with kindness, understanding, and acceptance during challenging times. Recognizing that setbacks and difficulties are a part of life allows individuals to extend compassion towards themselves and embrace the imperfections and mistakes that may occur along the way.

Additionally, maintaining a sense of purpose and meaning in life can contribute to resilience. Engaging in activities that align with one's values, setting goals, and finding meaning in everyday life can provide individuals with a sense of direction and motivation, even in the face of adversity.

Ultimately, nurturing resilience is an ongoing process that requires consistent effort and self-reflection. By cultivating a positive mindset, practicing self-care, seeking support, developing coping strategies, practicing self-compassion, and maintaining a sense of purpose, individuals can build their resilience and navigate challenges with strength and perseverance.

Finding Meaning and Purpose in Everyday Life

Finding meaning and purpose in everyday life is a transformative journey that brings a sense of fulfillment and direction. This section focuses on exploring and clarifying personal values, passions, and interests to align daily actions with a deeper sense of purpose and meaning.

One way to discover meaning and purpose is by engaging in self-reflection and introspection. Taking time to ponder on personal values, what truly matters, and what brings joy and fulfillment can provide valuable insights. Reflecting on past experiences, achievements, and moments of flow can also shed light on areas that resonate deeply and align with personal values.

Exploring passions and interests is another avenue for finding meaning and purpose. Engaging in activities that spark enthusiasm and curiosity can lead to a deeper understanding of one's passions and interests. This exploration may involve trying new hobbies, volunteering, or exploring different areas of knowledge. By pursuing activities that ignite a sense of joy and passion, individuals can align their daily lives with what brings them a sense of purpose and fulfillment.

Clarifying personal values is an essential step in finding meaning and purpose. Identifying core values helps individuals understand what they stand for and what is truly important to them. By living in alignment with these values, individuals can feel a deeper sense of purpose and authenticity. Reflecting on values such as compassion, integrity, growth, or creativity can guide decision-making and the actions taken in daily life.

Setting meaningful goals and intentions is another way to infuse daily life with purpose. By setting goals that align with personal values and aspirations, individuals can create a sense of direction and focus. These goals can be related to personal growth, relationships, career, or any area of life that holds significance. Working towards these goals provides a sense of purpose and a feeling of progress and accomplishment.

Incorporating acts of kindness and service into daily life is another means of finding meaning and purpose. Contributing to the well-being of others and making a positive impact in the world can bring a profound sense of fulfillment. This can be done through volunteering, supporting a cause, or simply engaging in acts of kindness towards others. By extending compassion and making a difference in the lives of others, individuals can find a deeper sense of purpose.

It is important to remember that finding meaning and purpose is a dynamic and evolving process. What brings meaning and purpose may change over time, and it is essential to regularly reassess and adapt to new insights and life circumstances. Embracing personal growth and being open to new experiences and perspectives allows individuals to continue evolving on their journey towards meaning and purpose.

By exploring passions, clarifying values, setting meaningful goals, engaging in acts of kindness, and remaining open to personal growth, individuals can find greater meaning and purpose in their everyday lives. This journey of self-discovery and alignment brings a deeper sense of fulfillment and allows individuals to live authentically and with a sense of purpose.

Cultivating Gratitude and Appreciation

Cultivating gratitude and appreciation is a transformative practice that enhances our well-being and outlook on life. This section focuses on techniques and practices for cultivating gratitude, such as keeping a gratitude journal, expressing appreciation, and being present in the moment.

One powerful practice for cultivating gratitude is keeping a gratitude journal. This involves regularly writing down things we are grateful for, whether big or small. It could be the people in our lives, moments of joy, achievements, or even the simple pleasures we often take for granted. By intentionally focusing on the positive aspects of our lives, we train our minds to recognize and appreciate the abundance around us. Writing in the gratitude journal daily or weekly helps develop a habit of gratitude and shifts our attention towards the blessings in our lives.

Expressing appreciation to others is another way to cultivate gratitude. Taking the time to express our gratitude and appreciation to the people who have made a positive impact in our lives can deepen our sense of connection and foster a positive atmosphere. It can be as simple as a heartfelt thank-you note, a kind word, or an act of kindness. By expressing our appreciation, we not only uplift others but also enhance our own sense of gratitude and well-being.

Being present in the moment is a powerful practice for cultivating gratitude. Often, we get caught up in the busyness of life and fail to notice the beauty and blessings that surround us. By intentionally practicing mindfulness and being fully present in the moment, we open ourselves to the richness of our experiences and develop a deeper appreciation for the present moment. Whether it's savoring a delicious meal, enjoying nature, or connecting with loved ones, being present allows us to fully experience and appreciate the joys and blessings in our lives.

In addition to these practices, it's important to cultivate a positive mindset and shift our focus towards gratitude throughout the day. This can involve reframing challenges and setbacks as opportunities for growth, acknowledging the lessons they bring, and finding gratitude even in difficult circumstances. By cultivating a mindset of gratitude, we become more resilient and open to the abundance and opportunities that life presents.

Practicing gratitude and appreciation is not about denying or minimizing the challenges and difficulties we may face. Instead, it's about shifting our perspective and focusing on the positive aspects of our lives. By regularly engaging in gratitude practices, we cultivate a positive mindset, enhance our overall well-being, and invite more joy and abundance into our lives.

By incorporating practices such as keeping a gratitude journal, expressing appreciation, being present in the moment, and cultivating a positive mindset, individuals can foster a deep sense of gratitude and appreciation. This practice brings a greater sense of contentment, joy, and fulfillment in their daily lives.

Sharing Your Journey and Inspiring Others

Sharing one's personal journey can have a profound impact on others. This section emphasizes the importance of sharing experiences, insights, and lessons learned with authenticity and vulnerability. By doing so, individuals have the opportunity to inspire and uplift others, creating a positive ripple effect and contributing to the growth and empowerment of those around them.

When we share our journey with others, we offer a glimpse into our unique experiences, challenges, and triumphs. By being open and vulnerable, we create a space for others to relate to our stories, find solace in knowing they are not alone, and gain insights and inspiration from our personal growth journey. Sharing our struggles and how we have overcome them can provide a sense of hope and encouragement to those who may be facing similar challenges.

Authenticity is key when sharing our journey. By being true to ourselves and sharing from the heart, we create a genuine connection with others. This means embracing both the highs and lows of our journey, acknowledging our vulnerabilities, and being willing to show our imperfections. Authentic sharing allows others to see our humanity and relate to our experiences on a deeper level.

In addition to sharing our personal stories, it's valuable to share the insights and lessons we have gained along the way. By offering wisdom and practical advice based on our own experiences, we can guide and support others in their own growth journeys. Sharing the strategies and tools that have helped us overcome challenges and cultivate personal empowerment can provide others with practical guidance and inspiration for their own paths.

It's important to remember that sharing our journey is not about seeking validation or attention. Instead, it's about creating a space for connection, understanding, and growth. By sharing our experiences and lessons learned, we contribute to a collective pool of wisdom and foster a sense of community and support.

Social media platforms, blogs, support groups, or even intimate conversations with friends and family can serve as avenues for sharing our journey. The medium we choose should align with our comfort level and the audience we wish to reach. Whether it's through written or spoken words, visual storytelling, or engaging in meaningful conversations, the key is to be authentic, respectful, and mindful of the impact our sharing can have on others.

By sharing our personal journey with authenticity and vulnerability, we have the power to inspire and uplift others. We create a positive ripple effect, fostering a community of growth, support, and empowerment. In the process, we not only contribute to the well-being and growth of others but also deepen our own understanding of our journey and the lessons we have learned along the way.

Creating a Personal Manifesto and Life Vision

Creating a personal manifesto and life vision is a powerful process that empowers individuals to live intentionally and with purpose. This section guides individuals in crafting their own personal manifesto and life vision, providing a guiding framework for living in alignment with their values, aspirations, and desired impact on the world.

A personal manifesto is a statement of beliefs, values, and intentions that reflects who we are and what we stand for. It serves as a compass, guiding our choices and actions in accordance with our core principles. When creating a personal manifesto, it is essential to reflect on our values, passions, and what truly matters to us. What are the principles and ideals that we want to embody in our lives? What kind of impact do we want to make in the world? Taking the time to explore these questions helps us articulate our beliefs and intentions, allowing us to live in greater alignment with our authentic selves.

A life vision, on the other hand, is a compelling and inspiring description of the future we envision for ourselves. It encapsulates our aspirations, dreams, and goals across various areas of life, such as career, relationships, personal growth, and contribution to society. Developing a life vision requires us to tap into our deepest desires and imagine what our ideal life would look like. What do we want to achieve? How do we want to grow and evolve? What kind of legacy do we want to leave behind? Crafting a vivid and detailed life vision enables us to set meaningful goals and take purposeful actions towards creating the life we truly desire.

To create a personal manifesto and life vision, consider the following steps:

Self-reflection: Take time to reflect on your values, passions, and what truly matters to you. Consider your strengths, interests, and the impact you want to make in the world. Journaling, meditation, or engaging in meaningful conversations can help in this process.

Identify core beliefs and values: Determine the principles and values that are most important to you. What are the guiding principles that you want to live by? What values do you want to honor in all aspects of your life?

Craft your personal manifesto: Write a statement that encompasses your core beliefs, values, and intentions. Make it concise, powerful, and authentic. Your personal manifesto should resonate with who you are and what you aspire to be. Review and refine it as needed to ensure it accurately reflects your evolving self.

Envision your ideal life: Imagine your life in the future and create a vivid vision of what you want to achieve and experience. Consider various areas of life, such as career, relationships, personal growth, and contribution to society. Write down your vision in detail, including specific goals, milestones, and the emotions associated with living that vision.

Align actions with your manifesto and life vision: Use your personal manifesto and life vision as a guide for decision-making and goal-setting. Regularly review them to ensure your actions are aligned with your beliefs, values, and aspirations. Make adjustments as needed to stay on course.

Share and revisit: Share your personal manifesto and life vision with trusted individuals who can support and hold you accountable. Regularly revisit and reassess them to ensure they continue to reflect your evolving self and aspirations.

Creating a personal manifesto and life vision provides a foundation for intentional living and empowers individuals to make choices aligned with their values and aspirations. By regularly revisiting and reaffirming these guiding statements, individuals can navigate their journey with clarity, purpose, and a deep sense of fulfillment.

Embracing Personal Evolution and Transformation

Embracing personal evolution and transformation is a vital aspect of the journey towards self-discovery and empowerment. This section emphasizes the importance of embracing the changes and transformations that naturally occur throughout our lives, recognizing that personal growth often involves letting go of old patterns, beliefs, and behaviors, and embracing new possibilities.

Personal evolution is a continuous process of growth, learning, and self-discovery. It involves becoming aware of our strengths, weaknesses, and areas for improvement, and actively working towards becoming the best version of ourselves. As we evolve, our perspectives may shift, our values may change, and our priorities may realign. Embracing personal evolution means being open to self-reflection, learning from our experiences, and making conscious choices that support our growth and well-being.

Transformation, on the other hand, is a more profound and radical change that can occur in our lives. It often involves a significant shift in our beliefs, identity, or life circumstances. Transformation can be catalyzed by major life events, challenges, or moments of deep insight and awakening. Embracing personal transformation requires a willingness to let go of old ways of being that no longer serve us, and embracing new paths, possibilities, and potentials.

To embrace personal evolution and transformation:

Embrace self-reflection: Take time for introspection and self-assessment. Reflect on your values, beliefs, and behaviors. Identify areas for growth and areas that no longer align with who you are becoming.

Embrace change and uncertainty: Recognize that change is a natural part of life. Embrace the unknown and embrace change as an opportunity for growth and self-discovery. Be willing to step out of your comfort zone and explore new possibilities.

Let go of limiting beliefs: Identify and challenge limiting beliefs that hold you back from embracing personal evolution and transformation. Replace them with empowering beliefs that support your growth and potential.

Cultivate a growth mindset: Adopt a growth mindset, which is the belief that our abilities and intelligence can be developed through dedication and effort. Embrace challenges as opportunities for learning and growth, and view setbacks as valuable lessons.

Seek new experiences and learning opportunities: Engage in activities and experiences that expand your horizons and expose you to new ideas and perspectives. Pursue lifelong learning and personal development through reading, courses, workshops, or engaging with mentors and role models.

Surround yourself with supportive individuals: Seek out a supportive community of like-minded individuals who are also committed to personal growth and transformation. Share your journey with them, exchange ideas, and support each other's growth.

Practice self-compassion: Be gentle and kind to yourself throughout your journey of personal evolution and transformation. Embrace self-compassion as you navigate challenges and setbacks, and celebrate your progress and achievements along the way.

Embrace the process: Personal evolution and transformation are ongoing processes that unfold over time. Embrace the journey itself, rather than focusing solely on the end result. Trust the process and have patience with yourself as you navigate the twists and turns of personal growth.

Embracing personal evolution and transformation is a courageous and empowering choice. By embracing change, letting go of what no longer serves us, and embracing new possibilities, we can create a life that is authentic, aligned with our true selves, and filled with purpose and meaning.

Seeking Support and Guidance when Needed

Seeking support and guidance when needed is an important aspect of personal growth and empowerment. It is a sign of strength, self-awareness, and a recognition that we don't have to navigate life's challenges alone. This section emphasizes the importance of reaching out for help and guidance, whether through personal relationships, mentors, coaches, or professional support.

Here are some key points to consider when seeking support and guidance:

Self-awareness: Develop self-awareness to recognize when you need support. Pay attention to your emotions, thoughts, and behaviors. If you're feeling overwhelmed, stuck, or uncertain, it may be a sign that seeking support could be beneficial.

Personal relationships: Reach out to trusted friends, family members, or loved ones who can provide a listening ear, emotional support, and different perspectives. Share your thoughts, concerns, and aspirations with them, and be open to their insights and advice.

Mentors and role models: Seek out mentors or role models who have expertise or experience in areas you want to grow in. They can provide guidance, share their wisdom, and offer valuable insights to support your personal and professional development.

Coaches and counselors: Consider working with a coach or counselor who specializes in the areas you want to focus on. They can provide guidance, tools, and strategies to help you overcome challenges, set goals, and navigate personal growth effectively.

Professional support: If you're facing specific challenges or struggling with mental health issues, consider seeking professional support from therapists, psychologists, or other healthcare professionals. They can provide a safe and confidential space for you to explore your concerns and receive expert guidance and treatment.

Online communities and support groups: Explore online communities or support groups that align with your interests or areas of personal growth. These communities can provide a sense of belonging, shared experiences, and valuable insights from others who are on a similar journey.

Be open and vulnerable: When seeking support, be open and honest about your needs, challenges, and aspirations. Vulnerability allows others to understand and connect with you on a deeper level, fostering meaningful support and guidance.

Take action on advice and insights: When you receive guidance or support, take proactive steps to implement the advice or insights you receive. Apply what resonates with you and take ownership of your growth process.

Remember, seeking support and guidance is not a sign of weakness, but rather a powerful step towards personal growth and empowerment. By reaching out to others and engaging in meaningful conversations, you can gain new perspectives, learn from the experiences of others, and receive the encouragement and support needed to overcome challenges and thrive on your journey of self-discovery and empowerment.

Cultivating a Growth-Oriented Community

Cultivating a growth-oriented community is crucial for personal development and empowerment. Surrounding yourself with like-minded individuals who share a commitment to growth can provide valuable support, inspiration, and accountability on your journey. *This section explores strategies for cultivating such a community:*

Seek out like-minded individuals: Look for individuals who are on a similar path of personal growth and share similar values and aspirations. Attend events, workshops, or conferences related to personal development, spirituality, or areas of interest to connect with like-minded people.

Join or create a mastermind group: A mastermind group is a small community of individuals who come together regularly to support each other's growth and success. These groups provide a space for sharing goals, challenges, and insights, and offer accountability and encouragement.

Engage in online communities: Join online communities, forums, or social media groups focused on personal growth and empowerment. Engage in discussions, ask questions, and share your experiences. Connect with others who resonate with your journey and actively participate in supporting and uplifting each other.

Attend workshops or retreats: Participate in workshops, seminars, or retreats that focus on personal development, self-discovery, or areas of interest. These events often attract individuals seeking growth and provide opportunities for deep connections and transformative experiences.

Foster supportive relationships: Nurture relationships with individuals who are supportive, positive, and growth-oriented. Surround yourself with people who inspire and challenge you to step out of your comfort zone and strive for your highest potential.

Share and collaborate: Share your knowledge, experiences, and insights with others. Offer support, guidance, and encouragement to those on their personal growth journey. Look for opportunities to collaborate on projects or initiatives that align with your values and goals.

Be open to diverse perspectives: Embrace diversity and seek out individuals with different backgrounds, experiences, and perspectives. Engaging with people who have different viewpoints can broaden your understanding, challenge your assumptions, and stimulate personal growth.

Create a supportive environment: Be intentional about creating a supportive and growth-oriented environment within your community. Encourage open and respectful communication, celebrate each other's achievements, and provide constructive feedback to help each other grow.

Remember, cultivating a growth-oriented community is a mutual process. It requires active participation, genuine connections, and a willingness to both give and receive support. By surrounding yourself with individuals who are committed to growth, you can create a powerful support system that fosters personal development, accountability, and inspiration on your journey of self-discovery and empowerment.

Embracing the Wholeness of Your Being

Embracing the wholeness of your being is a transformative and empowering journey of self-acceptance and self-love. It involves acknowledging and integrating all aspects of yourself—the positive and the negative, the light and the shadow. ***This section guides you on this path of embracing your authenticity and cultivating self-compassion:***

Practice self-acceptance: Recognize that you are a unique individual with a combination of strengths, weaknesses, talents, and imperfections.

Embrace all parts of yourself without judgment or criticism. Emphasize self-acceptance rather than striving for perfection.

Cultivate self-awareness: Engage in self-reflection to deepen your understanding of yourself. Explore your beliefs, values, desires, fears, and patterns of behavior. By becoming aware of who you are, you can consciously choose how you want to show up in the world.

Embrace authenticity: Honor and express your true self. Let go of the need to conform to societal expectations or others' opinions. Celebrate your individuality and allow your authentic voice and expression to shine through.

Practice self-compassion: Treat yourself with kindness, understanding, and compassion. Be gentle with yourself when facing challenges or setbacks. Offer the same level of care and support to yourself as you would to a dear friend.

Embrace your strengths and weaknesses: Recognize and appreciate your strengths, talents, and unique gifts. Celebrate your achievements and allow yourself to shine. Simultaneously, acknowledge your weaknesses and areas for growth. See them as opportunities for learning and development.

Explore your shadow aspects: Embrace and integrate your shadow aspects—the parts of yourself that you may have suppressed or denied. These shadow aspects often hold valuable lessons and hidden strengths. By acknowledging and integrating them, you can foster personal growth and wholeness.

Practice self-care: Prioritize self-care practices that nourish your mind, body, and spirit. Engage in activities that bring you joy, relaxation, and rejuvenation. Take time for yourself regularly to replenish and recharge.

Seek support: Reach out to supportive friends, family members, mentors, or professionals who can provide guidance, encouragement, and a safe space for self-exploration. Surround yourself with individuals who accept and celebrate your authentic self.

Release self-judgment: Let go of self-judgment and negative self-talk. Replace self-criticism with self-compassion and positive affirmations.

Treat yourself with love and kindness, understanding that you are deserving of acceptance and wholeness.

By embracing the wholeness of your being, you can experience a profound sense of self-acceptance, empowerment, and inner peace. Embracing all aspects of yourself allows you to live authentically and align with your true purpose and potential. Remember, this is an ongoing journey that requires patience, self-reflection, and self-care. With time and practice, you can cultivate a deep sense of wholeness and live a more fulfilling and authentic life.

Living Authentically and Aligning with Your Values

Living authentically and aligning with your values is a powerful way to cultivate a fulfilling and meaningful life. Here are strategies to support you in living authentically:

Know your values: Take time to identify your core values—those principles and qualities that are most important to you. Reflect on what truly matters to you in life, what brings you a sense of purpose and fulfillment. Understanding your values will provide a solid foundation for living authentically.

Set boundaries: Establish clear boundaries that honor and protect your values, needs, and well-being. Learn to say no to commitments, situations, or relationships that are not aligned with who you are and what you value. Setting boundaries helps you create space for authentic living and prevents the erosion of your sense of self.

Make conscious choices: Practice mindful decision-making by considering how each choice aligns with your values and authenticity. Prioritize choices that resonate with your true self and contribute to your overall well-being. Pause, reflect, and listen to your inner voice when making decisions.

Express your true self: Embrace and express your unique identity, opinions, and emotions. Allow yourself to be seen and heard authentically, without fear of judgment or rejection. Express yourself through creative outlets, honest conversations, or engaging in activities that reflect your passions and interests.

Practice self-acceptance: Accept and embrace all parts of yourself—the strengths, weaknesses, successes, and failures. Release the need to seek approval or validation from others. Celebrate your individuality and honor your journey, knowing that you are worthy of love and acceptance exactly as you are.

Seek alignment in relationships: Surround yourself with people who support and uplift your authentic self. Cultivate relationships where you can be open, vulnerable, and true to yourself. Avoid compromising your values or pretending to be someone you're not for the sake of fitting in or gaining acceptance.

Cultivate self-awareness: Engage in self-reflection and introspection to deepen your understanding of who you are and what drives you. Regularly check in with yourself and assess whether your thoughts, actions, and choices align with your values and authenticity. This ongoing self-awareness will help you stay true to yourself.

Practice self-care: Prioritize self-care practices that nourish your mind, body, and spirit. Engage in activities that bring you joy, relaxation, and fulfillment. Take care of your physical, emotional, and mental well-being, as it provides a solid foundation for living authentically.

Embrace vulnerability: Embrace vulnerability as a gateway to authentic living. Allow yourself to be open and honest, even if it means taking risks or facing discomfort. Vulnerability fosters connection, growth, and authenticity in relationships and self-expression.

Embrace growth and evolution: Recognize that living authentically is an ongoing journey of growth and evolution. Be open to learning, exploring new perspectives, and adapting as you gain new insights and experiences. Embrace the opportunity for personal growth and transformation on your authentic path.

By living authentically and aligning with your values, you cultivate a sense of inner harmony, fulfillment, and purpose. Embrace the courage to be true to yourself, and remember that authenticity is a lifelong practice. Trust in your unique journey and honor the essence of who you are.

About The Author

The author of this book is a passionate advocate for personal growth, self-discovery, and holistic well-being. Drawing from his own experiences and extensive research, David Olubiyi offers valuable insights, practical wisdom, and guidance to readers on their journey of self-discovery.

With a deep understanding of the challenges and opportunities that come with embarking on a path of self-discovery, David uses his own personal stories and struggles, creating a relatable and empathetic connection with readers. His authenticity and vulnerability allow readers to feel seen and understood, inspiring them to embrace their own journey of self-discovery with courage and self-compassion.

David's expertise extends beyond theory and knowledge, as they have dedicated significant time and effort to their own personal growth and self-discovery. Through his own exploration and transformation, he has gained valuable insights and tools that he generously share with readers.

David offers a well-rounded and integrative approach to self-discovery. He believes in the importance of addressing all aspects of human experience—mental, emotional, physical, and spiritual—to foster holistic well-being and personal growth.

David's writing style is engaging, insightful, and accessible, making complex concepts and practices easy to understand and apply in daily life. He provides practical exercises, reflective prompts, and actionable steps throughout the book, empowering readers to actively engage in their own self-discovery journey.

With a genuine desire to support and uplift others, David's mission is to inspire readers to embrace their authenticity, cultivate self-awareness, and live a life aligned with their values and purpose. Through his writing, he aims to create a positive and transformative impact, encouraging readers to tap into their inner wisdom and embrace the infinite possibilities of self-discovery.

Overall, David Olubiyi's passion, expertise, and compassionate approach make him a trusted guide and mentor for individuals seeking personal growth, self-empowerment, and a deeper connection with themselves. His authentic voice and genuine commitment to helping others make this book a valuable resource on the journey of self-discovery.